GRETA AND CECIL

Diana Souhami is the author of many widely acclaimed books, including *Gluck: Her Biography*, *Gertrude & Alice*, *Mrs Keppel and her Daughter* and *The Trials of Radcliffe Hall*, which was short-listed for the James Tait Black Memorial Prize for Biography.

GRETA AND CECIL

Diana Souhami

PHOENIX
PRESS

PHOENIX PRESS
5 UPPER SAINT MARTIN'S LANE
LONDON WC2H 9EA

A PHOENIX PRESS PAPERBACK

First published in Great Britain
by Jonathan Cape in 1994
This paperback edition published in 2000
by Phoenix Press,
a division of The Orion Publishing Group Ltd,
Orion House, 5 Upper St Martin's Lane,
London WC2H 9EA

A CIP catalogue record for this book
is available from the British Library.

Printed in Great Britain by
Butler & Tanner Ltd, Frome and London

ISBN 1 84212 160 X

Contents

Illustrations

A Personal Note

Two letters by Alice B. Toklas prompted me into this book. The first was written after Greta Garbo, Cecil Beaton and Mercedes de Acosta went to tea with her in November 1951. Alice, widowed from Gertrude Stein, lived alone at 5 rue Christine in Paris. Cecil, she told her friend Carl Van Vechten, was 'very tousled exhausted and worshipful'. Garbo she could not make out. 'Do explain her to me. She was not mysterious but I hadn't the answer. The French papers say they are to marry – but she doesn't look as if she would do anything as crassly innocent as that. *Expliquez moi* as Pablo [Picasso] used to say to Baby [Gertrude Stein].'

Her second letter, written when she was eighty-four, was to Anita Loos in May 1960. Alice had read Mercedes' memoirs with their revelations about her love affairs with women. 'You can't dismiss Mercedes lightly,' she wrote. 'She has had the two most important women in the United States – Garbo and Dietrich.'

I was intrigued. What was Greta Garbo doing with Cecil Beaton and why was Mercedes de Acosta with them? Images gave clues: Dorothy Wilding's photographs of Cecil dressed, so convincingly, as a woman; Garbo as *Queen Christina* dressed, less convincingly, as a man; Garbo so frequently shielding herself from the camera, Cecil so frequently posturing to the camera. Clarence Sinclair Bull's photographs of Garbo – her haunting androgyny and aloof beauty; Cecil's photographs of his own mirrored image – his flagrant narcissism.

I delved into the archives of films and photographs, diaries, memoirs, letters. I found, predictably, a superfluity of Cecil and an abiding desire for privacy from Greta. Cecil, the most self-revelatory of men, moved greedily into print. He turned fleeting impressions into published prose. Like his photographs, his writing grasped at transient things. All of it was autobiographical. His diary account of his relationship with Greta Garbo, *The Happy Years*, was published while she was still alive. My problem was of selection, focus and tone; to preserve Garbo's inwardness and find a meaning in Cecil's gush.

Letters written by Garbo have survived and I have made use of these. I watched videos of her films in the hope that her shadow would touch my work. I thank Kevin Gough-Yates for help on all aspects of her films, and the librarians in the Department of Film at the Museum of Modern Art, New York for private screenings of *The Gösta Berling Saga* and *The Kiss*.

I have drawn from material at the following archives: The library of St John's College, Cambridge, where Beaton's manuscript diaries and letters are housed (the gift, in August 1986, of his appointed literary executor the late Eileen Hose). Copyright of this material rests with the Beaton estate.

The Archive of Art and Design at the Victoria and Albert Museum, London. Beaton bequeathed his 'Scrapbooks' – forty-nine volumes of his press cuttings – to the Museum.

The film archives at the Museum of Modern Art, New York.

The British Film Institute Library, London. (And with special thanks to the anonymous donor to the Institute of the 'Garbo Scrapbook'.)

The Rosenbach Museum and Library, Philadelphia, which holds the papers of Mercedes de Acosta and Eva Le Gallienne.

Georgetown University Library, Washington.

The Swedish Film Institute, Stockholm.

The National Library of Sweden, Stockholm.

I thank the following people for information and permission to quote from letters and memoirs: Lady Hutchinston of Lullington; Stephen Tennant's nephew the Honourable Toby Tennant; Salka Viertel's son Peter Viertel; Sven Broman, author of *Garbo on Garbo*; David Diamond; Toni del Renzio; Richard Buckle and Pat Battle.

My thanks, too, to Terence Pepper at the National Portrait Gallery, London, for help with photographs from that collection, to Peter Campbell for designing the jacket, to my editor, Philippa Brewster and to Rebecca Wilson, Publishing Director at Weidenfeld.

The Divine

'I love you as one adores sacred things –
God, country, honour, you.'
'I come last?'
'You come before anything.'
Mata Hari

An image of Garbo's gaze, like a moon breaking through darkness, was used on the cover of *Photoplay* in January 1930 at the height of her fame. Her gaze is incorporeal, photogenic in the sense of emitting light. Caricatured figures struggle vainly to reach her. The image makes a metaphor of the cinema's darkness and her luminous beauty. It prints on the mind as essence, not form.

She came to cinema at a time when stars were idolised. Audiences revered the image of her face. They could, said the French critic Roland Barthes, simply sink into it as if into a philtre. She 'offered to one's gaze a sort of Platonic idea of the human creature . . . descended from a heaven where all things are formed and perfected in the clearest light.' The planes of her face were such that there was nothing to be overcome with lighting effects and preferred angles. William Daniels, cameraman for most of her films, called her face 'perfection itself'. Still photographs by Arnold Genthe, Edward Steichen, Ruth Harriet Louise and Clarence Sinclair Bull testify to the range of her beauty. The imagist poet Hilda Doolittle compared her beauty to the masterpieces of the renaissance and antiquity.

It was said of her screen performances that she could turn the worst turnip into a masterpiece, that she created out of the thinnest material the 'complex, enchanting shadow of a soul upon the screen'.

The themes of most of her twenty-four Hollywood films were nugatory, but she invested herself in them and redeemed them. She said she made a fantasy of each part, disliked rehearsal in case her performance might stale, and took little notice of direction or her co-stars whose performances were unmemorable and irrelevant to hers.

Her supreme quality was an inwardness – sentience and feeling expressed through silence – and for this she was called The Divine. Clarence Brown, who directed four of her films, called it the photography of thought:

> she had something behind the eyes that you couldn't see until you photographed it close up. If she had to look at one person with jealousy and another with love, she didn't have to change her expression. You could see it in her eyes.

Fifteen of her films were silent, and silence and her inwardness entwined. Hollywood turned her image into legend. A publicity photograph showed her face superimposed on the Sphinx with the desert beyond. With the advent of talkies she found emotion in the interstices between words, the inflectional look and a sub-text of suggestion. When she said 'hello-oo' into a phone her voice was plangent with the sorrows of history and the hope of the world. If the words assigned to her were terrible she delivered them without thinking about them and conveyed something else.

Fourteen of her twenty-four films have an unhappy ending. In *Inspiration* she leaves Robert Montgomery when he is asleep rather than ruin his life. In *Romance* she persuades a priest to give up his love for her. In *Woman of Affairs* she kills herself to avoid breaking a marriage. In *Camille* she dies of consumption in Robert Taylor's arms. In *Anna Karenina* she throws herself under a train. In *Queen Christina* she sails into the unknown with the corpse of John Gilbert. In *Grand Hotel*, unknown to her, John Barrymore has been murdered. In *Mata Hari* she goes to the firing squad. It was not what happened to her that concerned her audience, but the emotions for her they found in themselves.

In her early movies MGM merchandised her as an object of desire. 'I am a woman', she said of her performances, 'who is unfaithful to a million men.' She was cast as the *femme fatale* whose moods and appetites wreck ordinary lives: 'Always the bad woman. What can I do? In the end I fall through the ice so the play can go on. They want me out of the way. That is the kind of part I have.' Of *The Temptress*, where she makes a banker, a bandit, a bridge builder and all men her slaves, she said to the press: 'I do not want to be a silly temptress. I cannot see any sense in getting dressed up and doing nothing but tempting men in pictures.'

After 1932, when MGM were in awe of her box-office power and when she had become, like royalty, an icon, she was cast as heroines of European history, regal and remote, in expensive costume melodramas. By devices of direction audiences were coerced to revere her on film. Her entrance was delayed then heralded by music as she descended flights of stairs in trailing gowns. Heroes suffered the *coup de foudre* at first glance. When she first appears in *Anna Karenina* she steps from a train, wreathed in steam which slowly disperses. In *Ninotchka* she waits alone on a railway platform. In *Queen Christina* she thunders on horseback across dangerous terrain.

She said, with disdain for the profession, that she was not much of an actress and had no particular technique. She asked for retakes if she felt a scene was false, could not work if there were distractions on set, ate a frugal lunch, brought from home, in her dressing-room, for years had a nervous blink that caused torment to cameramen and directors, and went home drained and depressed after each day's filming.

Neither physically nor spiritually could Hollywood make her into a type. She came from peasant stock and her shoulders were broad, her feet large – often she wore men's shoes – her breasts matter-of-fact, her stride like a sailor's with a pelvic thrust. Dismissive of name and gender, she chose, as aliases, Harriet Brown, Mr Smith, Mr Thompson, Mr Toscar. From childhood on she referred to herself as 'he' or 'boy' or 'little old man'. Her men friends or escorts were often homosexual and her sexuality as intriguing to women as men. She seemed to suggest an emotional hinterland, beyond gender, place or time. On film her men were shadowy and irrelevant, like trees blowing in the wind. When she saw the Japanese National Theatre's *Grand Kabuki*, on its first American tour, she asked if she might go backstage to watch the onnagata (the specialist in female roles) effect his transformation from man into woman.

Her mere presence on celluloid confounded the censor who could not excise her suggested androgyny or intrinsic subversion. She had a way of 'cupping her man's head in both hands and seeming very nearly to drink from it'. Women, too, she kissed straight on the mouth. Her kissing was open-mouthed, 'precise and lascivious' and was in time banned by the Hays Code of Decency. The moral right dredged evidence to show that she corrupted the young, quoting the testimony of high-school girls: 'I practised love scenes either with myself or with a girlfriend. We sometimes think we could beat Greta Garbo but I doubt it.'

She wished she could have had two lives, one for the cinema and one for herself. 'The story of my life', she said toward the end of it, 'is about back entrances, side doors, secret elevators and other ways of getting in and out of places so that people won't bother me.' She could not walk down a road without being followed, photographed and questioned, nor sign her name without the penmark being coveted. Each day brought orchids from unknown admirers, long-distance phone calls from strangers hoping to hear her voice. Each week her fan letters, unopened, were burned by the sackful on the studio lot.

Her off-set persona tantalised. The public wanted a commensurate story about her private life. But she was shy and conversationally erratic, by turns direct, defensive, humorous, rejecting, silent or odd. She showed, both in her acting and in her private persona, no plausible anchor to the world beyond herself, not of home nor of partner nor creed. She appeared before the camera in some spiritual sense naked, in a curious tension between Nordic profundity and Hollywood splash. No one was more displaced in Hollywood all who met her averred. On film she promised the ultimate in intimacy. In life she never went to a wedding, christening or ball.

Her elusiveness became a resource for journalists. They wrote columns about not interviewing her, about her aloofness, perversity, restraint. Her remarks to the press when she made them were dark: 'Dead? I have been dead for many years', 'I am a wanderer, just a wanderer', 'Everyone whom I loves dies.' 'Love comes, love goes, who can help it?' Her secretiveness and aloneness frustrated. Love, fame and fortune were offered to her, yet she chose privacy, a spartan regime of early nights and up at dawn, a frugal diet of spinach, yoghurt, bread and cheese, a nomad's home within her rented Beverly Hills house – only two rooms used, sparsely furnished, an unpretentious, mannish garb – trousers, flat shoes, severe hats. If given jewels or expensive lighters she put them away in a drawer, saying that they oppressed her.

Captured memories of her were kept by many. Louise Brooks described walking down Santa Monica Boulevard in Beverly Hills in 1936 and seeing an 'old town car' driving toward her:

I had never seen it before but I *knew* it was Garbo's. It was going slow, but it got *very* slow as it got up to me. Then I saw Garbo. She was sitting very straight in the shadows of the interior, black coat, black turban. Her expression did not change at all when she looked at me, but her eyes said, 'I will stop and take you with me.'

I played like I did not see and walked to the Villa Italia while the car picked up speed on its way to Beverly Hills.

Such memories were like photographs, printed on the mind.

Stardom threatened to destroy her. She resisted by keeping intact an integrity to a notion of self, but the cost of resistance was high. Always a reluctant icon she became, in time, her own iconoclast. 'I have made enough faces,' she said at the age of thirty-six, in 1941, when she gave up acting and tried to be private.

In her years of retirement her camera image came to haunt her, for she had to live with the actual face from which the perfect image was derived. And her actual face, unlike its arrested image, altered and aged with time. As she grew older, photographs taken against her will seemed savage. They implied that her life was of less value than the split second image of passed time.

Her face in *Photoplay*, though it cannot age, seems ethereal, ready to fade when the lights go up, or the day breaks, or the page is turned. Troubled by her reflection and the perception of its beauty Cecil Beaton pursued her. Like a quest for the Holy Grail.

Cecil's Quest

'O chéri, *why don't you answer the* phone? Please!'
Grand Hotel

'How I long to get at Garbo,' Cecil Beaton wrote in his diary in December 1929. He was in Hollywood, photographing the famous, rich and beautiful for *Vogue* and for his projected *Book of Beauty* which, he said, 'would show feminine beauty in all its phases'.

It was to be an imitation of the Victorian Albums in which lovely young ladies swooned over doves, read love-letters, or admired trails of convolvulus, while they faced a page of glowing descriptive text. This contemporary version was to be illustrated with my photographs and ornamented with purple prose written by myself.

Though the roll of Cecil's lovely young ladies included filmstars, tycoons' wives, Graces, Viscountesses, Marchionesses and at least one Highness, none of them, in his view, could compare in glamour with Greta Garbo and it frustrated him that she would not agree to be photographed, drawn, spoken to or even glimpsed by him.

He had seen her in her early silent movies: *The Torrent, The Temptress, Love, The Divine Woman, The Kiss*, and had read tantalising articles about her in the movie magazines. He kept publicity photographs of her and a scrapbook of her cuttings, called himself her 'breathless victim', said there was no one with a more exotic, magnetic or romantic personality and that her mystery and allure surpassed that of all women.

> She is at once simple, subtle and the acme of sophistication and by her never appearing in public and by her being utterly impregnable, no one can find out the truth about her.

Cecil, aged twenty-five at the time of this visit to Hollywood, had already in London become an authority on female beauty, style and glamour. His pictures of debutantes and their mothers had made him, young as he was, the darling photographer of the glittering class. He was the most noticed of the bright young things and present at all the lunches and balls. His hand-held Kodak did not highlight unkind wrinkles and he excised double chins and warts from his prints with a penknife and a pen. He made all his ladies look beautiful in a cosmetic sense of the word, or else filled the background to his pictures with balloons, cellophane, or cement sacks and did tricksy things with mirrors, so that it was difficult to notice if they were not.

His work appeared regularly in the society magazines – *The Sketch, Gentlewoman, Graphic* and *Vogue*. He photographed Lady Louis Mountbatten as the figurehead of a ship, Lady Brecknock in a white fringed dress, Lady Loughborough in black jet, Lady Diana Cooper as a statue of the Madonna, the Marquise de Casa Maury 'formerly Miss Paula Gellibrand', peering from behind the wrought-iron gates of her Grosvenor Street home, Edith Sitwell breakfasting in bed, Emmeline de Broglie in a plastic mac with a background of crumpled cellophane. His mother Etty and his sisters Baba and Nancy were his favourite subjects and he designed their clothes then told them how to pose. He dressed his mother in eau-de-Nil trimmed with diamante, or like a dowager duchess in 'two shades of orchid mauve with mauve Bangkok picture hat'. Bedecked as Madame Pompadour, her picture appeared on the cover of

Gentlewoman. His sisters he dressed as Gainsborough's daughters, or festooned them with balloons, or draped them in eighteenth-century silver brocade. He took them reflected in mirrors or water, fragmented, presented and superimposed. His portraits of them appeared again and again in *Eve*, the *Sketch*, the *Graphic*, bearing the caption that they were descended from Lady Mary Beaton, lady-in-waiting to Mary Queen of Scots.

In October 1927, when Cecil was a callow twenty-three, *The Graphic* described him as an elegant first nighter who 'designs pretty frocks for his friends, takes exquisite photographs and is generally artistic as well as being popular at tea parties'. A month later *The Sunday Herald* called him Wonder Boy, artist and photographer and commended him on his fantastic angles.

His energy, output and tenacity were formidable. By the time he got to Hollywood at Christmas 1929, intent on Greta Garbo, he had produced a body of work that appealed to stylists in London's West End and in Manhattan. An exhibition of his photographs, held at the Cooling Gallery, New Bond Street, in Spring 1927 was described as the most crowded private view of the 'little season'. The interior designer Elsie de Wolfe then staged it at her Gallery on Fifth Avenue and Edna Chase, American editor of *Vogue*, offered him work. His costume and set designs, first for the Cambridge Footlights, when he was an undergraduate there, then for fancy dress parties and charity pageants, shocked and amused. *Eve* featured his interior decorations for the Beaton family home.

As well as photographing the rich and designing their party clothes, Cecil drew and wrote. By 1929 *Vogue* regularly used his spidery, weak, almost satirical drawings to illustrate articles of a Who's About Town or What to Wear sort. He wrote such articles too. In 'What is Beauty', for *Vogue*, November 1928, he commended taut toes and arched insteps, restrained self-consciousness and an awareness of elbows. He maintained that true beauty lay with the privileged class and said he did not believe that 'the loveliest blooms of humanity have withered in the slums, that the most brilliant geniuses have died without a chance'. He wrote that he adored fashion because it was made up of everything that was most successful at that moment, expressed a preference for flat chests and schoolboy figures, over bosoms and 'hips like watermelons', said that he liked high foreheads, bones and thin necks and that he adored make-up and 'the gilded lily'.

The suggestion that he might gild his own lily earned him a caution in December 1928 from Beverley Nichols, author of *The Star Spangled Manner*. At lunch a young woman remarked to Beverley that Cecil was heavily made-up. Cecil bridled at the idea:

> it's absolutely untrue that I have used make-up for years now and haven't in my possession any powder or any paint whatsoever . . .
>
> I adore maquillage and so wish that young men could paint their faces but they definitely can't without being branded as social nuisances and if one renounces all things social one misses so much.

Though Cecil renounced powder and paint, his interest in taut toes, arched insteps, restrained self-consciousness and an awareness of elbows was acute. In his student days he had received acclaim for his skill in acting female roles for the Cambridge Footlights. Reviewers described him as an exquisite heroine and a successful female impersonator. Years later, in 1947, when he was forty-three, he told Greta Garbo of how, even as a boy, he had loved women's clothes. He told her that on family outings to musical comedies and pantomimes he looked through opera glasses to see precisely how actresses painted their eyelids turquoise blue and put dots of scarlet in the corners of their eyes. He told her of his love for his mother's dressing-table and of the time, on the family annual summer holiday in Norfolk, when he painted his face with her make-up. His perturbed father shut him in the bedroom for the day. It was no punishment. Cecil spent the time painting a watercolour of his theatrical love, the actress Lily Elsie.

Anita Loos introduced Cecil to Hollywood's high life at Christmas 1929. She was writing a book about Hollywood characters for which Cecil was to do the drawings. 'We clicked immediately,' she said. 'It was one of those instant things . . . Yes, he met people through me, but he was popular. He soon didn't need that.' Her husband, John Emerson, who claimed to co-author much of her work, was less sure of Cecil and called him 'that snotty peacock'.

The trio stayed at The Roosevelt Hotel, 'Home of the Stars', on Hollywood Boulevard, 'a mock Moorish conceit with patio, fountain, and shawl-draped balconies, its lobby crowded by desperate blondes in black satin, osprey and furs'. The Boulevard was lined with huge Christmas trees 'all tarted up by vari-coloured lamps'. The New York stockmarket had crashed the previous month, but life went on. The success of Anita Loos's novel *Gentlemen Prefer Blondes*, written in 1926, earned her over a million dollars by 1929.

On Christmas Eve she took Cecil to a party at John Gilbert's house in Tower Road. Gilbert was Greta Garbo's erstwhile lover and co-star in *Flesh and the Devil* and *Love* and had wanted, dramatically, to marry her, but she failed to turn up for the much-publicised wedding in September 1926.

To her Swedish friend Mimi Pollak Garbo wrote, 'I have been very naughty.' She admitted she had promised Gilbert all manner of things which she could not follow through; that she was too uneven in mood ever to marry, and that Gilbert was angry. He had offered her all the luxury she had never known: swimming pool, servants, a magnificent house. For reasons that mystified even herself she felt compelled to go home alone to her ugly hotel room.

During the long aftermath of their affair he was sent to jail for threatening her with a gun. Shortly before Cecil met him, he married Ina Claire, the third of his four wives.

Gilbert showed Cecil the loggia and waterfall he had built for Greta, the pine trees he had planted to remind her of Sweden, the sun parlour, the swimming-pool and the indoor court where he taught her to play tennis. Cecil thought he showed too many white teeth when he smiled and that Ina Claire overacted the part of the jubilant newly-wed. After the party he wrote in his diary of rumours that the marriage was 'already somewhat turbulent' and that the bridegroom had a reputation for violence when excessively drunk.

On New Year's Eve, Anita Loos took Cecil to the ultimate party at the San Simeon ranch of William Randolph Hearst, the newspaper magnate. They travelled in Hearst's special train, then were chauffeured to the ranch. They drove past high mountains, herds of buffalo, zebra, deer and antelope and exotic birds.

> . . . at the top of a tree-spotted mountain, we caught sight of a vast, sparkling white castle in Spain. It was right out of a fairy story.
>
> The sun poured down with theatrical brilliance on tons of white marble and white stone. There seemed to be a thousand marble statues, pedestals, urns . . . Hearst stood smiling at the top of one of the many flights of garden steps.

Cecil's room had a carved gilt ceiling, Jacobean beds with gold brocade covers, tinselled velvet wall-hangings and a view of pale green mountains, blue hills and a silver sea. The glitterati of filmland were at this party, but not Greta Garbo.

In the first week of January 1930, Anita took him to the Paramount film studio and introduced him to those whose names he knew from the movie magazines. '"Meet Mr Lubitsch" – a fat birdlike little jew with a pointed mouth without any teeth . . . "Meet Mr Richard Arlen", a nice, clean-looking young man wrinkled his forehead and smiled. "This is George Bancroft" the twinkling tadpole eyes didn't seem a bit thuggish off the screen.' Cecil photographed Mary Astor, Buster Keaton, Irving Berlin, Joan Crawford, Anita Page.

On 6 January he met Howard Strickling, MGM's head of publicity and implored him to help him meet Garbo. Strickling agreed to phone her and ask if she would be photographed. Cecil stayed on tenterhooks waiting for her reply.

Strickling gave him a wad of stills of Garbo from *Anna Christie*, in which she had just starred and which marked her transition from silent to talking movies. Cecil had heard it rumoured that her voice was no good and that her downfall would be as rapid as her rise. But her first world-weary words, drawled in a husky voice with a heavy accent, etched their way into cinema history: 'Gimme a whisky, ginger ale on the side, and don't be stingy baby.' 'Shall I serve it in a pail?' says the waiter. 'That'd suit me down to the ground.'

Strickling told Cecil that Garbo simply did not want to meet her fans. 'She is so casual and dreamy,' wrote Cecil, 'she doesn't give a damn and the fact that she doesn't give a damn and will not come out of hiding only increases the frenzy and as with me they are almost driven insane with desire to see her.'

By midday he felt that the odds against her agreeing to be photographed had narrowed from 1000 to 1, to 6 to 1. Then he heard the news. Strickling had spoken to her on the phone and she had said to him: Oh she didn't know about it, oh well. The following day Cecil arranged to photograph more accessible stars, like Norma Shearer. But all he wanted to hear about was Garbo's decision. He had, he wrote, 'worked himself into a frenzy of adoration of her'. He kept phoning: 'Mr Strickling is not in his office just now and I'm afraid I don't know about Miss Garbo's decision.' Cecil went without lunch and felt 'frantic' with exasperation and tiredness. He finally got through to Strickling. What about getting Garbo? he asked. Not a chance, was the reply.

'Hell, Damn Blast the Bitch,' Cecil wrote in his diary. 'I almost wept with fury, exhaustion, pique. Hell. It was too awful to be so taunted by the Bitch. She's got nothing else to do.' He went back to the studios and shouted 'Where in Hell is Miss Shearer? If she doesn't arrive in three minutes I go.' Oh Miss Shearer is on her way, he was told.

Anita took him to meet Elsie Janis who had been one of his 'hottest boyhood enthusiasms'. When he was ten, he loved hearing her sing, at the Palace Theatre, London, 'Give me the moonlight, give me the girl and leave the rest to me'. He had amused his sisters with impersonations of her and felt that she had great chic. Now she lived in a 'niceish little house with awful Japanese-style furniture', wrote Hollywood scenarios and looked 'pretty terrible' in cinnamon satin and brocade pyjamas with a rope of crystal beads round her neck.

She and Anita tormented him with talk of Garbo:

It is really too awful that she is so impregnable. I have pulled a hundred wires to try and see her, to photograph and draw her but without success and everywhere I go I hear the most palpitatingly exciting things about her beauty and her intelligence and Mother Janis today heaped on torments, one after another, about her movements being more beautiful than a panther's, her skin more ivory than ivory, teeth more pearly than pearls, and eyelashes which when her eyes look down spread across her cheeks like peacocks' tails. She is the only glamorous Hollywood star today and a hermit.

He was so agitated by his failure that Elsie Janis tried to intercede for him. Someone got through to Garbo's maid: 'Mees Garbo ees away for weekend.' Elsie Janis assured Cecil she would pull all strings to try to fix a meeting, but he doubted her chance of success.

In New York Cecil had heard that Garbo's only friend was 'a man named Adrien ... a dressmaker and a pansy'. Due to leave Hollywood the following day, Cecil wrote an ingratiating note to Adrian saying how much he would like to photograph him. 'Well he appeared, a scraggy queer, and I took some pictures of him.' Cecil arranged that same evening to go and see Adrian's home and his drawings. He hoped that this would lead to an introduction to Garbo.

Anita wanted to meet Adrian too. He arrived at the Roosevelt wearing a bright suit, jade green scarf and with rouged cheeks. Cecil thought it all for his benefit, so he showed him his own drawings, about which Adrian was polite but lukewarm.

They set off in Adrian's car. Cecil and Anita sat in the back 'and pinched one another and poked each other and nudged with pursed lips. This pick-up was a riot.' But Cecil felt chastened when he saw Adrian's exquisite house, an 'oasis' in the desert of bad taste of Hollywood. It rivalled his own boldness of style.

They went into a room with white satin curtains, urns of white daisies on marble columns and wall paintings by Adrian of gold and silver tropical plants in a white jungle. Beyond this was a patio with trees, giant plants growing against high white walls, three monkeys and a parrot. Adrian then showed his drawings and Cecil was impressed: 'No wonder he had not enthused over my amateur efforts.' He thought Adrian's work witty, decadent, decorative and superbly drawn, in the manner of Aubrey Beardsley. He described him as a sensitive and subtle person with a 'phallus mania'. Never before had Cecil seen so many images of phalluses. Jungle flowers and cacti looked like them, palm trees were sprouting them, hats were trimmed with them and the 'central parts' of all the figure drawings ruled supreme.

Adrian told him that he was well-paid for costume design, which allowed him to live in his exquisite house and to draw and paint his pictures. Cecil mocked his manner and his 'pansy voice', but admired his work, style and individuality.

He plied him with questions about Garbo. He received only

vague answers, though Adrian said she was by far the most interesting person in Hollywood. Cecil would have liked to have stayed with him for hours. Adrian drove them home in pouring rain. Anita was equally impressed and both were intrigued by Garbo's friendship with him. 'So much more credit to her,' said Cecil.

Adrian was with Metro Goldwyn Mayer from 1928 until 1942 and became the most famous costume designer in Hollywood's history. He designed for Joan Crawford, Jean Harlow, Myrna Loy and Janet Gaynor – with whom he eloped in 1939. Their marriage was referred to as a 'twilight tandem', a 'lavender cover-up', where public image and private life were at odds.

Adrian projected Garbo's androgynous image and his designs for her had a huge impact on commercial fashion. The little velvet hat trimmed with ostrich feathers and worn over one eye, which he devised for her in *Romance* in 1930, set a vogue for the decade for the Empress Eugénie hat. His costumes for *Mata Hari* were toured round the States. The large, face-framing linen collars, heavy velvet jackets and leather jerkins which she wore in *Queen Christina* were adapted for retail and sold at Macy's, Gimbel's and Saks, Fifth Avenue. *Vogue* printed his sketches for *Camille* in 1936. When Garbo quit Hollywood in 1941, so did he, saying that with her departure, glamour went too.

He was always her discreet friend. As a gesture of admiration, when dressing her for *Camille*, he had the initials GG embroidered in seed pearls inside the cuffs of her silk-lined mauve kid gloves. In 1935, he gave an interview for *Photoplay*, in which he tried to explain her temperament without infringing her privacy. He said she often told him she would give anything in the world to have the privilege of walking about, shopping and travelling, without being noticed, that she hated being stared at and fussed over and liked to live quietly. He said that a crowd would gather to look at an elephant walking up a gangplank as readily as it would to see a movie star, and that if you happened not to like being stared at, or photographed and talked to against your will, you did what you could to avoid the discomfort. Twenty years later Greta told Cecil that photographers who took pictures against people's wills, violated the privacy of human beings.

Adrian, in 1935, described her as shy, full of fun, and beautiful in a spiritual way. He said her eyes were extraordinary, her body slender and athletic from exercise and walking, that she was usually tanned by the sun, rarely arrived at fittings with her hair combed, and used no make-up except for a pencil line at the edge of her eyelids. Her preferred clothes were tailored suits, sweaters, slacks, berets and sports' shoes and he did not think she had an evening dress and if she had, he was sure she had never worn it.

He called her a woman apart, an individualist who ruthlessly defended her own code of living by ignoring the mores of the world outside. He said that anyone who kept away from group thinking was usually disliked, mistrusted, or considered odd. He described her as simple, direct and truthful and as having not one ounce of affectation. 'She is at no moment the actress and never gives the illusion of being one until she is on the set before the lights, actually in the part.'

Cecil left Hollywood on 8 January 1930 without having set eyes on Greta Garbo. In an interview for the *Chicago Daily News* he said, 'I went out there purposely to take her picture. I will never go again unless I am assured that she will pose for me.' He travelled by train to Palm Beach with Anita Loos and John Emerson and stayed with them in their house in Sea Spray Avenue for sixteen days. For *Vogue* he took photographs of those seen in the sun at Palm Beach, and wrote of the 'fabulous vulgarity in this operetta town'. On 14 January, on his twenty-sixth birthday, Anita gave a dinner party for him. There were joke cigarettes, buzzing matchboxes and biscuits that squeaked.

Back in New York at the end of January, he stayed at the Barclay Hotel. *Vogue* were lukewarm about the technical merits of his photographs – for which he was paid $50 each – said that he knew nothing about lighting and recommended that he take photography classes at nightschool. *Cosmopolitan* derided his drawings for Anita's book on Hollywood, called them amateur and naïve and sent her a telegram: 'Beaton's work definitely not up to *Cosmopolitan* standard.' She compounded the criticism in a letter to Cecil:

> I feel you are on the crossways between being an artist and being a dilettante . . . Your drawings would be funnier if backed by a thorough knowledge of anatomy . . . Even though you are winning more and more social and professional friends all the time, what a nonsensical career in comparison with winning respect for your work . . . I long to see you pulling a Garbo and giving everyone the air.

On Sunday 2 February he lunched with Mercedes de Acosta at her house. She was a playwright and socialite, known for her lesbian lifestyle. Cecil thought her appearance 'outrageous and formidable'. Her hair was short and she wore men's clothes – a tie, trousers, buckled shoes and a cloak. But she was enthusiastic about his work and he liked her company and called her 'enchanting and naïve', 'charming and birdlike' and 'vividly quick'.

They gossiped about and made fun of the 'dreary crowd of New York lesbians . . . their earnestness, squalor, poverty and complete lack of humour'. She talked at length about Garbo which thrilled Cecil so much he felt like taking the train back to Hollywood to make another attempt to see her. Mercedes had, at this time, only seen Garbo from afar. This was in Constantinople, in 1924, when Garbo was there with Mauritz Stiller, working on a film called *The Odalisque from Smyrna*, which foundered through lack of funds.

'One day in the lobby of the Pera Palace Hotel,' Mercedes wrote in her memoirs of that first sight:

> I saw one of the most hauntingly beautiful women . . . The porter said he did not know her name but he thought she was a Swedish

actress who had come to Constantinople with the Swedish film director, Mauritz Stiller.

Several times after this I saw her in the street. I was terribly troubled by her eyes and I longed to speak to her, but I did not have the courage. Also I did not even know what language to use. She gave me the impression of great loneliness which only added to my own already melancholy state of mind. I hated to leave Constantinople without speaking to her, but sometimes destiny is kinder than we think, or maybe it is just that we cannot escape our destiny . . ., as the train pulled out of the station which carried me away from Constantinople I had a strong premonition that I might again see that beautiful and haunting face on some other shore.

At the time of this sighting, Mercedes was entrenched in an affair with the Broadway actress Eva Le Gallienne.* Mercedes was thirty-one (though on her passport she gave her year of birth as 1900), Miss Le G, as she called herself, was twenty-five. They wore rings inscribed with messages of devotion and wrote of being married to each other in a sense they called 'beautiful and poignant'.

The affair lasted until 1926. In February of that year Mercedes sat alone in the Capitol Theatre on Broadway and watched Garbo in her first Hollywood film, *The Torrent*. She thought that Garbo, like Eleonora Duse whom she knew, was a great actor and that the character she played 'took hold of her and not she of it'. She saw the film through twice and felt that she might, in her secret heart, draw Garbo to her.

On that Sunday lunchtime, with Cecil, she gave him all the gossip and half-truths she had heard about Garbo. She told him how, in Sweden when Garbo was still a girl, Mauritz Stiller who was already 'already quite fifty years old' and who stood for glamour and all that

* Richard Le Gallienne, her father, was a poet and friend of Oscar Wilde. 'I hope the laurels are not too thick across your brow for me to kiss your eyelids,' Wilde wrote to him in 1890.

was intellectually exciting in life, found her, educated her, fell in love with her and took her to Hollywood. She told him of Garbo's affair with John Gilbert, said that Stiller, outraged, returned to Sweden then died and that Garbo almost killed herself from remorse and grief.

She said Garbo talked very little and never looked in a mirror, walked like a boy, with long strides, was not so far a lesbian, but might easily be one and had rushed about showing everyone when the tailor sent her a new pair of riding breeches with fly buttons. 'Well that was Mercedes' story, gleaned from a great friend of Garbo's,' said Cecil.

The next day, Monday 3 February, he and Mercedes met again, dined together and went to the opening of a play in which Mercedes' friend Hope Williams was acting. Cecil was embarrassed at being seen with Mercedes. He felt that people were sneering at him for being with a 'furious lesbian'. Back in her kitchen, after the show, they both talked for hours of love and courage and of how there could be 'no grovelling when one felt a great passion'. That night he wrote in his diary that he liked her thin, brittle arms and intelligence and would have liked to have gone to bed with her.

Off-guard, he confided to her that he had had an affair with Adèle Astaire. Later, when alone, he regretted the admission, was afflicted by a sense of self-betrayal and chided himself for a serious mistake. He took pride in his secretiveness about his sexual encounters. He wrote in his diary that Mercedes knew the affair meant little to him and that he could have killed himself for having told her.

Perhaps his anger with himself was because the news was too cool to be true. He needed to boast that he had been to bed with a woman. The event had taken place the previous December in New York and left him feeling 'hysterical', deathly tired and unable to work. He and Adèle had shared a bed, held hands in the cinema, tap-danced together and she had bitten him on the chin 'unendurably hard'. But his truer interest was in the relationship between Adèle and her brother Fred, which mirrored something of his own preoccupations with his sisters and with merged male and female identity.

His photographs of the Astaires, whom he first saw dancing together in 1924, show them as a single entity. 'I'd like to change my whole self,' he wrote after seeing them dance. 'I adored the Astaires so much that I nearly died in my stall.' It was always his desire to be other than he was, the performer, not the photographer, the viewed and not the voyeur.

On Tuesday 4 February 1930, after his 'confession' to Mercedes, he woke up with the feeling that he had done something foul – like 'going to bed with a nigger or something disgusting'. He had, he felt, been untrue to himself and was furious at his weakness.

Quite what being true to himself entailed for Cecil, when it came to sex, was no direct matter. A fortnight later, through Adèle, he met a boxer, Jimmy, a drawing of whom he wanted to include in Anita's book. He began by taking dull photographs of him. Then it was agreed Jimmy should call back for a session of more realistic boxing poses. He left his gear in Cecil's rooms at the Barclay Hotel.

He returned after a few days, tanned from lying under a sunray lamp. Cecil thought him a 'real Adonis', with huge shoulders, narrow hips, marble skin and solid neck. He photographed him, they drank whisky, and Jimmy regaled him with accounts of the women he had sent to hospital because of 'the size of a certain part of his formation'.

The next day Jimmy returned, yet again, for more pictures – though not ones that were offered to *Vogue* – 'complete nuders this time'. Cecil smeared him with cold cream and was thrilled by his body, 'in the bright lights it shone like wet stone and he is, my gosh, "well built" to the point of being a monstrosity.' Cecil wrote in his diary that he had never known anything like it and could readily believe all that Jimmy told him about the twelve inches and the huge thickness.

They had a long talk about Jimmy's appetites, with Cecil lying on the bed and Jimmy sitting beside him. He told Cecil that for breakfast he had porridge, four eggs, fifteen rashers of bacon, sausages and twenty slices of toast. At night he had two steaks and saltpetre in his coffee. The talk became ribald and obscene. 'We talked dirty details for hours,' wrote Cecil. Jimmy told him that he had sex eight times a night with women whom he left crying for mercy and that pansies beseeched him for sex but that 'he would not do that because he was a real man'. He could, he said, spot 'lesbians and faggots a mile off' by the way they smoked their cigarettes. He knew from Garbo's smoking, in her love films with John Gilbert, that she was 'at any rate a prospective lessy'. Jimmy left at two in the morning, with Cecil pleading with him to stay.

He kept coming back and Cecil took to lending him money for the weekly bills of rent and groceries, and $50 to find a new room. One night he stayed over, which left Cecil feeling frayed, nervy, sleepy and sad. He read Cecil's palm and told him that by the age of thirty-five he would be an entirely different person, but that he would never be happy. 'Frankly Seesil you'll never be happy.' He took him to his gymnasium but Cecil did not like the 'demented looking pugilists', the language of the black attendants and the smell in the corridors. They dined at Dinty Moore's on 46th Street, a haunt of gays and transvestites, where the waiters treated Jimmy like a god. They had oysters, vegetable stew and steak. Cecil wished in vain that Jimmy would at least offer to pay for the taxis on these outings. Jimmy punctuated silences with 'What a Life, Cecil. Isn't it a Life.' Back at the Barclay, he drank Cecil's whisky and insinuated that sexual delights were in store, 'but enough of that until it happens', wrote Cecil.

Whatever it was, it almost happened on 13 March 1930, Cecil's last night in New York.

It was hard to get him talking about what I wanted. He is an independent bastard and so am I and after a terrific struggle I won and it was not worth the bother and once I had won the delight had left . . . I feel very triumphant at having been the first person to overcome him for he's a tough proposition.

Cecil then lent him 'another batch of money', and, after he had gone, went to sleep at once.

Cecil's diary entries on this conquest conveyed no trace of the shame he felt at admitting to Mercedes de Acosta that he had gone to bed with Adèle Astaire. It was an off-beat encounter for London's elegant first nighter and well-paid advocate in *Vogue*, *Gentlewoman* and *Eve* of taut toes, arched insteps, restrained self-consciousness and an awareness of elbows.

The next day, on 14 March 1930, Cecil sailed for England, his quest for Garbo unfulfilled. He was as far as ever from realising his wish to meet and photograph her. It was a wish compounded of strange ambitions and desires. Like Narcissus who loved no one until he saw his own reflection in water and fell in love with that, Cecil saw himself reflected in his photographs of women. Often, by contrivance with mirrors, he appeared in the photographs with them, confounding the reality of who was the viewer and who the viewed. With unconventional zeal he liked to dress as a woman. He thought photographs of himself in dresses for a Cambridge production of *All the Vogue* 'simply marvellous, just as I had expected them to be'. He 'adored maquillage'. In 1930, writing in *Screenland*, he called Hollywood the most artificial place in the world. He said that because it was artificial he enjoyed it a thousand times more.

But with Garbo illusion moved to a different dimension. She acted so convincingly that she seemed more real than reality. She seemed to be the essence from which the image of beauty came. But she wanted to stay hidden. He had heard that she neither looked in mirrors nor viewed rushes of her films. She was glamorous, but eschewed the trappings of glamour, a woman apart, who cherished her solitude and walked in the mountains alone.

He had seen from her films that when she acted love, she cupped men's faces and kissed them thirstily, that she kissed women open-mouthed on the lips, but it was only acting, only a tease. Off-set he had heard that she was friends with men like Adrian, men who were maybe like himself. From Mercedes he learned that she might be lesbian and that she liked to wear trousers, if not in quite the same way as he liked to wear skirts. Behind his photographs of women was a need to reveal something of himself. Were he to track Garbo down and capture her with his camera, what would those images reflect back, in the mirror of his illusions and the flamboyance of his dreams?

3

Mercedes Meets Greta

'Little sister you mustn't waste your tears on me.'
Mata Hari

Mercedes got to Greta Garbo before Cecil. The meeting happened on a Friday in June 1931 on Mercedes' third day in Hollywood. She had gone there with a commission from RKO to write a filmscript called *East River* for Pola Negri. The weekend before she left New York she stayed on Long Island with her actress friends Hope Williams and Tallulah Bankhead and the dancer Marjorie Moss. Tallulah Bankhead proffered a pack of cards and invited them all to make a secret wish. Mercedes wished that she might meet Greta.

Mercedes, who studied cosmic astrology and psychic phenomena, believed herself gifted with prognosticative powers. She was given to having premonitions of impending love, sore throats and financial disaster. She read the *Bhagavad Gita* 'like a parched camel who suddenly comes upon a spring at which he can quench his thirst', and took instruction on mystical matters from an artist called Kahlil Gibran.

Her formative years were turbulent. Her mother, Micaela Hernandez de Alba y de Alba, was descended from the Dukes of Alba, spoke fractured English and was devoutly religious. Her father, a failed Cuban revolutionary, fled to New York as a penniless immigrant, made his money in steamships and married Micaela who had inherited $4 million from a great-uncle. When drunk, he would lament that he had lived his life on a false basis. While Mercedes was still a child, he jumped to his death from a rock face in the Adirondack Mountains.

Mercedes was brought up in America and France. She was the eighth child – there were three boys and five girls – and until she was seven she thought she was a boy:

> Nothing occurred in my life to make me think otherwise. My hair was cut short, I was dressed as a boy and no one ever referred to me as a girl. Judging from some of my photographs at that age and earlier, my family must have had a keen sense of humour about me or none at all. I suspect the latter.

When she realised she was not a boy, she said she raged in bed for three days and ran a high temperature. The family doctor tried to reassure her. As a girl, he said, she had more in common with her – and Cecil's – favourite actress, Lily Elsie. Mercedes was not consoled. Disappointment made her turn to religion and she was sent to a day school run by nuns.

Apart from this confusion over gender, she recounted her childhood as free, undisciplined and surrounded by servants. Bedtimes were arbitrary and dinner might be served at ten at night. She never played with dolls, liked reading and 'unquestionably had a mother complex, a complex often found in boys but less common in girls'. Her attraction to women surfaced early and she left the school under the haze of a scandal involving Sister Isabel, Sister Clara and a fire alarm bell.

A depressive streak moved through her family. Her brother Enriqué gassed himself while kneeling by his bed holding a crucifix. He had aspired to be a poet, was reclusive, dropped out of law school and worked in a bank. And Mercedes suffered from anxiety attacks, toyed with the idea of escape through suicide and kept a small Colt revolver for the day when things became too much.

In her twenties, to please her mother, she married. Her husband Abram Poole, was an artist and an army captain. He was rich, dilettantish and conventional, half-English, half-Dutch and brought up in Chicago. Before they married she told him that she would keep her own name. She spent her wedding night in bed with her mother and then, in the autumn of 1921, fell in love with Eva Le Gallienne.

Eva was twenty and playing Julie in a New York Theater Guild production of Ferenc Molnar's *Liliom*. Her performance was praised by the critics who compared her to Eleonora Duse, whom Mercedes revered. Mercedes wrote a fan note and suggested dinner. A month later Eva wrote to Mercedes that each time she saw her she loved her more and that, 'You is with me always.'

Liliom toured America and their love was fuelled by separation, passionate letters, curtailed meetings, jealousy and a sense of merged identity. In July 1922 Eva wrote of how they had 'poured' themselves into each other so entirely that she had lost the defining boundaries of self. From New Haven she wrote thanking Mercedes for the most wonderful year she had ever had.

In her memoirs Mercedes made scant mention of her husband other than to say that she threw at him a lapis lazuli and sapphire clock from Cartier's. There was, though, painful subterfuge and there were jealous scenes. On 18 October 1923 Eva wrote angrily of the charade that controlled and circumscribed their private lives. It seemed to her, she said, unfair, ridiculous and stupid that Abram should be accepted as Mercedes' partner, 'legally and by right and in the face of the world', while she, Eva, was marginalised and hidden away, unable to show any emotional connection. It made her want to 'proclaim loudly from the housetops' that she belonged 'wholly and utterly' to Mercedes and to flout the conventions that consigned their relationship to silence.

Mercedes, like Cecil in later years, aspired to succeed as a playwright. In Paris, in June 1925, Eva starred in her play *Jehanne d'Arc.* But by March the following year she had come up against Mercedes' insecurity and invasiveness. She cancelled meetings, watched what she said, took another lover, and wrote of her misery at Mercedes' pain. She would, she said, have given anything not to make her suffer.

After the affair ended, Eva gave up her career as a Broadway star, bought a country house at Weston, Connecticut, and, in 1926, founded the Civic Repertory Theater in New York, where she staged classics at popular prices.

Such was the backdrop to Mercedes' dream of meeting Greta. On her second day in Hollywood, in 1931, she lunched at Pickfair, the fantasy home of All the World's Darling, Mary Pickford and of Douglas Fairbanks. She wore white trousers and a white sweater and Elsie Janis drew her aside and said, 'You'll get a bad reputation if you dress this way out here. People are already scandalised at seeing you . . .' The next day Mercedes woke up with

a feeling in my bones that something out of the ordinary was going to happen. The telephone rang. It was an invitation to tea that day at Salka Viertel's. I had heard of her vaguely through Hope Williams . . . She remarked that if I went to tea I might have a 'surprise'. Feeling a bit lost alone in my hotel, I accepted.

Salka Viertel lived at 165 Mabery Road, Santa Monica, with her filmmaker husband Berthold, whom she had married in 1918, and their three sons. From her house she could see the Pacific Ocean, hear the waves hitting the shore, see the hills across the canyon. The atmosphere of her home was a haven for intellectual Europeans who passed through Hollywood between the two world wars. Most of them had short-term contracts in Hollywood, found its commercialism and vulgarity inimical, made a bit of money and got out. Brecht visited: 'Every morning to earn my bread I go to the market where they buy lies,' he said to Salka. Stravinsky, Schoenberg, Max

Reinhardt, Sergei Eisenstein, Lion Feuchtwanger, Thomas Mann, Upton Sinclair, Christopher Isherwood – all worked for the studios and were friends with the Viertels.

Born in Poland in Galicia on the Russian border, Salka Viertel studied acting in Vienna, worked in theatre in Berlin, then went to Hollywood. She first met Greta Garbo in 1930 at a party given by Ernst Lubitsch, who directed *Ninotchka* nine years later. Greta was then twenty-five. The party was for a visiting German filmstar, married to a producer known to Berthold. The women gathered at one end of the room and the men talked shop at the other. Salka saw Greta sitting on a couch next to the star: 'Books have been written about Garbo's beauty, mystery and talent,' she wrote in her memoirs, *The Kindness of Strangers*:

> Her films confirm her magic. There is something unexpected in the loveliness of this face; it is always as if one were seeing it for the first time. She was then at the peak of her success, the critics comparing her to Duse and Sarah Bernhardt.

She was the only woman wearing a plain black suit. The Belgian film director, Jacques Feyder, introduced her to Salka and, as the German star had a billowing dress which took up most of the couch, the three of them went out on the veranda with a bottle of champagne.

Salka had only seen the first of Greta's films, *The Gösta Berling Saga*, made in Sweden in 1924 by Mauritz Stiller. They talked about its premier in Berlin, and of Salka's work in the theatre. Greta was, said Salka,

> intelligent, simple, completely without pose, with a great sense of humor, joking about her inadequate German and English, although she expressed herself very well. Berthold joined us and we talked until late, while Feyder kept refilling our glasses . . .
>
> The next day we had just finished lunch, when the doorbell rang

and in the open window of the entrance appeared the unforgetta-
ble face. In the bright daylight she was even more beautiful. She
wore no make-up, not even powder, only the famous long
eyelashes were blackened with mascara. Her fine skin had a
childlike smoothness; the slender hands were sunburned and
contrary to her reputation I found her well-dressed: the slacks
and shirtwaist were beautifully cut and well-fitting. Gaily she
announced that she had come to continue the conversation of last
night and stayed all afternoon. We went for a short walk on the
beach and then sat in my room. She told me she was pleased that I
had only seen her in *Gösta Berling*, as she did not care much for
her other films. She was very funny, caricaturing the repetitious-
ness of the seduction techniques.

She lived not far from us, and in the evening Berthold and I
walked her home. After we had said goodnight to her, we
exchanged our impressions. What had charmed us was her great
politeness and attentiveness. She seemed hypersensitive, although
of a steely resilience. The observations she made about people
were very just, sharp and objective. 'Probably all that fame
prevents her from living her real life,' I said.

'It's a high price to pay,' said Berthold. She came very often
early in the morning when the beach was deserted, and we took
long walks together.

Later in 1930 Salka acted with Garbo in the German version of
Anna Christie, directed by Jacques Feyder. She was Marty, the
kindhearted drunk, played by Marie Dressler in the American
version of the film. She described Garbo as a 'patient, appreciative
and considerate colleague', who worked hard and precisely, conquered the problem of acting in yet another language and spoke
German without accent.

During shooting Salka came across a biography in German of
Queen Christina of Sweden. She thought the life of Christina would

be an apt role for Greta, who was tired of being cast as a vamp. Christina was brought up as a man, dressed in men's clothes and held heretical views. Greta wanted Salka to write the film. So Salka Viertel's career as her favoured scriptwriter began.

Greta confided in her, thought her wonderful, called her Darling Salka or Salka lilla, depended on her for help and said that the only delightful thing about Hollywood was the fact that Salka was there. 'I am very fond of you to put it very mildly,' she wrote.

Mercedes dressed for tea with Salka in June 1931 in trousers and a sweater. She put on a steel bracelet she had bought in Berlin. Buying it, she had fantasised that it was for Garbo who, she had read, liked heavy bracelets. She took a taxi to Mabery Road and for a while talked alone to Salka. They discussed a mutual actress friend, Eleonora von Mendelssohn, grandchild of the composer and goddaughter of Eleonora Duse, who lived in a castle near Salzburg filled with art treasures and had 'violent fixations on both women and men'.

They were joined by Berthold. Then Salka told Mercedes that Greta Garbo had said she wanted to meet her and was coming round.

Suddenly the doorbell rang. Salka went to open it. I heard a very low voice speaking in German. Of course it was unmistakable although I had only heard it once before – in *Anna Christie*. Salka brought her into the room and introduced me.

It is strange how something that in imagination seems extraordinary can suddenly become very natural when it really happens. To have Greta in the flesh before me instantly seemed the most natural thing in the world. As we shook hands and she smiled at me I felt that I had known her all my life; in fact, in many previous incarnations.

Mercedes thought her more beautiful than in her films. Greta was wearing a white jumper and blue trousers, her feet were bare, her hair straight and shoulder length and she had a white tennis visor pulled down over her eyes. She said to Salka 'I trotteled down to see you,' a line used by Marie Dressler, acting drunk in *Anna Christie*.

'I do not recall too well what we talked about that day', Mercedes wrote in her memoir:

> I was too overwhelmed to record the conversation. I remember discussing Duse with Greta and Salka, and then Salka went upstairs to telephone. Berthold had gone out to the garden to read to Tommy. Greta and I were left on our own. There was a silence, a silence which she could manage with great ease. Greta can always manage a silence. But I felt awkward. Then suddenly she looked at my bracelet and said, 'What a nice bracelet.' I took it off my wrist and handed it to her. 'I bought it for you in Berlin,' I said.

Greta did not stay long. She was in the middle of filming *Susan Lenox, Her Fall and Rise*, with Clark Gable. As usual her presence redeemed a demeaning tale. Her part had all the components that wearied her. She was the abused and exploited daughter, the attraction of all attractions in the circus, the inarticulate and misunderstood lover. She told Mercedes she never went out when working on a film, 'or perhaps I just never go out'. She told her that when she got home she had her dinner in bed.

Mercedes wanted to ask if they might meet again but did not have the courage. From Salka's house she went on to Ivor Novello's. He, Marjorie Moss and others, were sitting on the terrace overlooking the sea.

> Ivor ran down to meet me and putting his arms round me said, 'You look as though you are walking on air.' Upstairs, before dinner, Marjorie said to me, 'What has happened to you? You look different.' 'It is probably the California air,' I answered.

Two days later, on a Sunday, Salka rang Mercedes early in the morning and invited her, at Greta's suggestion, to breakfast at nine thirty. Greta was wearing white shorts and the visor and her legs were brown from the sun. Mercedes noticed that the hairs on her legs were bleached to gold. 'At this second meeting she was more beautiful than I had ever dreamed she could be.' After breakfast Berthold was having a meeting at the Mabery Road house with a producer. Greta and Mercedes wanted to be alone, so they walked to the empty house of Oliver Garrett, a friend of Salka's. It was the corner house on Mabery Road, overlooking the Pacific. Garrett, a scriptwriter for Paramount, was away with his wife and child.

Mercedes described the progress of her affair with Greta in her memoirs, which she gave a title of unconscious ambiguity *Here Lies the Heart*. She made several drafts and it was published in 1960. Of her revelations about Greta she said, 'It gives me great frustration. I couldn't let myself go. I tried to say nothing that she would object to too much . . .' None the less, in it she declared her love for Greta.

At Garrett's house they pushed back the rug in the sitting-room, put his records on the phonograph and danced to 'Daisy You're Driving Me Crazy', 'Ramona', 'Goodnight Sweetheart' and 'Schöne Gigolo'. Mercedes used the Russian word 'toscar', meaning 'yearning' to Greta, and Greta told her the Swedish equivalent. Greta asked Mercedes to go home with her to have lunch, but Mercedes had already agreed to lunch with Pola Negri. 'She tried to detain me but I begged her not to. Just one push and I won't go, I said.' As Mercedes left, Greta picked a flower from the front garden and gave it to her.

The lunch at Pola Negri's house was for a hundred people on a terrace looking out over the sea. Mercedes sat between Basil Rathbone, who was to star with Greta in *Anna Karenina* and Ramon Navarro who starred with her in *Mata Hari*. In the middle of the afternoon a butler told Mercedes she was wanted on the phone by a Mr Toscar. Greta told her to come to her house at 1717

San Vincente Boulevard. Mercedes left Pola Negri's lunch party without explanation and without saying goodbye.

Greta, wearing a black silk dressing-gown and men's bedroom slippers, was waiting for her in the driveway of her home. Her mood was flat.

Only a few hours ago I had seen her radiant. When I came to know her well, I realised how easily her moods and looks could change. She could be gay and look well and within five minutes she would be desperately depressed.

Her mood change was because in the morning she had to go to the studio and continue filming *Susan Lenox*. She could not both work and socialise. 'People take energy from me and I need it for pictures.' She said it was useless talking and trying to explain things and that she wanted simply to sit with Mercedes in silence in the garden by the eucalyptus trees. When the sun went down she told her to go home.

This day she created a pattern between us that we have ever since carried out. Whenever I go to see her and it becomes time to leave she asks me to go home as she did this day. It is a joke between us. She always has to remind me to go home.

The following week Greta finished filming *Susan Lenox* and so invited Mercedes to her house. 'She plucked a handful of blossoms from a small tree, threw them at my feet and opened the door.' Most of the rooms in the house were closed and she occupied only the bedroom, which was simple and without anything personal. 'It seemed a chaste room. It was more like a man's room. I thought it was a sad room.' There was a bed, a desk, a dressing-table and a few straight-backed chairs in heavy oak. Outside the window was a leafless tree which she called her 'winter tree', saying that it comforted her when her homesickness for Sweden became unbearable. She imagined that the cold had made it leafless and that soon it would be covered in snow.

They ate bread and cheese and drank milk by moonlight in the room, then drove in Greta's old Packard car to the coast at Casa del Mare. They walked in the mountains, looked out over the moonlit sea and stayed until dawn, then went back to Greta's house.

Forty-eight hours later Greta asked Mercedes to visit her early in the morning. She told her she was tired after filming and was going alone to a remote house on an island on a lake in the Sierra Nevadas, and that she did not want people to know where she had gone.

'But what shall I do without you?' I asked. 'Take me with you. I'll chuck the studio.' She shook her head. 'I am ready to leave and we have to do at least 200 miles today.'

James was going to drive Greta to the island. She had at first hired him to clean her windows and because he was silent and uninvasive she employed him as her driver and handyman. He was tall, thin and taciturn, evinced no curiosity, passed no comment and drove slowly. The smallest of jobs took him a long time to complete. Greta would say, 'James you're very lazy' and his reply was 'Yes ma'am,' in a drawling voice.

Mercedes watched them drive away then, disconsolate, went home. She was living at that time at 121842 Rockingham Road on the corner of Sunset Avenue in a house with four bedrooms, a big living-room, two servants' rooms, a large garden and no charm. She shared it with John Colton, a scriptwriter drawn to a sleazy side of homosexual life. Mercedes would rescue him from speak-easies and dives:

In the dead of night I would get out of bed, take a taxi and go out to find him. I walked where angels fear to tread and sometimes I had to argue with gangsters to persuade them to let me take John home.

After Greta left, Mercedes heard that MGM were shelving *East River* and that she should stop work on the script. She would be kept on the payroll for ten weeks until her contract expired.

Two days later Greta phoned to say that she had seen the island, that the scenery of the mountains, lake and hut were beautiful beyond words, but that she did not want to enjoy it all alone. She was, she said, coming back for Mercedes. So, with James, she motored for three days back to Beverly Hills from Nevada, through the Mojave desert with the heat at 120 degrees.

John Colton made a supper of roast chicken and champagne for Greta and the next day she and Mercedes set off again in Mercedes' car, with James driving. They planned to cross the desert at night to avoid the heat. The temperature went as high as 140 degrees and the sand in the desert wind cut their faces. They stopped two nights at small hotels along the route, and on the third day began the climb into the Sierra Nevada mountains.

From high in the range they saw Silver Lake between two mountain peaks. Greta pointed out their little island and the simple log cabin on it. It belonged to Wallace Beery (who was to act with her in *Grand Hotel* in 1932) and he had given her the keys for six weeks. The lake was fourteen miles long and three miles wide and the island was half a mile out from the west shore and surrounded by snow-covered mountains. They reached it by rowing-boat which James helped them load with provisions. Greta rowed. James drove back across the desert with instructions to return in six weeks and to tell no one where they were.

'How to describe the next six enchanted weeks?' Mercedes wrote, 'Even recapturing them in memory makes me realize how lucky I am to have had them. Six perfect weeks out of a lifetime. This is indeed much.'

They spent the time swimming, rowing, sunbathing and walking in the mountains. Sometimes at night they went out in the boat and drifted on the lake in the silence. They bought their provisions from a lumbercamp a few miles away and the lumberjacks thought they were schoolgirls on a holiday. Mercedes wrote in eulogious prose about these six perfect weeks:

No one can really know Greta unless they have seen her as I saw her there in Silver Lake. She is a creature of the elements. A creature of wind and storms and rocks and trees and water . . .

There in the Sierra Nevadas she used to climb ahead of me, and with her hair blown back, her face turned to the wind and sun, she would leap from rock to rock on her bare Hellenic feet. I would see her above me, her face and body outlined against the sky, looking like some radiant, elemental, glorious god and goddess melted into one.

She wrote about them towards the end of her life when Greta had refused all contact with her. She said that there were no cross words between them and that Greta was happy. Her snapshots showed Greta wearing only shorts and a beret, looking sunburned and strapping, or pegging out bits of washing on a line. Perhaps they were perfect weeks for Greta too. She was free from the unreality of Hollywood, the politicking and the commercialism, the constrictions of wigs, ornate costumes and face paint. She did not have to pretend to be in love with Clark Gable or Charles Bickford, or be a vamp, or get her tongue round lines from *Susan Lenox* like 'Rodney when will this painful love of ours ever end?' There were no photographers hiding in the trees to plague her, or journalists among the lumberjacks. And Mercedes was besotted, protective, determined to please and to do whatever she was bid.

I want to defend her, to protect her, to take her part. This may be

because there is a strange sadness in her, underlying everything she does. This sadness is lurking beneath the surface, even at her gayest moments . . . It awakens in me a great sense of compassion – a readiness to forgive her any shortcoming – a desire to take upon my own shoulders her slightest pain or sorrow.

'Wasn't one summer all you wanted?' Garbo says to Robert Taylor in *Camille*. To which, of course, the implicit answer is no. Mercedes' words, 'Six perfect weeks out of a lifetime. This is indeed much,' were written thirty years after that summer at Silver Lake. But six weeks are not very many out of a lifetime, when it comes to love.

The terms were Greta's. She had no desire to share the substance of Mercedes' life. Nor did she invite her to share the substance of her own. Her dislike of invasiveness was absolute and she responded to the sense of it with silence and exclusion. 'To write of Greta,' wrote Mercedes

and things connected with her is the most difficult task . . . No one knows better than I how much she dislikes being discussed but I cannot write my life and leave her out of it. I have deeply considered and weighed the problem and it has caused me untold anguish and anxiety . . . But no one can write an autobiography without bringing back on the stage of her life people who have played major roles.

James came to take them back to Hollywood. Greta panicked at the thought of returning to the studios. She was going back to star, after a brief interval, in *Mata Hari*. She left Silver Lake as if for the firing squad. James sounded the car horn from across the lake. She packed her things and rowed Mercedes to the mainland.

Mercedes merged into Greta's life as much as was allowed. She helped her move from San Vincente Boulevard to a large house in

Rockingham Road, half a block away from her own. There was a tennis court, a large garden, with pear trees in the front and a wire fence all round it and a clear view over the hills and the Canyon. The dining-room was panelled in dark wood and in the living-room was a picture of a caged lion. Salka thought the house gloomy.

Greta spent time with Mercedes in the brief interval before work on *Mata Hari*, her fifteenth film, began. Their days started early. Soon after sunrise she walked down to Mercedes' house and whistled under her window. They played tennis, swam, took picnic lunches to the beach near Malibu, hired horses from the Bel Air Riding School and rode in the hills. Most days they walked six or seven miles and sometimes ten, through wild country to the San Fernando Valley. James then came and picked them up in the car. They went to bed early, never much later than nine. 'We used to laugh when we read and heard about the so-called night life of Hollywood.'

Mercedes then rented the house next to Greta's. It had the same view looking toward the hills and over the Canyon. Her ostensible reason for moving was that she did not like the 'speak-easy proprietors and various underworld characters' whom John Colton brought back to Sunset Avenue. She felt unsafe, had no privacy and did not want Greta to be in such company. Jobless, she had no reason to be in Hollywood apart from her desire to be with Greta. She went with her to Adrian's strange house on Whitley Heights, liked his looks and found him sympathetic. They dined on the patio with its tropical plants, parrot and monkeys. They looked at the sketches for Greta's costumes for *Mata Hari* and Mercedes suggested that in the final scene, where Mata Hari is shot, Greta should wear a long black cape and draw her hair straight back.

She sought, in matters large and small, to appear intrinsic to Greta's life. In the drafts of her memoirs she gave many examples of her apparently beneficent influence:

[Greta] had an appalling habit of burning insects she found in the house or in the grass . . . The first time I saw her do this we were sitting on her lawn and she found a tick on her leg. It was trying to dig in and bury its head as they do. I saw her pick it off her leg, strike a match and burn it. My stomach turned over. 'How can you take a life so easily?' I asked. 'These insects have just as much right to live as you have. Why don't you just carry them off to some other part of the grass? You don't have to kill them, much less torture them by burning. They probably have a large family waiting for them somewhere. Have you ever thought of that?'

Greta said she had never thought much about the insect world at all, but that now she would change her ways. Not long after this she telephoned me quite late one night to say she had found a spider in her bed and had carefully picked it up and put it out of the window. 'Bravo,' I said. 'Now you are a reformed murderer.'

Mercedes saw Greta as masculine, Amazonian, heroic, with a genius for acting and a beauty that disturbed. She wanted it to be known that she chose Greta's clothes and acting roles and influenced her career and thinking. She wanted to serve her in every way, to wield influence with a kind of giving that was more like taking.

'Garbo In Pants', declared a newspaper article in 1931. It showed a picture of Greta and Mercedes in Hollywood Boulevard wearing chappish clothes. 'Innocent bystanders gasped in amazement to see Greta Garbo and Mercedes de Acosta striding swiftly along Hollywood Boulevard dressed in men's clothes.' At her house Mercedes took snaps of Greta wearing men's shoes, a shirt and tie and serious trousers. She seemed to like the irony of suggesting to the world that its symbol of allure was lesbian.

Mercedes tried to live through Greta but her own career at that time was bleak. She had no work. Greta suggested to Irving Thalberg, MGM's production chief, that Mercedes should write a script for her. Thalberg gave Mercedes a tenuous contract for a script of her choice. She wrote in an office at the studio. At five in the evening she and Greta would meet and go to the beach or walk in the hills. Mostly Greta was uncommunicative and brooding over work. The films she starred in in the early thirties were shot in four or five weeks under great pressure.

Mercedes came up with *Desperate*, resonant with her preoccupations with gender and Greta. 'One must learn to live desperately,' is a line from Nietzsche, she told Thalberg. Greta was to be Erik Chanler, who outmans the men. Erik's divorced parents hate each other and vie for her love. Her father is American, her mother Norwegian and she must choose between them. Mother, fearing rejection, jumps from a cliff and is dying as Erik flies to her. 'We see Erik's face in the plane,' Mercedes wrote:

> One feels in her a strange wild nature with the conflicting struggles of her mother and father combined . . . One feels in her sadness and gaiety, sanity and neuroticism, vitality and listlessness, reticence and recklessness, shyness and daring, all these mixed in a contradiction that spends her strength and throws her back into herself . . . In her eyes one already sees the door that comes from the soul rather than from outward events – unmoved eyes, holding in their depths that look of eternity.

With mother dead, Erik turns into a tearaway, drives fast cars, climbs mountains and gambles for high stakes. She is served by a toyboy, Toto. 'Isn't he sweet?' she says to her father.

'Are you in love with him?' asks Sloane.

'Love? Love? What quaint Victorian terms you use, father.'

Mother is the only one she loves.

In lukewarm deference to Hollywood, Mercedes has Erik meet Stephen Train, 'a great athlete'. Erik tells him he is a 'very straight stick' and that 'only as one deviates from straightness does one find beauty'. She downs her brandy and carts him off, with Toto, to a squalid dive. Toto gets killed in a drugs' deal – scoring drugs with Erik's money. Erik is implicated and, to escape trouble, dresses in men's clothes. This cross-dressing was the dramatic significance of the story:

> In making herself into a boy, shedding her skin as it were, she dissolves her whole identity. From now on she is taken as a boy by everyone with whom she comes in contact.

Greta was to wear heavy corduroy trousers and boots, or 'perfect evening clothes, her hair brushed and varnished into smoothness'. Women were to sense her 'unfathomable allure'. It was a conundrum of disguise which Mercedes found compelling. She had wished to be a boy and was distressed at being a girl. She loved Greta and sought to merge into her life. Now she aspired to 'dissolve' Garbo's 'whole identity' and show her on screen as the irresistible boy she herself had wanted to be.

Thalberg hated *Desperate*. He ditched the script and fired Mercedes. He was not convinced that Garbo dressed as a man would boost box office takings and he foresaw interminable wrangles and complaints from the censor, the Hays office, the women's clubs and religious groups. There had already been trouble enough with Garbo's films. *Susan Lenox, Her Fall and Rise* was first banned by the British censor, then had 125 feet of film cut out of it. And *Mata Hari* was condemned as blasphemous when Ramon Navarro, in the part of a Russian general, says to Garbo:

> 'I love you as one adores sacred things – God, country, honour, you.'
> 'I come last?'
> 'No.'
> 'That's how you said it.'
> 'You come before anything.'

'Anything?'

'Yes.'

Such hubris was as nothing compared to parading her as a man.

Mercedes got nowhere in Hollywood. She could not distance herself sufficiently from her own preoccupations to play the Hollywood game. Something mawkish and humourless stymied all she wrote. And yet she tried in her script to serve Garbo's haunting, cool androgyny, her aloofness which mirrored the elusive, border-lines of self, neither male nor female, which was at the heart of her allure.

After the *Desperate* debacle, Greta told her she would like to play Dorian Gray. The theme was not pursued with Thalberg. As Mercedes' career chances waned, she took to fasting and going off into the hills to meditate on spiritual matters. Greta called her 'a crazy mystic Spaniard'.

They spent Christmas 1931 together. Greta drew the curtains on the bright Californian sky and pretended that snow and Sweden were outside. They decorated a Christmas tree, ate roast goose by candlelight and exchanged presents. Greta gave Mercedes a raincoat, rubber boots and a sou'wester so that they could walk together in stormy weather. On 30 December 1931 Greta began filming in *Grand Hotel*. Filming lasted until 19 February 1932. Retakes were completed by 29 March 1932 and then Cecil met her for the first time.

4

Cecil Meets Greta

'Last night I didn't know you at all. Who are you really?'
Grand Hotel

That March, Cecil was again in Hollywood photographing stars: Marlene Dietrich, the Marx Brothers, Joan Crawford. He again implored Howard Strickling to arrange for him to photograph Garbo. Strickling told him that she had gone into the mountains to rest, that she had left no address, that when she came back she would be busy with retakes on *Grand Hotel*.

Once more Cecil resigned himself to disappointment. She was as ever elusive and Strickling seemed to have no influence over her. Then, for his last weekend in Hollywood, Edmund Goulding, the director of *Grand Hotel*, invited him to stay at his house. Cecil jumped at the offer. He had heard that sometimes, on a Sunday, Greta called there for supper.

A few months previously Goulding had married Mercedes' friend, Marjorie Moss. John Gilbert was best man at the wedding. The marriage lasted a year. Before it, Goulding lived alone in a house by the sea. He was British and wrote novels, had a play, *Dancing Mothers*, on Broadway for eighteen months and arrived in Hollywood as an MGM scriptwriter in 1925. In 1927 he directed Garbo, with John Gilbert, in *Love*, the silent movie of *Anna Karenina*. He called her 'director proof'. 'No director has any right to take any bows for any performance of Garbo's . . . she knows better what to do in a scene than all the directors rolled into one.' He said that in the studio she was nervous, 'actually trembling, hating onlookers', but that at the first click of the camera she 'poured forth Garbo into the lens'. He said that in conversation she laughed frequently, but talked seriously, with long silences, 'looking at you and expecting you to know what she means without speaking'. She was always on time, certain of every scene, required little rehearsal or reshooting, was businesslike, untemperamental and had a capacity for taking pains and concentrating.

Joan Crawford co-starred in *Grand Hotel* and their dressing-rooms adjoined. They do not speak in the film and they spoke only once during the making of it. 'We would pass in the corridor,' Joan Crawford said in a later interview:

but we were all told by publicity that she was terribly shy and she'd rather go through the bushes than take the path to her dressing-room. And she worked until five every day on the set and then I started at six. I'd go and rehearse when she'd leave the set and I'd work until, oh, one or two in the morning . . . Anyway, we overlapped and she was coming up the steps and I was standing there with a friend of mine . . . and I said, 'Oh here she comes. Stand back, she doesn't like to have anyone on the stairway with her.' And we stood back like two kids hiding in the corridor! And she came up and I thought I'll scoot by her real fast when she turns the corner and I misjudged it. I mistimed it. I got down two steps too soon and she just came round and she *grabbed* me and this *magnificent face* looked into mine and I looked up at her and she held my face in her hands and she said, 'I am so sorry we are not working together. It's so sad; in the same film and no scenes. Wha-at a peety. Perhaps some day soon.' My knees got so weak, being so close to this *magnificent* woman . . . Oh golly, it's the only time we ever spoke.

She said that if ever she was going to be a lesbian, that was the moment.

Cast in *Grand Hotel* as Gruskinskaya, a faded Russian ballerina, Garbo, with her tombstone shoulders, angular body and large feet, looked odd in a tutu. The part was intended to suggest the passing of the Russian Imperial Ballet and of all that was Tsarist and Grand in Russia. She said she wanted to try to be an ageing ballerina but the constraints of Hollywood insisted that she remain beautiful and young.

Clark Gable, who had acted with her in *Susan Lenox*, was originally cast as the hotel thief, the Baron Gaigern who saves her life and with whom she falls in love. He dropped out at the last minute and the part was taken by John Barrymore who made an unconvincing villain. He had his chin strapped, Greta told Cecil, to make his profile look taut. He called on Mercedes one night during the making of the film and told her he was in awe of Garbo.

In the Gouldings' Spanish-style house, Cecil was given a turret bedroom, reached by circular stairs. On the Saturday before he met Greta, he drove a hired car to the Army and Navy Stores, bought a white kid jacket and 'vast quantities', at negligible cost, of football vests, exotic shoes and scanty little shorts in all colours and in white sharkskin.

On the Sunday, Greta phoned Goulding. She heard Cecil was there and did not want to meet him. 'He talks to newspapers,' she said. That week in the syndicated papers, Cecil had written about her temperamental moods, her solitariness, her simplicity, her lack of make-up and her legs. Crushed with defeat and dejection, at this latest rebuff, he tried many times to phone Mercedes so that they might meet and at least talk about their idol. Mercedes was out. Cecil slept, took a long bath and dressed himself in the white kid jacket, the scanty sharkskin shorts and new white shoes and socks. When he looked out of the bedroom window he saw Greta sitting cross-legged on a white garden seat, smoking a cigarette and talking to the Gouldings. She was suntanned and wearing all white too – a thick sweater, shorts, and an eggshell cap on her head with her hair tucked under it.

If a unicorn had suddenly appeared in the later afternoon light of this ugly, ordinary garden, I could have been neither more surprised nor more amazed by the beauty of this exotic creature.

He said his heart was thumping as he went down the turret stairs to meet her.

In the months preceding this longed-for meeting with Greta Garbo, Cecil's heart had thumped for different reasons. To his private diary he confided details of another love, unaired in *Gentlewoman, Eve* and *Vogue*.

To the world, however, he paraded his fascination with beautiful women and with Greta Garbo above all. Beauty, he wrote, 'the most important word in the dictionary . . . is art, endeavour, perfection, the right, the true, the good.' His *Book of Beauty*, 'a collection of the loveliest ladies I have ever seen', was published by Duckworth in November 1930. In it he said that his earliest childhood recollection was of a lady dancing on a table at Maxims. He reiterated his obsession with dresses and with his sisters: 'I stare a lot, watching the varying light of day and night upon them.' He wrote of Bab's small pointed breasts and 'did not know that anyone could look so liltingly lyrical in a bathing costume as she'.

But the saccharine in his *Book of Beauty* was laced with more than a dash of vitriol. He did a drawing of Lady Lavery without a nose, said of Lady Cunard that she had 'perfect legs and sparrow-small feet', that Tallulah Bankhead had eyes like a snake, cheeks like huge acid-pink peonies, eyelashes like burnt matches and a mouth like an 'evil rosebud as shining as Tiptree's strawberry jam'. He talked about eyebrows like tapering mousetails, knotty noses made up of little lumps and said that the Countess Howe had a complexion like icing sugar on a birthday cake. He said that Gladys Cooper had nostrils like a horse and that Mrs Dudley Ward had the ludicrous charm of a male impersonator. Virginia Woolf he called frail and crisp like a dead leaf, which is what his drawing of her resembled. He said she wore cotton gloves and hatpins and exuded an atmosphere of musk and old lace.

Greta Garbo he described as perfection beside whom all other beauties paled. 'There is no one with a more magnetic, romantic or exotic personality . . . all the beauties of today grow their hair like hers . . .' But his admiration seemed mixed with contempt. He said that she had pointed features in a round face, that her mouth was wide and knife-like, her teeth large and square and that she had a slightly insane look.

The deluxe edition of the book cost three guineas, the ordinary, twenty-five shillings. Duckworth targeted customers and sent Mayfair dwellers a circular of the names of those who appeared in it. The reviewer in the *Observer* said the book would please all those who ate chocolates during the performance of grand opera. The artist, John Piper, in *The Nation and Athenaeum* called it immoral, the drawings insensitive, the photographs cluttered with 'modern' fragments and the whole thing 'a monument of vulgar advertising'. Virginia Woolf, more alert to misogyny than most of the women on whom Cecil focused, wrote of her perturbation in the same paper:

Sir – I hope you will acquit me of any desire to ventilate a merely personal grievance if I ask you to publish the following facts. A book has just been issued of drawings and photographs by Cecil Beaton. To my surprise I find that two sketches of myself are included. My permission was not asked. I have never had the honour of meeting Mr Beaton. He has twice kindly asked me to sit to him and I have twice, I hope politely, refused. The matter is insignificant in itself, but I venture to ask you to give publicity to these facts by way of protest against a method of book-making which seems to me as questionable as it is highly disagreeable to one at least of its victims.

Yours &c

Virginia Woolf

29 November 1930

In a letter to a friend she called him a hateful man who gatecrashed smart parties. Cecil's reply did not improve her opinion of him:

Sir – I regret that the inclusion of two sketches of Mrs Virginia Woolf in *The Book of Beauty* should have been disagreeable to her, since I have an equal admiration for her gifts and beauty.

I must point out however that in such matters the victim is seldom – and should never – be consulted. Which caricaturist ever asks his victim for permission to include him in a book of caricatures – all the less reason to protect against inclusion in a Book of Beauty?

In fact, Mrs Woolf's complaint should be addressed to her Creator, who made her, rather than to me. Since possibly I am the last from church, may I remind her—

All things bright and beautiful

All creatures great and small

All things wise and wonderful

The Lord God made them all

Yours &c

Cecil Beaton

4 December 1930

But it was Cecil, not the Lord God, who had drawn the brittle pictures and written the malicious prose. He purported to be presenting beauty, not caricature. And what Virginia Woolf was protesting about and recoiling from was not the fact of her own existence, but of being crudely portrayed against her wish. It was the same sense of invasion as cut into Greta Garbo's life and made her say to the photographers waiting at jetties and to the journalists hungry for crumbs of news, that she wanted to be left alone.

Beverley Nichols gave Cecil's *Book of Beauty* a page of comment in the *Daily Mail*. He seemed as muddled as Cecil as to quite why it was that women should be deemed beautiful:

> Why should an oval surface, surmounted with a matty substance, pierced with two dark holes, slashed with a red opening, decorated with a thing so odd that 'nose' is the only word for it – why should this singular collection of shapes and colour arouse men to a frenzy of delight or despair? Why should this astounding patch-work be capable of launching a thousand ships?

Beverley was another of those with whom Cecil liked to talk, in the dark hours, in New York hotel rooms, where 'intimacies spread like fire in a wind'. Beverley had a face twitch and liked a drink or three. He was the author of *Down the Garden Path* and *A Thatched Roof* and a regular contributor to page 2 of the *Sunday Chronicle*. He wrote such articles as 'I Danced with the Queen', 'Why did the Lord Chamberlain tell me to watch my step?' and 'Fear drives a Novelist from her bath'. He had confided his loneliness to Cecil and his unfulfilled desire for love with someone of his own sex. In the meantime he went to male brothels and various 'suitable' parts of town to pick up sailors, marines and guardsmen. He went into poetical effusions about an electrician who when naked looked like a Greek god. He said that Cecil's rival as a stage designer, Oliver Messel, was homosexual, as were Noël Coward, Somerset Maugham, Avery Hopwood and Edward Knoblock and nearly all of Cecil's friends.

'I'm not ashamed of it, I'm proud of it,' Beverley told him. 'Sex is everything in life – the trees, the flowers, everything exists through sex.' Some people, he said, were born one way and others another. He told Cecil that he adored his sexual experiences, that they were the most thrilling thing in his life, that all his work was influenced by sex and that were he castrated, he would lose all will to live. Cecil, Beverley thought, was not living life to the full.

This was something Cecil tried to do when he fell in love with Peter Watson in the summer of 1930 – a love he confided to his diary, letters, and to 'nearly all his friends'. In that summer he also signed the lease on a two hundred-year-old farmhouse, built of lilac-coloured brick, in three acres of ground in an isolated part of Wiltshire at Berwick St John, five miles from Shaftesbury. Set in a combe, protected by an arcade of beech trees with the downs beyond like a vast park, the house was in disrepair, with crumbling rafters, no floors or plumbing and covered in weeds and nettles. The rent was £50 a year.

An Austrian architect, Michael Rosenauer, a friend of Anita Loos, helped Cecil carry out the renovations. Over the months and years that followed Cecil created a stage-set of a home that reflected the camp, inspired gaiety at which he so excelled. 'Ashcombe – such a *lovely* name! It sounds sequestered – the haunt of wild birds and strange sad Dawn skylines . . . I *ache* to show you my orchids,' Cecil's strange, sad friend, Stephen Tennant, wrote to him that year.

Cecil had two bathrooms and four bedrooms put in. There was a separate cottage, a separate studio, glasshouses, a tennis court, a kitchen garden, a rose garden. The house demanded from him a labour of love and reflected back to him his best perception of himself. He filled the place with life-sized cupids, silver and gilt candlesticks, silver bird cages, glass balls, engraved mirrors, shell pictures, crumbling Italian console tables, stone statues called Castor and Pollux, and plaster casts of bits of his own anatomy. The studio curtains were of Hessian covered with three hundred thousand pearl buttons. They were more expensive than antique Genoese velvet. He saw the decor as a revolt from the conventionality of his childhood home in which no colour seemed clean and bright. He described one perfect June day when he rested in the grass on the downs and surveyed his house and grounds: 'I sat gazing and enjoying the knowledge that this small treasure was my own and that at any rate one dream had come true.'

Other dreams were of making love with Peter Watson, photographing the British royal family and marrying Greta Garbo.

His *pièce de resistance* was his bedroom. He called it the circus room. It was in garish colours and filled with baroque emblems and flowered mirrors. Larger than life-size paintings of circus performers featured in its niches. Oliver Messel, Rex Whistler and Gerald Berners helped paint them one weekend. Rex Whistler painted a fat woman, Lord Berners a Columbine with performing dogs, Oliver Messel a naked black man with a pink ostrich feather on his head. Whistler also designed Cecil's four-poster bed which was then made by Savages of King's Lynn, circus roundabout makers. Neptune was at the bedhead, 'flanked by Cupids and subaqueous plants', the canopy was supported by brass barley-sugar posts. Cecil regretted that the bed could not be made to revolve to the sound of steam-organ music.

The room delighted him. On that Sunday in 1932 when he met Greta Garbo at the Gouldings' house he showed her pictures of it in the hope that she would one day share it with him.

Cecil found rich, successful people irresistible and courted them as friends. Art and life were part of the same surface. He never lived at Ashcombe, or anywhere, in an intimate relationship with anyone, but parties were perpetual. The famous flitted through and he led the gaiety and masquerade.

At weekends he arrived with his car stacked with flowers, bought from Covent Garden, for the house and prepared the menus with Mrs Noble, his housekeeper. 'The place is a paradise for me,' he wrote, 'and I have loved each party more than the last.' It was all that he adored – pretty people, charades, impersonations and dressing-up

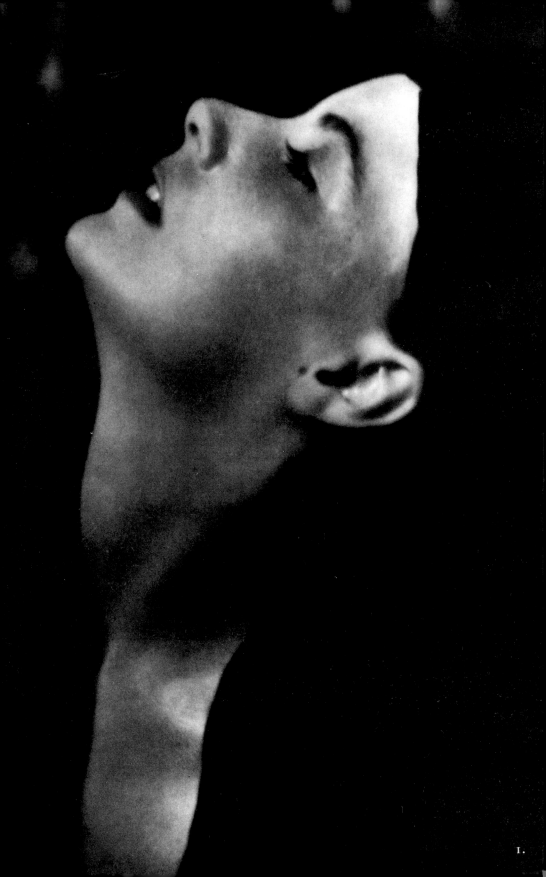

2.

CECIL'S 'GREATEST AMBITION' WAS TO PHOTO-
GRAPH GRETA. HERS WAS THE PERFECT GAZE,
THE IMAGE OF BEAUTY HE SOUGHT TO REFLECT.

1. Greta Garbo.
Photo by Arnold Genthe, New York, 1925.

2. Double enigma. Self-portrait by Cecil with
mirror and camera, c.1935

3. Greta Garbo for *The Kiss.*
Photo by Clarence Sinclair Bull, 1927.

4. Greta Garbo.
Photo by Arnold Genthe, New York, 1925.

4.

6.

CECIL TEASED WITH SELF-IMAGES OF DISPLAYED
AND CONCEALED IDENTITY. GRETA DEFIED THE
CAMERA'S INTRUSION INTO THE WORLD BEHIND
HER EYES.

5. 'Cecil Beaton by himself'.
Self-portrait as pierrot, c. 1920.

6. Greta Garbo for *Susan Lenox*.
Photo by Clarence Sinclair Bull, 1931.

7. Cecil festooned with photos of himself.
Study by Paul Tanqueray, 1937.

8. Greta as pierrot. Dressed and photographed
by Cecil at the Plaza Hotel, New York, 1946.

games. At his parties he changed his costume half a doze
evening. Ashcombe became a stage set for the *fêtes-cha*
entertainments of Cecil's set in the years that led up to
World War. Conventional neighbours wondered what
was coming to.

But though Cecil created the setting, he could not provide a
commensurate script. Nothing much happened at Ashcombe when
the finery was back in the dressing-up chest and the *fêtes-champêtres*
were through. No everyday life could equal the decor, nor other
identity impinge. There were scenes in the circus bed, but no real
passion. Strange people came and went, but they were only passing
through. When Cecil tried, on several occasions and with real
ambition, to write plays he failed – the characters wooden, the
content fragile, the dialogue false. And in his life when, on four
occasions – once with Greta Garbo – he tried to find a partner, the
attempts failed.

In the summer of 1930, while builders worked on Ashcombe, he
joined Anita Loos in Vienna for his summer holidays. Oliver Messel
who had been working with Rex Whistler on C. B. Cochran's Revue
was there, accompanied by Peter Watson, a gangling young man
with, said Cecil, the face of a charming codfish. Going down in the
hotel lift, Peter gave Cecil a look – 'a glance of sympathy, of
amusement, it may have been a wink, but it did its work, it went
straight to my heart and from that moment I was hypnotized by
him, watching every gesture of his heavy hands, the casual languid
way he walked.'

Though Cecil wanted the world to know of his quest for Greta
Garbo, his private desire was for Peter Watson. He felt himself to be
terribly in love, 'Oh how I doted!' The form of this love, which
lasted for four years, was a kind of sexual hankering, a longing for
lovemaking that never happened. He wore the same clothes and
scent as Watson, copied his mannerisms and voice and spirited away

his socks and handkerchiefs so that he might have them as his own. His love became another dimension of mirror image, reflection and self-reflection. He wrote screeds about his tortured feelings for Peter Watson, from which no picture of the other man emerged.

Peter Watson was tall, aesthetic, world-weary and rich. (In November 1930, Nancy Mitford wrote to her brother 'Peter Watson has bought a coral-coloured Rolls Royce inlaid with gems & with *fur* seats. I love him quite a lot but it is no use.') His father, Sir George, marketed margarine and made a fortune – which Peter inherited shortly before Cecil met him. Peter grew up in a large house by the river Thames, went to Eton and Oxford and at the time of his involvement with Cecil led a lightweight life. After a few years Cecil's *Book of Beauty* world bored him, and he withdrew from it and used his fortune to support the contemporary arts. With Cyril Connolly and Stephen Spender, he started *Horizon* in 1939 and he gave financial backing to the founding of London's Institute of Contemporary Arts. 'What had formerly been spent chez Charvet, Cartier, or in the Rolls-Royce salerooms, now went towards sponsoring *Horizon*, the ICA and similar causes.' Early in their careers, he bought paintings by Graham Sutherland, John Craxton, Lucian Freud, Jankel Adler, Robert Colquhoun and Robert MacBryde. Pavel Tchelitchew, Christian Bérard and Francis Bacon were among his friends. His portrait, by Giacometti, is in the Museum of Modern Art in New York. He was fond of Cecil, but not attracted to him, physically or intellectually.

After the thunderbolt of Peter Watson's glance or wink, Cecil travelled with him and Oliver Messel to Venice. Anita Loos stayed in Vienna. Peter caught a cold. Cecil brought him flowers and fussed over him, but it was Oliver who shared Peter's bed. Back in England they all spent weekends at Ashcombe. 'You have infused your domain with a very special kind of cynicism and atmosphere,' wrote Peter to Cecil. There were 'tragedies of jealousy' with Peter and

Oliver behind a locked bedroom door and Cecil speechless with pain and unable to breathe. Determined to lure Peter away from Oliver, he asked him to travel to New York, Mexico and Hollywood. Peter had not been to America and agreed. Cecil was to take photographs for Condé Nast and to write about such matters as the six most beautiful women in the movies, to finance his own side of the trip.

They sailed from Southampton in January 1931 on the SS *Aquitania*. The trip lasted three months and began as it was to continue. Peter almost missed the boat because he had spent the night with Oliver, and Cecil waited by the quayside, anxious and weepy. 'Titania was never so besotted of her Bottom than I with my travelling companion,' he wrote of the sea voyage. He watched Peter night and day, observing every detail of his appearance – his tiny hips, his long 'flagpole' legs, his flat wide shoulders. He documented his every move with an obsession that he was later to transfer to Greta Garbo. It was, he professed in his diary, heaven on earth to share a cabin with Peter, to dress together in the mornings and evenings, to play the gramophone, to have baths together.

He wished that the sea voyage would last for ever. But Bottom, though captive, was not in the least besotted with Titania. He spent most of the journey asleep. There was tussling on the bunks, shared baths and friendly goodnight kisses, but that was it. 'No real spark except on my side,' wrote Cecil. Once, he gave careless voice to his wishes and said, ' "One day when we are lovers" . . . Peter was obviously annoyed. It rankled.'

Cecil described himself as 'the proverbial unrequited lovelorn governess, quivering and blanching' at the mention of Peter's name. His self-portrayal, in his diary entries about his love for Peter Watson, was on a par with how he looked when dressed as the leading lady for the Cambridge Footlights revue – a girl with all the social graces but not every man's dream of a sexy time. He wrote of the danger of giving 'everything'. 'The more you do, the more they loathe and despise you.' He thanked God that he had not gone the full length in 'abandoning' himself to his man.

Peter Watson had no particular interest in Titanias, or governesses, or girls of any sort. He liked going to bed with men. And nor was Cecil's gender bending as simplistic as it seemed. He also wanted to *become* Peter Watson as in time, when he transferred his obsession, he sought in a sense to become Greta Garbo.

Alone in the state cabin of the SS *Aquitania* Cecil postured in front of the mirror wearing Peter's clothes . . . 'his jacket is displayed on me. I feel the thickness of the bulge of his handkerchief in the breast pocket.' In many of his photographs, Cecil's narcissism depended on merged image. In photos, using mirrors, he appeared to blend with his ostensible sitters. In the mirror in the ship's cabin it was a salve to unrequited love to see himself reflected as Peter whom he adored.

In New York they had a grand suite at the Ambassador Hotel. Flowers arrived for Peter from Cecil – lilies of the valley and violets. Cecil introduced him to Fred and Adèle Astaire and to the people whom he knew. But Peter kept his distance. He ducked from dinner parties at the last minute, leaving Cecil to go alone, went out on his own without saying where, picked up men leaving Cecil to stew with jealousy and spoke of his social plans in the singular, whereas Cecil always said 'we'.

In Mexico Cecil doted, wept and got on Peter's nerves. Peter intimated that he was falling in love, but would not say with whom. He walked ahead on the beach. Cecil ran to catch up. He bathed alone in the sea. Cecil followed him. Sometimes they shared a bed with butterfly kisses, tickling, wrestling and hugging, but one night they fought in earnest over who should put out the light. Cecil asked Peter, 'Please put out the light. I always do it.' Peter would not. They fought on the floor, wrecked the room in a battle that lasted much of the night and the management of the hotel complained. Peter threatened to return to Oliver and the mood the next day was sour. 'We are not very friendly in spite of and partly because of my doting,' wrote Cecil.

'And then the torment of the last night in Mexico.' As Cecil was packing to leave for Hollywood, Peter said that he could not make the morning plane trip. Cecil, unlike Peter, could not afford to waste the £25 for the ticket. In an 'agony' of depression, he packed and left alone in the cold light of dawn. Four days later Peter arrived in Hollywood by train. Cecil drunkenly told of his suffering from unrequited love. Peter stroked Cecil's hair in sympathy, but insisted on separate hotel rooms.

Despite these dramas Cecil produced innovative work for *Vogue*. In Hollywood, when photographing filmstars, he incorporated the technical structures of the studios into his portraits – the asbestos-lined doors, the scaffolding, the festoons of chains and electric wires. But such work as he did was escape from the tensions with Peter who confided to Greta's costume designer Adrian, how wearing he found Cecil's obsession to be, and how he wanted to get back to England. Cecil was jealous of Adrian's parrot, when Peter said it was the most kissable thing.

Peter returned to England two weeks ahead of Cecil, who went to New York to secure new contracts with *Vogue*. These were for 'London Letters' telling of lunches, balls and chic, and for spreads of photographs of beautiful English women in tweeds. When Cecil arrived at Southampton his sisters and Peter were there to meet him. Peter asked 'How are ye?' and, wrote Cecil, 'once more I knew I was as in love as ever.' The flirtations continued, but Peter resumed his relationship with Oliver, which kept Cecil on tenterhooks. Cecil asked Oliver to give Peter up, but Oliver said no. Cecil wept alone in his bedroom. Oliver, his 'terrible rival', seemed triumphant.

Ashcombe was Cecil's refuge: the cupids, the curtains, the heavenly parties, the charades in fancy dress. On a weekend in October 1931, Peter arrived late in the evening. He was wearing a loose overcoat, his hat slouched over one eye, his scarf hanging loose. After the other guests had gone to bed, he and Cecil walked for miles on the downs, arm in arm, then returned and raided the fridge. Cecil suggested Camembert, but Peter thought not, as they were going to share a bed. They had ginger cake. Cecil then had a hot bath and they got into the circus bed which looked 'fantastic' in the candlelight. They upset the bedclothes with tickling and fighting and Cecil was almost completely happy 'as completely as I ever will be with this poppet because he is the most unperturbed bastard and I shall never alas become his lover.'

The next night Peter went out alone. Cecil lay, ready, in the circus bed with candles lit. He stayed awake for as long as he could. He slept, woke, then looked in the Pink Room. There was the poppet, 'like a suckling pig' naked and asleep in the Pink Room bed. 'I sadly return to the circus bed,' wrote Cecil, 'hoping for at any rate the pleasure of kissing my poppet awake in the morning and handing him his pyjamas.'

And so it went on – a curious, chaste charade of provocation, tease, inhibition and rejection. 'I'll give you a dinner when you fall in love with someone else,' Peter said to Cecil in October 1931.

Thus it was that when Cecil, in March 1932, bathed, manicured and wearing his brand new scanty sharkskin shorts and kid jacket, tripped gaily down the turret steps of the Gouldings' Spanish style Hollywood house to meet Greta Garbo, he was not entirely eligible, nor his heart entirely free.

He 'catwalked' into the drawing-room. Greta and the Gouldings were sitting on a sofa drinking Bellinis – champagne with peach juice. Cecil said 'Oh sorry,' and made as if to return to his room. Marjorie called him back and told him to join them. He felt stage fright, but introductions were made and Greta told him to sit next to her on a leather pouf and Marjorie gave him a large drink. Greta said to him, 'But you're so yorng! How do you stay so yorng? Are you like one of those people that never grow up? I know a man who is fifty who still looks so yorng.' She told him he was beautiful and that he was wearing the nicest Indian shoes she had ever seen. Cecil told her that *she* was beautiful, but she rebuked him for returning the compliment.

They talked inconsequentially and there was much friendly hand squeezing. Marjorie told Cecil to show Greta his manicured hands, with their long fingernails. Greta laughed at their perfection and said that hers were kitchenette hands. 'I play the most sophisticated women with rough hands,' she said. They drank quantities of Bellinis and it seems became quite drunk. From a vase of yellow roses on the bar, sprayed with water, Greta picked one out, kissed it, and said, 'A rose that lives and dies and never again returns.' Cecil took the rose home to Ashcombe, framed it in silver, inscribed it 'Greta's rose' and hung it above his circus bed. After his death in 1980 it was bought by a New Zealand photographer for £750.

They ate lobster, chicken and salad. Greta served Cecil with lettuce and speculated on the sex of the two cold chickens on the buffet table. There was more drinking and then she went to his turret room and looked at photographs of Ashcombe where he wished she would live with him for ever. He said that he kissed her, that she smelled like new-mown hay and that her skin was soft and flawless. She told him he was like a young Grecian boy. 'If I were a young boy I would do such things to you,' she said. She asked him if he was happy and he told her that he was. Perhaps he had for the moment forgotten Peter Watson. She said that she felt as if she was an onlooker in life and that Hollywood made her feel dead.

Back downstairs they danced to the 'rardio'. Greta imitated Douglas Fairbanks and swung from the Spanish rafters. Marjorie did a ballroom dance, Cecil a Strauss waltz. At dawn Greta drove off in her black Packard. Cecil asked her if she would see him again. He asked if he might go to the studio and eat spinach with her for lunch that day. She said No. There was a feather duster with a long handle on the passenger seat of her car and he asked if he might keep it as a memento. She again said No.

'Then this is goodbye?'

'Yes I'm afraid so. C'est la vie.'

They did not meet again for fourteen years. Cecil described this first evening together as 'violent and intimate', as if he and Greta 'had known each other for ever'. He soon let the world know, in his magazine articles, of the milestone of this meeting. When he met Greta again in 1946, she remembered little of their Sunday at the Gouldings' and had not thought about it.

He did not tell Mercedes about the evening, though he knew of her obsession with Greta. She learned of it a year later from Greta when they were discussing the suicide of Cecil's brother Reggie. She wrote to Cecil on 18 December 1933:

558 N. Bristol Heights, California

I wanted to write you many times as Anita told me some months ago that your brother had killed himself and I was so sad for you. I wish I could see you . . . By the way Greta told me yesterday that she had met you when you were out here last. You didn't tell me about it.

Not to tell her was a strange omission, for they had confided to each other about their hearts' desires. And Anita Loos had let him know of problems between Greta and Mercedes, as a letter dated September 1932 made clear:

The Garbo Mercedes business has been too amazing. They had terrific battles and Garb left without saying goodbye. Then Mercedes flew to New York to see her and Garb wouldn't. Mercedes flew back despondent – lost her job with MGM and is in the most awful state. Also says she's broke – can't get a break and it's too terrible. The story is as long as the dictionary but much more amazing, so will hope you get together with Mercedes one day and hear it from her own lips. I am really terribly sorry for her. She just never seems to have any luck. And if she really is broke, I don't know what she'll do because this is a tough racket and I doubt she can get by in it.

Hollywood knew of the tensions between the two women. Greta complained often to Salka Viertel of Mercedes' wrecking persistency. The previous month she sent a telegram thanking Salka for all she had done to help over the dramas with 'black and white' (her allusive name for Mercedes who dressed in black or white and wore pale make-up). She fervently hoped that Salka had managed to get money to Mercedes to tide her over the latest storm.

Mercedes, an intense and insecure lover, was not good at observing emotional boundaries. Even Eva Le Gallienne, who had promised total commitment to her, lifelong and declared, found her too invasive. Ten years earlier Eva wrote of how she minded Mercedes wanting to share her 'every happening' and 'every thought'. She had, she said, 'a terror of losing her individual personal life' and her freedom. She wanted to do as she pleased without being questioned or made to feel guilty, or having to answer for her actions.

Greta was even more reluctant to share her happenings or thoughts. Many a time she would not answer the phone to Mercedes – or in his turn to Cecil – or acknowledge her letters. But Mercedes could not let go of her love for Greta, even when reduced to waiting for phone calls she did not receive, or to begging friends like Cecil for scraps of information which satisfied nothing but made her hunger for more.

Four years on, in December 1936, Greta was writing with tired irony to friends in Sweden that nothing new had happened in her life apart from Mercedes wanting her to ring. She was not, she said, in any hurry to oblige. 'Poor Mercedes – she has got an extraordinary ability to make people nervous. Even people who are not quite as unkind as I am.' And in November 1939, Gayelord Hauser, a dietitian who wrote popular books about losing weight, plastic surgery and healthy living, and who was Greta's escort for a while, wrote to Mercedes: 'Do take my advice and not write to her address, as that is one of her "pet peeves".'

In May 1932 the First National Bank of Beverly Hills failed. Greta had a million dollars in account with them. Mercedes claimed to have had premonitory dreams about the bank's collapse, but these did not prove helpful. At the same time Greta's contract with MGM was due to end. Her disaffection with Hollywood, her homesickness for Sweden, her hatred of the invasion of her privacy by the press, were all well known. She sailed for Gothenburg on the SS *Gripsholm* in the summer of 1932 amid speculation that she had left Hollywood never to return. To the hordes of journalists who were at the quayside to quiz her when the ship docked, she said that she wanted to find a secluded corner where she could stay without being disturbed, that she did not know how long she would remain in Sweden, that she would tell them nothing of her plans, that she did not know if she would return to Hollywood.

In fact she had signed a contract with MGM three weeks before she sailed. She felt that the loss of her savings obliged her to continue working despite her desire to leave acting for ever. Her new contract gave her $250,000 for each film which made her the highest paid woman in the USA. It gave her, too, imperious powers over the selection of her directors, the content of her scripts and over other actors.

She spent the summer of 1932 swimming in the sea and hiking in the hills with her friend the Countess Wachtmeister who lived with her husband and daughter at Tistad Castle, Nyköping, some hours from Stockholm. There was a farm, orchards and vast tracts of land. When she returned to Hollywood eight months later, it was to star as Queen Christina. The days of playing a vamp, of being used by Hollywood, of kowtowing to Louis B. Mayer were through. Contractually, the terms of engagement were hers from that point on and her roles were commanding and grand.

Greta's Wandering Years

'We don't make our own hearts'
Camille

Nothing in Garbo's childhood prepared her for fame and fortune. In the early 1930s she gave a few reluctant interviews which, without design, turned the particulars of childhood into the universal, resonant with melancholy:

> I was born. I grew up. I have lived like every other person. Why must people talk about me? We all do the same things in ways that are just a little different. We go to school, we learn, we are bad at times, good at others. But we grow up, one the same as the other. We find our life's work and we do it. That's all there is to anyone's life story, isn't it? . . .
>
> Some people were born in red brick houses, others in plain white board ones. What is the difference? We were all born in houses. I will not have it printed that I was born in this house or that, that my mother was this or my father that. They were my mother and father, just as yours were your mother and father. To me that is what counts. Why should the world talk about them? I don't want the world to talk about my mother and father.

But the world did talk, its interest aroused by her image on screen. And the more she was questioned the more she retreated, told her maid to say Miss Garbo is away, and encouraged her family to conceal their connection to her and reveal nothing about her. So the world constructed a life history from scant fact, the recollections of acquaintances and the betrayal of friends. In his diaries Cecil recorded the anecdotes and shadowy insights she divulged.

When they were on holiday in Sweden in 1935, Greta took Mercedes to see the apartment block in Stockholm, at 32 Blekinge Street in a poor district on the south side of the city, where her family lived when she was a child. It was a three-room flat without hot water. She and her friends used the public baths. Life was constrained by lack of money. Mercedes wrote:

> She had no opportunity to experience the things that are part of many children's and young women's lives – a good education, going to parties, dances, having good clothes, going to the theatre, to the opera, to concerts, learning sports – tennis, skiing, riding, fencing and above all travelling.

She was born Greta Lovisa Gustafsson on 18 September 1905. Both her parents came from farmworking families in southern Sweden and the occupation of most of her forebears was given in official records as 'bonde', meaning peasant. Her parents, Carl Alfrid Gustafsson and Anna Lovisa Karlsson, married in Stockholm in 1898 and the ceremony legitimised the birth of their first child, Sven, born ten weeks later. Greta's sister, Alva, was born in 1903. Their father's occupation was variously given as street cleaner, grocer, merchant, handyman, factory worker. His health was poor and he took such work as he could find. An extant photograph shows him standing in an abbatoir in front of carcasses of meat, wearing a bloodstained overall, with a knife at his belt and a bludgeon in a pail and with a cow awaiting slaughter. Greta told Cecil that when she was a child she saw some men kill a lamb and pour its blood into a basin and that the incident stayed with her for life as an image of terror.

Garbo resisted conjecture about her formative years: 'Your joys and sorrows. You can never tell them. You cheapen the inside of yourself if you do tell them.' She admitted though, in an interview for the Swedish magazine *Lektyr*, in 1931, that there was an atmosphere of anxiety in the home 'as if there is danger in the air' and that their lives were ruled by lack of money. In later years she wrote to Salka Viertel of the sadness she felt in the company of her family, of how though she was close to them they darkened her mood and made her feel heavy inside.

In the cramped family apartment, without anywhere to be physically alone, she developed the trick of being alone in her mind. She said that although she was the youngest, her parents looked on her as the oldest. Tall as a child, fully grown by the time she was twelve, she could not remember a time when she was ever very little or as little as other children. 'I don't think anyone ever regarded me as a child.' Her height made her self-conscious and she avoided group photographs. She described herself as a spectator of her own life, said that her moods swung from elation to depression, that she always detested crowds, liked only a few people and for as long as she could remember sought solitude. Cecil would urge her to change: to make plans, have projects, participate in a multitude of interesting things. Her response was tautological and fatalistic: 'I am what I am. C'est la vie.' It was as if life acted upon her, and that was her reality which she could not change. The aspect of being an outsider, of living in a closed inner world, of understood but unexpressed feeling, imbued her acting talent and made her a star.

Despite her unprivileged childhood, she retained a longing for Sweden and what she perceived as the simplicity of Swedish life. She felt that fame severed her roots. When she moved to America she spoke of living in exile 'for the sake of Mammon'.

To Mercedes she recounted inconsequential anecdotes about her childhood, anecdotes that Mercedes treasured, like snippets from the Holy Shroud. She told of a time when she was six and her uncle was reading his newspaper. Greta asked him, Does uncle care a lot about Jesus? He replied absentmindedly, Yes, uncle cares a lot about Jesus. She played, then asked again, Does uncle really care about Jesus? He said Yes, uncle really cares about Jesus. She went away, then returned to the subject. Are you quite sure that uncle cares about Jesus? Uncle stopped reading and shouted, Uncle doesn't give a damn about Jesus. It became a byline for years between Merecedes and Greta when they were uninterested in something: 'Uncle doesn't give a damn about Jesus.'

She went to the Katarina Elementary School from 1912 to 1919. Her grades were good – mostly As – in all subjects, including 'diligence, behaviour and maturity'. In her seven years of school she missed eleven days through illness and played hooky one day in the spring of 1918:

School? There isn't much to tell of my school years. I went to public school and hated it. I hated its confinement, its repression. I dare say all children feel this way even if they do not dare be frank about it. History interested me most. Geography I detested. I could never understand maps.

She was nine at the outbreak of the First World War. To get enough food, the family grew fruit and vegetables on an allotment at Enskede south of Stockholm and sold any surplus for cash. When she became rich, she had a reputation for meanness, her attitude to money shaped by her early years. She did not spend, except on advised investment, never adapted to living in more than a couple of rooms, would deliberate over any mundane purchase and was discomfited by the presence of servants and unwilling to give them instruction. But she also sought the company of the rich and the protection from public scrutiny they were able to provide: Georges

Schlee, Eric and Cécile de Rothschild, Aristotle Onassis. Ram Gopal, an Indian dancer, wrote to Mercedes in 1956:

> I see from the papers that the Divine One, your Greta, is in the South of France hobnobbing with Onassis . . . All this roving about with the big money people is from her subconscious poverty in far off Stockholm but it's rather overdone now and a bit tiresome. After all what Swedes call *poverty* there . . . is *riches* compared to poverty as I've seen it and known it in India.

In 1919, when she was thirteen, her father became mortally ill. She went with him to the district clinic and learned that if you had money you received treatment and if you had not, then you waited in line. He died of kidney failure when he was forty-seven. 'God what a feeling. Someone you love is there, then he is not there.' It was the first of several bereavements that seemed like abandonment.

Childhood ended and she and the rest of the family worked to pay the bills. Their mother cleaned in a local canning factory, delivered early morning newspapers and took in sewing. Sven, who was father to a child, worked in a sweet shop. Alva was a clerk. A neighbour found Greta a job in a barber's shop – lathering men's faces and cleaning the razors. While the barber shaved one customer, she soaped the next one's stubble. 'I soon conquered my initial shyness and a certain feeling of degradation . . . I had never been as proud as of my first day's wages.' She gave her earnings to her mother and spent tips on chocolate.

As for acting, she 'carried it inside her' from childhood on as a fantasy of escape from a circumscribed life. She and a friend, Eva Blomkvist, used to hang around backstage at the Mosebacke Theatre hoping for opportunity to strike. In letters to Eva, written when she was fourteen, she described her own nature as arrogant and impatient. She was possessive of her girlfriends and high-handed when Eva assumed intimacy with them too. She warned her to keep away from them 'if you and I are to remain friends'. Eva was acceptably contrite, but voiced resentment at being treated like a child. 'I only do that when you behave like a child,' Greta replied.

In August 1920, a month before her fifteenth birthday, Greta got a job selling ladies' coats in PUB, Stockholm's main department store, owned by Paul V. Bergström. She was paid 125 kronor a month, about £12. Her mother thought it the best of birthday presents, called PUB 'paradise' and hoped her daughter's future was assured.

Greta viewed the job as proof of maturity and liked the interest evinced in her by Bergström's son. But she confided that she longed for the theatre. 'There's everything I want there.' She wanted to act, to have some fun and to meet someone for whom she could really care. She said she did not see herself as a teenager, but felt as if she had been alive for all time.

She was thought pretty at PUB, promoted from coats to hats and chosen to model for the store's mail-order catalogue. It pictured her in hats ranging from 10 to 25 kronor in styles called Clary, Ethel, Jane, Helny and Solveig.

She worked in the store for two years and while there had an affair with a customer, Max Gumpel, a wealthy construction engineer, sixteen years older than she, flashy, patronising and rich. He lived in Drottning Street in a smart apartment with brass taps which, he said in a privately published memoir *Tales and Reality*, she thought were made of gold. He served artichokes for dinner, which confounded her, and gave her a gold ring set with a small diamond which, he wrote, 'she thought was as beautiful as a diamond in the English Royal Crown'.

But the ring had no binding significance and in August 1921, afflicted by a kind of *cafard*, by one of the bouts of melancholy that dogged her life and by some unspecified illness, she went alone to the country at Nykroppa.

From there she wrote to Eva with the kind of closed melancholy that marked her life. She signed herself with her nickname 'Katha'.

She said that she felt unwell and indifferent to life and to people and had chosen to go away alone where she would meet no one whom she knew. She found solitude acceptable and had no particular desire to return to Stockholm. She invited Eva to write if she wished, but if not, so be it.

A producer of advertising films, Ragnar Ring, provided her next career opportunity. PUB was the first Swedish store to use filmed advertisements and in 1922 Ring produced a promotional film for the store's fortieth anniversary. Called *From Top to Toe* it was the saga of a family who, their home razed by fire, replaced all their clothes at PUB. Greta, cast as one of the daughters, chose lots of dresses and hats.

Ring employed her in three more commercials. In *How Not to Wear Clothes* she buffooned with buttons and baggy trousers in a man's voluminous check suit and in *Our Daily Bread*, made for the Co-operative Stores, she and other girls ate cakes.

These inconsequential appearances gave substance to her ambition and led a small-time producer, Erik Petschler, to give her a part the following year as a bathing belle in a slapstick comedy. Petschler was in Bergström's store choosing costume items for the film and Greta asked 'boldly and outright if there was a chance for her to play a role in my film. She had acting experience, she said, adding that she had done film commercials for PUB.' Bergström would not give her unpaid leave, so to her mother's alarm she quit the store on 7 July 1922 and gave as her reason: 'To enter the films.' Her contract with Petschler was for fourteen days' work at ten kronor a day.

Called *Peter the Hobo*, the film required her to fall in the water, shake itching powder over the villain and slap him with a wet fish. She appeared, using her family name of Greta Gustafsson, as plump, happy and giggling. This debut screen performance went unremarked except for faint praise from a reviewer in a boxing magazine, *Swing*:

As Miss Gustafsson has so far had only the doubtful pleasure of playing a Bathing Beauty for Mr Petschler, we have no real impression of her capabilities. It pleases us though to have the opportunity of noting a new name in Swedish film and we hope to have a chance to mention it again.

On Petschler's advice she applied for admission to Stockholm's Royal Dramatic Theatre's Training School and was coached for the entrance tests. Out of fifty applicants, six were given places and she was one. 'I thought I would die of joy when I learned that I had got in,' she said years later when she got to Hollywood. 'And it still makes me breathless when I remember that moment.'

She began at the School at 9 am on her seventeenth birthday. The curriculum was formal and included elocution, diction, posture and movement, fencing and theatre history. Her student notebook, in Stockholm's Filminstitutet archive, shows the theories and techniques she learned. Teaching was influenced by the Delsart system – an approach to acting and movement based on the interrelationship of body, mind and emotion:

> Bending the head forward means submission to somebody else's will, or confession of a truth, can also express tiredness, sympathy, sincere understanding.
>
> Head back means the opposite – proudness and haughtiness. Head held high means calmness and persistence.

She played Hermione in *The Winter's Tale*, a maid in *The Admirable Crichton* by J. M. Barrie, Ellida in Ibsen's *The Lady from the Sea* and she supplemented her grant by modelling in advertising – a 1923 photograph shows her at the wheel of a Lancia Lambda with Vera Schmiterlöw in the driving seat.

She was poorer than other students and from the wrong side of the tracks. Her close friend, Mimi Pollak, recounted how her own landlady, a 'snooty' woman from Östermalm who wore a pearl necklace, said she would prefer not to have Greta Gustafsson from the South Island visiting the house. An Academy photograph, taken in 1924, shows other students looking at the camera and Greta looking at Mimi Pollak. When Mimi married, Greta wrote to her that she felt left out. She said she always thought they belonged to each other in some special way. 'I cannot believe that everything has changed.'

In Greta's second year Sweden's leading director, Mauritz Stiller, put through an audition call to the School for the part of the Countess Dohna in his silent movie *The Gösta Berling Saga*. Stiller had won praise with his films *St Arne's Treasure* in 1919 and *Erotikon* in 1920, which Ernst Lubitsch said was the inspiration for his own screen comedies. For *Gösta Berling*, he wanted unknown actors with intrinsic quality, not learned technique:

> When an actor has become famous he continuously tries to simplify his technique, to recapture his unaffected simplicity from the time when he knew nothing about acting. And that is difficult.

At Greta's audition he told her to lie on a bed and be very ill:

> I came off the street, they made me up and then took me in and told me to lie in a bed and be sick. Very sick. I didn't know what it was all about. It seemed to me like a big joke . . . I was embarrassed to try and put myself over . . .
>
> Stiller waited a few moments and then said, 'My God can't you be sick? Don't you know what it is to be sick? Then I knew it wasn't play and it wasn't funny. I knew it was necessary in the movies and I became a very sick lady.
>
> The stage is so different from the movies. On the stage you have your voice but in the movies only your face.

Stiller gave her the part of the Countess Dohna who, young, beautiful, Italian and married, falls in love with Gösta Berling, a disgraced pastor. He told her to lose ten kilos. She dieted and bandaged her legs each night in an effort to make them thinner. Vera Schmiterlöw wrote to Mimi, then in theatre in Helsingborg:

Greta and I are taking Turkish baths together, partly to diet. I'm not getting anywhere. I've actually put on nine pounds. But Greta just gets thinner and thinner. You can't see her breasts any more. They're just two buttons.

Greta was eighteen. Her contract ran for six months from 23 July 1923 and, as she was underage, was countersigned by her mother. With the 3,000 kronors she received, she bought a pearl necklace and a ring for her mother and furniture for the family home. On 9 November she applied to change her name. Stiller thought Gustafsson too clumsy for fame. He was himself his own creation, from a drab, unhopeful childhood and he wanted a similar spectacular metamorphosis for her, his female counterpart. For Greta, he wanted a name that was modern, elegant and international, 'that says just as clearly who she is in London and Paris as in Budapest and New York'. The change to Garbo was formally made on 4 December.

Twenty-two years older than Greta, Stiller was a flamboyant, epicurean individual with a sexual preference for men. He wore an ankle-length yellow fur coat, had his suits tailored in London, wore rings set with diamonds, sapphires and pearls, and diamond studs in his shirt, kept a French bulldog called Charlie – after Charlie Chaplin – and drove a yellow Italian sports car.

Born Moshe Katzmann in Helsinki, his father, a Russian Jew, was an army musician, his mother the daughter of a Polish doctor. She killed herself when Stiller was three. His father died soon after and Stiller was fostered by a milliner. Like Greta, his childhood was haphazard and his education rudimentary. He started as an actor when he was sixteen, went to Sweden on a faked passport to escape military service, directed in a small experimental theatre, then began making films for a studio called Magnusson's Svenska Bio in Stockholm. He made thirty films before *Gösta Berling*.

He directed on a grand scale with a painter's eye and a genius for atmosphere. It was his aim to shape Garbo as an artistic ideal – a star for whom the world would irresistibly fall. 'I am merciless as I force her into her role,' he wrote in his diary. 'But wait until I am through with her. She is going to please the very gods.'

He became her manager, protector, director and creator, told her how to dress, how to move, how to feel. She was to be beautiful, sorrowful, sophisticated, innocent. She told the Swedish press that acting in *Gösta Berling* was like passing through a terrible fire: 'Stiller', she said, 'creates people and shapes them according to his will.' He wrote of how easily he could dominate her by looking into her eyes and how she was as wax in his hands.

A letter written in 1922 from Selma Lagerlöf, author of *The Atonement of Gösta Berling* – the story from which the film was made – complained of his creative ruthlessness:

> you consider my book should only be a source of inspiration and that the contents should be changed to something new, exclusively for film . . .
> I understand that with your great ability you are trying to raise film to a new branch of art, like music to the eye, but in order to do this it is certainly necessary that the story be meant for the film from the beginning.

The press nicknamed Garbo and Stiller 'Beauty and the Beast'. The film took a year to make and he provoked Garbo during shooting. 'Damn you, Stiller, I hate you,' she is quoted as saying, as he criticised her and cajoled her. He demanded total concentration. The film camera, he said, registers everything with merciless clarity.

More than four hours long, *Gösta Berling* premièred in two parts: on 10 and 28 March 1924. 'In a few years I expect the name of Greta Garbo will be known all over the world,' 'She has the gift of beauty, of unique beauty,' 'Greta Garbo's way to stardom seems clear,' wrote the critics. Trianon Films in Berlin then bought the film for 100,000 marks and Stiller and Garbo went over for the première and were fêted and praised.

Trianon then agreed to finance the next film of Stiller's choice and gave them both four-year contracts. Stiller proposed a blockbuster, filmed on location in Turkey, called *The Odalisque from Smyrna*, and starring Garbo. It was the story of a girl intent on reaching her lover, who smuggles herself aboard a ship, gets sold to a harem and then dramatically escapes.

Greta was nineteen when, in December 1924, she travelled with Stiller to Constantinople on the Orient Express. He drove her to see the sights and scenery and the sunsets over the Bosphorus. For Christmas, he gave her a fur coat and a costume in brick-red silk with yellow flowers. They stayed at the Pera Palace Hotel, where Mercedes caught a glimpse of her and felt her heart turn.

He aimed to shoot the film in three months, but everything went wrong. Cameras and props were held at customs for eighteen days. Filming was forbidden outside a mosque where the lovers were to reunite. Telegrams asking for funds went unanswered. Trianon went bankrupt and no other company would finance the project. An industrialist who had lent money impounded the cameras and various embassies and legations had to get the crew out of Turkey. Greta wrote home, in January 1925, that despite the trials it had been a good beginning. In two days she would be back in Berlin and would see what would happen then. Everything, she said, would be all right.

She was more prudent and realistic than Stiller. There were rumours that the fur coat turned up in a pawn shop, and that she now had reservations about his business acumen. In Berlin G. W. Pabst, impressed by her performance in *Gösta Berling*, wanted her for a part in his film *Die Freudlose Gasse (Joyless Street)*. Stiller negotiated her terms, arranged for her salary and all living expenses to be paid in dollars and booked himself and her into a luxury suite at the Esplanade Hotel.

Pabst filmed in thirty-four days. Greta found the work schedule daunting, the brightness of the studio lights exacerbated her nervous blink and only by speeding the camera could the cameraman, Guido Sieber, home in on her face without the twitch being visible. But Pabst was enthralled by her. He wanted her to stay in Berlin and to sign a long-term contract with him. 'Such a face you see only once in a century,' he said. When Louise Brooks met him, three years later, in 1928, he 'raved' about Garbo:

> we had tea in his apartment. Heinrich Mann and other people. Very intellectual tea and very boring. But he took me to a big cupboard and he had just hundreds of stills of Garbo. Oh he thought she was so marvellous! And he showed me all these stills and he talked about her, and talked about her and talked about her.

Jealous of Pabst's interest, Stiller accused Greta of ingratitude. He planned the formation of a European filmmaking and distribution consortium on a par with MGM in which she was to be the principal star and he the principal director. He roused the interest of UFA in Germany, Pathé in France and financiers in Sweden.

But then, in spring 1925, Louis B. Mayer, vice-president of Metro-Goldwyn-Mayer, arrived in Berlin from Rome where he had been checking overrun costs on his $6 million production of *Ben Hur*. He was on the look out for European talent to import into Hollywood. Emil Jannings, Conrad Veidt, Ernst Lubitsch and the

Swedish director Victor Sjöstrom, had already been enticed there by him.

Mayer saw and admired *Gösta Berling* and wired Sjöstrom to ask what he thought of Stiller. 'All the good that can be put in a cable' Sjöstrom replied. Mayer dined with Stiller at the Adlon Hotel. Stiller set the scene. Creatively, he felt inseparable from Greta. The dinner table was arranged and lit to show her to advantage. Communication was problematic as Stiller spoke no English. Mayer offered him a three-year contract, starting 1 July 1925, at $1500 a week. Stiller would not accept it unless Greta went with him. Mayer thought her ankles too thick and her chest too flat. He offered $350 a week for her and said she must lose more weight. 'American men don't like fat women,' he said. According to Greta he took no notice of her. 'I suspect he looked at me out of the corner of his eye, but I can't be sure he gave me even that much attention.'

As soon as the deal was struck, Stiller panicked, felt uncertain of the wisdom of severing himself from Europe and talked to a lawyer about how to break the contract. He was, a friend wrote to Sjöstrom, 'so nervous it was almost frightening'. He told Greta they would go to New York and decide there whether or not to go on to Hollywood.

Greta was equally tense and uncertain. Pabst wanted to work with her again. Mayer had hardly enthused over her. There were bureaucratic problems because of her age. Her sister Alva, herself an actress, was ill, with her career in jeopardy. Her mother needed help, and all her friends were in Stockholm. She left, she said, as an unhappy young lady. She confided her fears to Mimi Pollak, her 'darling Mimosa', and implored her to write though they were far apart.

She and Stiller sailed from Gothenburg on the SS *Drottningholm* and arrived in New York on 6 July 1925 in sweltering heat. MGM sent two personnel to meet them, a standard press photo was printed in the New York *Herald Tribune*, but their arrival went for the most part unremarked and for weeks they were both ignored.

Marooned in a stifling hotel on Forty-Second Street, Greta studied English, dieted, permed her hair and took cold water baths. She wrote home that everything was a mess, that she felt suicidal, and would either drown herself in the bath, jump out of the window, or take the next boat back.

Stiller hectored the MGM offices but drew no response. He too wanted to sail home. Then a friend of his, a Swedish singer, Martha Hedman, took Greta to the photographer Arnold Genthe. He was keen to photograph her. They spoke in German because she knew so little English. She protested about her hair and clothes. 'Never mind that,' Genthe said. 'I am more interested in your eyes and in what is behind that extraordinary forehead.'

In an hour he produced a sequence of photographs, 'all so different it was hard to believe they were of the same girl'. He used dramatic lighting, pictured her as passionate and wild, then took a selection of the prints to Frank Crowninshield, the editor of *Vanity Fair*. One of the photographs was used on the magazine's cover in August. Mayer saw it and told Sjöstrom to get her to Hollywood right away. He had not recognised her as the girl he had met in Berlin.

Greta's first Hollywood film was *The Torrent*. She played a Spanish opera singer, degraded by her lover. Louise Brooks described the effect on the studios:

> From the moment *The Torrent* went into production, no actress was ever again to be quite happy in herself. The whole MGM studio, including Monta Bell, the director, watched the daily rushes with amazement as Garbo created out of the stalest, thinnest material the complex, enchanting shadow of a soul upon the screen.

La Bohème with Lillian Gish and John Gilbert, directed by King Vidor, opened in February 1926 at the Embassy Theatre on Broadway. Business was average. The same week *The Torrent* opened to capacity audiences at the Capitol, the biggest cinema in New York. The queue for tickets stretched down Fiftieth and Fifty-First Streets and the show was extended for a second week. Loew's State Theater in Los Angeles also broke box-office records.

Reviews were good. 'The girl has everything, with looks, acting ability and personality,' *Variety* wrote. Garbo did not view the rushes of the film. She was twenty-two, separated from her country and friends, unable to speak much English, and homesick. To Vera Schmiterlöw and Mimi Pollak she wrote of how at times on set she was so despairing, she sat down and wept and ruined her make-up while the assistants stared uncomprehendingly at her.

Unhappiness was, she said, unacceptable in the studios. She was obliged to smile and to pretend that she had done so all her life. She worked from nine in the morning until six at night, went to no parties, wore no smart clothes. She would go out alone, look at the sky and the sea and say to herself 'time passes' and that soon she might go home.

America seemed to her ugly and soul-destroying; the Californian sun made her tired; Hollywood denied her the chance to travel, have fun and be young. Most of all she pined for news from home. She wanted to hear about Sturabadet (where they all used to go to the public baths), about Nordiska Kompamet (the shopping centre), about the cinema and the theatre, and whether Vera had had her hair cut and all the daily trivia of the life she had lost.

Nor did she think she had done well in the film. The public and critics had, she said, been wonderfully kind, but she did not think she deserved their praise. With the self-disparagement that defined her life she reduced her success to the fact that Hollywood did not have a 'type' like her. She supposed that if she could not, as she put it, 'learn to act', the studios would tire of her soon.

MGM worked to manufacture her image. She was to be Nordic and Amazonian. She was photographed seemingly caged with the Metro lion. 'Brave daughter of Vikings visits lion in its den' the caption read. Other publicity stills showed her having her biceps squeezed by a gymnast; shaking hands with a world-famous boxer; crouched on a chalk line waiting for a starting pistol to be fired. 'I will be glad when I am a beeg star like Lillian Gish,' *Photoplay* quoted her as saying in May 1926. 'Then I will not need publicity and to have peectures taken shaking hands with a prize fighter.'

She stayed in a hotel apartment at Santa Monica and the only person she felt close to was Stiller. Each evening they had dinner together at seven. He alone among the Hollywood directors, she told Mimi Pollak, understood the soul and feelings. Other directors just gave instructions. They were not like Moje who lived and breathed his films. He was, she said, the only man in Hollywood who mattered to her.

Stiller could not, as a director, adapt his talent to Hollywood. Greta succeeded from the start there, but he failed. He called the place Hollow Wood, openly criticised the studio's commercialism, expediency and compromise, pitted himself against the MGM hierarchy and was disliked for the nuisance he caused. Greta defended him publicly, though privately she suffered his ways of making life difficult.

When he was assigned to direct her in her second MGM film, *The Temptress*, there was trouble from the start. He was tyrannical, tempestuous, dismissive of the crew, unable to express himself in English and unheeding of schedule and budget. He antagonised the leading man, Antonio Morena, by telling him to shave off his 'silly' moustache and to wear shoes that were too large, to make Greta's feet appear smaller.

Though the best scenes of the film, an opening masked ball and banquet, remain his, Irving Thalberg and Mayer looked at early rushes, criticised his treatment as confusing and his progress as slow and expensive and, after ten days' shooting, fired him. Fred Niblo, who had directed *Ben Hur* the previous year, was told to complete the film. Greta wrote home to Axel Nilson, a Swedish friend of Stiller's and of hers, that when this happened to Moje she thought that the sun would never rise again.

Without Stiller she felt abandoned. Then news reached her, in July 1926, that her sister Alva had died of cancer of the lymph glands. MGM would not release her from filming so that she could go home for the funeral. She could not leave until she had made three films.

To her friend Lars Saxon she wrote that it was as if a part of her had been cut away and as if life had died within her. Separated from her family she was denied the chance to help them, and had no one to help her. She became afflicted by feelings of guilt and depression, a sense that God was punishing her for having been unhappy without sufficient reason. She had, she said, been given what millions envied, but the surprises life held, now made her afraid.

Stiller's fortunes plummeted. He directed *Hotel Imperial* for Paramount which proved popular, but he was ill with rheumatism, tired and depressed. He said he would direct one more film for them: 'It will be genuine garbage, but I'll do that one and go home with the money.' Greta hoped to leave with him.

He made two more films for Paramount and both were panned. When he heard that MGM planned to cast Garbo as *The Divine Woman*, based on the life of Sarah Bernhardt, with Las Hanson as the leading man, he asked Thalberg and Mayer if he might direct the film. They gave it to Sjöstrom. It was the final blow and he left Hollywood in November 1927. Greta saw him off from Los Angeles station.

Back in Stockholm he produced and directed a popular musical, *Broadway*, which boosted his morale and set him planning to make another film. But his health had broken. Greta asked Mimi if she had seen poor dear Moje and what America had done to him. He collapsed in the autumn of that year and was taken to the Red Cross Hospital with fluid on his lungs which surgeons tried unsuccessfully to drain. He died on 8 November aged forty-five.

Sjöström wired the news to Greta who was working on *Wild Orchids* with Nils Asther. She leaned against a wall, pressed her hands to her eyes, then continued the scene. Mayer left a phial of brandy in her dressing-room and a note: 'My sympathy with your sorrow, but the show must go on.' To be alone, she took the train to New York. Mayer sent a wire, 'Come back, you are risking the entire film.'

That Christmas, under an alias, she sailed for Sweden. It was her first trip home from Hollywood. She had been away three years. She returned as a star. The press and crowds thronged the boat when it docked. She was reunited with her mother, her brother Sven and Mimi Pollak.

Before Stiller's belongings were auctioned, she asked to see them and spent some time touching them and commenting on them – the suitcase he had taken to America, the rugs he bought on their trip to Constantinople. She acquired a large plain table of his and had it shipped to New York. Cecil admired it when he saw it in the 1950s. She said of Stiller that he was the 'best of persons' and that she had wanted him to become a leading Hollywood director, 'perhaps the leading one'. Alone, she went to his grave at the Jewish cemetery on the outskirts of Stockholm.

She was twenty-three and had lost her father, her sister, her place in her country and her true mentor. Stiller had taught her all she knew. He dominated her and tried to control her, but she had perceived his artistic integrity as he perceived hers. She was now under contract to the Hollywood factory which did not concern itself with the realities of vulnerability and grief. She followed her career with steely professionalism, negotiated fantastic contracts and iron terms and put her life into perfecting the art of projecting herself on screen. In the ensuing years she had lovers, protectors and unlimited admirers, but she had passed through fire and her youth, her freedom and her trust in life had died.

6

Cecil's Wandering Years

'I'm not always sincere.
One can't be in this world, you know.'
Camille

Cecil was born in London in leafy Hampstead, where his preoccupations surfaced early:

> When I was three years old, I used to be allowed to scramble into my mother's large bed, and nestle close to her while she sipped an early morning cup of tea and opened her letters. One morning during this customary treat, my eyes fell upon a postcard lying in front of me on the pink silk eiderdown, and the beauty of it caused my heart to leap. The photograph was of Miss Lily Elsie . . . her neck, in its full swanlike glory, was surrounded by an elaborate filigree of diamonds, while her hair was piled in billowing clusters of curls. To make the whole effect more unbearably beautiful, the photograph had been tinted, the cheeks and lips of this divine creature were of a translucent pink that I could never hope to acquire from my box of crayons, and the tulle corsage of her pale yellow dress was spangled with tinsel stardust. My passion for Miss Lily Elsie and my interest in photography were thus engendered at the same moment.

It was a startling admission of career choice. A desire to enter his mother's quintessentially pink and female world.

Mercedes as a girl, found no consolation when told that she was the same gender as Lily Elsie. She continued to 'examine herself each morning' to see if 'the miracle had happened'. Cecil's relationship to the unwitting Lily was easier. He collected postcards, playbills and images of her until he was old enough to create her, with his Kodak, from his own mind's eye.

Among my nightly prayers was the supplication that in next Tuesday's *Sketch* there might be a double-page photograph of, if not Miss Lily Elsie, then please, O Lord, let there be a simply scrumptious one of Miss Florence Smithson, or, failing her, of Mademoiselle Gaby Deslys!

His description of himself, aged three, in bed with mother had, like his photographs, the textures that he loved – pink silk, feathers, diamonds, billowing curls, yellow tulle, stardust – all adorning a female face that revealed nothing but a mirror gaze. 'My inward child's eye,' he wrote, 'even as my adult vision, always sought out the detail rather than the conception as a whole.' Adorned women reflected his own preoccupations. He pursued their superficiality tirelessly and turned it into art.

He was born Cecil Walter Hardy Beaton on 14 January 1904, at 21 Langland Gardens, Hampstead. His parents, Ernest Walter Hardy Beaton and Esther Sisson, married nine months previously and honeymooned at the Hotel Hermitage, Monte Carlo, where Cecil was conceived. His father, a timber merchant, specialising in European and Baltic softwoods, was one-time Secretary of the Thespis Dramatic Society, editor of *Timber and Plywood*, President of the Council of the Timber Trade Federation and a member of the Middlesex Cricket Club. His mother, the eighth daughter of a village blacksmith, was his joy. He loved the soft fabric of her dresses, the artificial roses and violets pinned at her waist, her dressing-table, powder and perfumes, the hours she spent curling her hair. He cherished the illusion that she was a woman of social standing and, when disabused, concocted status for her. From an early age he sent his photographs of her to society magazines.

The eldest of four children, Cecil had a brother Reginald who was born in 1905 and two much-loved sisters, Nancy and Barbara – 'Baba' – born in 1909 and 1912. Mother came first in Cecil's affections, but he was also devoted to her sister, Jessie. She married a Bolivian diplomat and had two sons who died in childhood. She indulged Cecil's childhood taste for chinchilla fur, pots of face cream and hats with osprey feathers. In her house were 'gilded baskets with silk bows, filled with pineapples and mangoes, custard apples and Brazil nuts, while the air was redolent with white lilacs out of season'. Aunt Jessie let Cecil watch as she painted her eyelids mauve, her cheeks carnation pink, her lips cerise, and as she stood in front of the cheval glass fixing the plumes of her hat into her dyed red hair. She spent hours languishing with her face covered in cold cream or chicken fat and sweated off excess weight by playing strenuous games of tennis wearing a rubber corset. Cecil loved it all.

In 1911, aged seven, he was plunged into the world of boys. He was sent to Heath Mount Preparatory School:

> Suddenly out of nowhere the bullies arrived. They had recognised their quarry in me. Growling like wire-haired terriers, they were large and solid, with hairy stockings and rough tweeds.

Their clothes were as menacing to him as their intentions. They stuck pins in him and bent back his arms. He learned the lesson that though terrified he must never show fear, for it marked him as a victim. Leader of the pack was Evelyn Waugh. An intense dislike began that lasted a lifetime. In a memoir Waugh wrote of Cecil: 'The tears on his long eyelashes used to provoke the sadism of youth and my cronies and I tormented him.' In adult life, in letters to friends, Waugh called Cecil 'Sexy Beaton', and 'trash' and said that his drawings gave him goose flesh. Cecil called Waugh a nasty piece of goods.

After Heath Mount there followed a worse reality – St Cyprian's school at Eastbourne. Cecil was sent there as a boarder in 1915 in the middle of the First World War. The experience marked the end of his idyllic childhood and severance from the soft and scented world of mother, Aunt Jessie and his sisters. The school was snobbish, the fees high, the regime cruel. It was cramming ground for Eton and Harrow and for the rigours of manly life. The only woman there was Mrs Vaughan-Wilkes, the headmaster's wife. She was stocky, square built, red-cheeked and capricious with punishment. The boys addressed her as Mum and nicknamed her Flip. She fascinated and terrified Cecil. Her husband, 'Sambo', beat the boys, except if their parents were rich, with a bone-handled riding crop or a rattan cane. The food was bad and insufficient, the communal plunge bath cold and dirty, the rooms unheated, the lavatories smelly and without locks.

Cecil cried at unsuitable times, suffered from chilblains and verrucas, found the gymnasium a torture and learned to suck up. He pretended to read books that would impress Flip. He mowed the school lawn and painted Christmas cards for her. 'I became such a positive favourite that she often took me down into the town of Eastbourne on her domestic shopping visits, and gave me a mid-morning coconut cake.' She let him practise the piano in her private sitting-room and there he sneaked looks at the weekly magazines and returned to the girlie world he loved of cosmetics, millinery, frocks and artefact.

Cyril Connolly and George Orwell were his contemporaries. Orwell wrote of the horrors of St Cyprian's in an essay *Such, Such Were The Joys*. Connolly liked Cecil's dreamy face and long eyelashes. (Greta too, was complimented on the length of her eyelashes. Her mother said their advantage was that she need see only what she chose.) In end of term shows Cecil sang 'Willow-Tit-

Willow' and 'A Wandering Minstrel I'. Connolly remembered in particular his rendition of 'If you were the only girl in the world and I was the only boy'. The audience felt, said Connolly,

> there could be no other boy in the world for them, the beetling chaplain forgot hell-fire and masturbation, the Irish drill-sergeant his bayonet practice, the staff refrained from disapproving and for a moment the whole structure of character and duty tottered.

Holidays were Cecil's solace. At home he burgeoned as a fashion photographer. He inveigled his sisters into his camp, satiric world. They posed, 'with monumental patience' while he photographed them, as Pavlova, Gladys Cooper, medieval princesses, nymphs and brides. He dressed them in dust sheets, towels, chiffon and the curtains and achieved a blurred background by getting one of them to shake a rug behind the other. He learned the rudiments of printing from their nanny, Alice Collard, whose hobby was photography and who washed her snapshots in the spare room basin and mounted them in albums with the captions 'We'll All Go A-bathing', 'Doing Their Bit' and 'Peek-a-Boo'.

Cecil declared himself glad to have been born into Edwardian England which bridged Victorian bourgeois security and 'the febrile modernity that was to follow'.

> The manners and morals of the time, though still strict, were beginning to yield and a taste for spice could be detected. Balls and entertainments became ever more lavish . . . Life was so inexpensive that a dandy with four hundred pounds a year could go out dancing most nights of the week wearing lavender gloves . . . Theatre stalls cost half a guinea, operetta was in its heyday and chorus girls . . . began to marry into the peerage.

Cecil's youth coincided with the coming of cars, electric lights and, most important of all, the mass production of cheap, easy-to-use home cameras. On his twelfth birthday his parents gave him a No 3A folding pocket Kodak to replace his box brownie.

He sent his early photographs to magazines and endured frequent receipt of the printed slip 'The Editor's thanks and regrets'.

I felt uncomfortable at continually sending photographs of my own sisters to the magazines, but since they were my only sitters I had no choice and would post them from various addresses under different assumed names. There was great excitement when a rather baffled aunt telephoned to say she had received at her address a note informing her that Liadov's Portrait of Miss Nancy Beaton had been accepted for publication in a forthcoming issue of *Britannia & Eve*.

Photography interested him more than school, where he showed no academic ability. He got into Harrow by writing dates and facts on little pieces of paper and cribbing with these in the entrance exam. But Harrow suited him. He liked the blazers and top hats and thought himself 'so marvellous, so witty and bright'. He wore silk pyjamas, painted his room mauve and his lips red and always used to powder his nose. 'I must have been rather awful at Harrow,' he wrote in 1924, three years after he had left.

He acquired an Automatic Self-Portrait Release accessory for his camera, which allowed him to take photographs of himself. He was good at art and he took the female lead in drama society productions. He shunned sport and drill, read the poetry of Rupert Brooke and described himself as quiet and effeminate and with an unearned reputation for sexual escapade: 'wretched people thought just because I was frightfully pretty and luscious that I must be a little tart and just dressed nicely to get off with people. It just makes me sick and everything I did was taken in the wrong way.'

But it was for his own delight in costume, posture and show that he dressed flamboyantly and painted his face. He regarded himself as 'unphysical', thought the promiscuous boys 'frightfully naughty', and only went to bed with a boy called Gordon.

Though he could not pass the Cambridge entrance exams, the intervention of his father and housemaster secured him a place at St John's College. His housemaster wrote a candid reference for him on 21 July 1922:

As an artist he is quite exceptional and he is also good at English. During his time here he won the Senior Reading Prize. With the ordinary school subjects such as Mathematics and Latin, he is very weak indeed, in fact, bad. He left Harrow at Easter to be coached for the 'Little Go' but I regret to say he has failed to get through. But he is a very nice boy and I feel sure you would not regret admitting him to the College for a degree. I believe he would read English and French, perhaps, if one is able to take such a degree. During his last term, he was a House Monitor, and was able to enforce his authority. At games he is quite useless and they do not appeal to him.

'The only thing you have,' said Greta, 'is the fundamental thing inside you, whether you take it into a monastery or onto a soapbox.' Cecil took himself to Cambridge, on 4 October 1922, wearing an evening jacket, red shoes, black and white trousers and a huge blue cravat. He worried about his hair, which he felt was cut too short. When he complained to his mother she said, 'I'm sick of you worrying about your hair. There's every chance of it growing again. You're getting very conceited.'

He grew it into a shingle, varnished his fingernails, wore gauntlet gloves and a medieval cloak, kept a scrapbook and a journal and 'set about becoming a rabid aesthete'. His rooms were described as the most perfect in Cambridge, with tall, twisted wooden candlesticks, emerald green curtains, green cushions, green china, cerise paint and carved gilt furniture. He kept a green lovebird and when it disappeared offered a reward in the local paper if it was returned alive. For the Footlights, he designed costumes, wigs, props and sets and acted in plays and comic revues. *The Times* commended him for his dazzling silver raiment as Princess Teela in *The Gyp's Princess*. He was Princess Angelica in *The Rose and the Ring*, and Lady Would Be in the Marlowe Society's *Volpone*. The *Sketch* photographed him in choker pearls, heels and a train, wearing a crown and holding lilies, as the marchioness Matilda Spina in Pirandello's *Henry IV*. For his performance in *All the Vogue* in June 1925 the *New Cambridge* called him 'one of the best leading ladies the Footlights have had', with ravishing costumes. (Greta at the time was working in Pabst's *Joyless Street*, a story of prostitution and exploitation in poverty-stricken Vienna.) Photographs by Dorothy Wilding showed Cecil in a cartwheel hat and ruched frock with bouffant hair and pointed stilettoes. Photographs by Carlo Crivelli showed him with plunging necklines and roses pinned to his dress.

Pictures of him and by him began to appear regularly in the papers. A 1922 photograph of his friend and rival, Boy Le Bas – who shared Cecil's interest in theatre, men and pretty clothes – in *Photograms of the Year* was one of his early successes. In 1924 *Vogue* published his 'Duchess of Malfi' not knowing it to be a transvestite study of a friend, George Rylands. He was commended in the *Cambridge Review* for his self-portrait, shown at the Drawing Society. He acquired a studio above an electrician's shop where he photographed 'the more artistic of the Dons' wives with their Spanish shawls and daring Eton crops'. Ostensibly he was studying art, history and architecture, but he seldom went to lectures or tutorials and felt sleepy when he tried to write essays or to read of Chaucer's life. His landlord complained at the extra work created by his elaborate tea parties.

In college exams he could not answer any of the questions and spent the hours writing rot, or letters, or sitting doing nothing, without the courage to leave the hall. For one paper he realised he did not know who Edward II or Edward III were. At home in the vacation his father asked him 'awful' questions about Cambridge which he could not answer: How many St John's people are there in the rugger fifteen? How many St John's people in the cricket eleven? What are the St John's colours?

Frequently he visited London for parties, plays and exhibitions and for days of taking photographs. When he was twenty-one, in January 1925, his mother gave a dance which drew comment in the society columns. She wore a gown of eau-de-Nil trimmed with diamante and the family house was decorated with lilies, lilac and carnations. Cecil designed his sisters' silver-brocade frocks. Guests included Prince Ferdinand of Lichtenstein and Daphne du Maurier.

In pursuit of photography, art and high society Cecil's vitality was huge. His leisured façade concealed inordinate ambition to make his mark. Sexually, he liked to appear outrageous, but like a nice girl he tried not to go too far. He kissed, flirted and danced with his gay friends and to his private diary confided his feelings about desire. In October 1923 he wrote that he was really 'a terrible, terrible homosexualist' but tried very hard not to be. He tried, he said, to pretend to everyone that he was above 'horridness'. He wanted to behave affectionately toward the men he fancied and to sleep in the same bed with them, but that was all. 'Everything else is repulsive to me and yet it's awfully difficult!'

As for women

I adore to dance with them and take them to theatres and private views and talk about dresses and plays and women, but I'm really much more fond of men. My friendships with men are much more wonderful than with women. I've never been in love with women and I don't think I ever shall in the way that I have been in love with men.

He wrote that he did not want people to know him as he 'really really' was, but as how he was trying to pretend to be. His confessional diary was, he said, his real self.

Forty years later, at the time of the Wolfenden Report, when some sex between men was deemed legal, he wrote of how he wished that 'this marvellous step forward' could have been taken when he was young. 'It is not that I would have wished to avail myself of further licence, but to feel that one was not a felon and an outcast could have helped enormously during the difficult young years.'

He left Cambridge in 1925 without a degree and with nothing clear about his future but his desire to shine and his ambition to succeed. For a while he lounged at home doing very little apart from smoking Pera cigarettes and taking long hot baths and with no idea of how to earn his living. Then his father gave an ultimatum that he find work within six weeks or start as a clerk in the City office. The Hyde Park family house was expensive to run, business was poor and money short.

Cecil made a few desultory attempts to find work. He showed his designs to the theatre impresario, C. B. Cochran and drew a jacket cover for a travel book written by a Cambridge friend. He did a drawing of a black felt hat under a glass dome, for which he was paid three guineas – then he escaped to a fancy dress party in Cambridge, wearing pink chiffon and a bustle. He drank cocktails and champagne, was stroked, licked and smothered with kisses by boys called Philip and John, and was sick over Anthony Jenkinson's couch. In November 1925 – two months after Greta had arrived in Hollywood – he began as a ledger clerk in his father's office for £2 a week.

He travelled by underground to an office that he said was overheated and smelled like an underground lavatory. His father kept a rubber wrapped in a piece of paper in a drawer and unwrapped and rewrapped it every time he used it. Cecil thought it all petty, ridiculous and unprofitable, dreaded the opinion of his friends, cried with rage when he got home and lasted eight days in the job. During those eight days he reduced the accounts' books to a chaos of mistakes, crossings out and omissions. His father hired a Dutch book keeper to redress the damage.

The family moved house to Sussex Gardens in 'a horrible neighbourhood of Paddington'. Cecil found brief respite from his career problems by supervising the decor for the new place. Nancy and Baba's bedrooms were peppermint pink and Botticelli blue, the drawing-room was apple green and gold, his own room was pink with hand-painted buff lilies and scarlet and gold bed-hangings. But he could not tolerate 'the squalor of being shut up with one's family like cabbages'. After Cambridge, he longed for a better world. He called his mother's circle dowdy, common and brainless – 'the worst sort of people'. He loathed his parents' unremarkable, uncreative lives – the fact that they travelled by bus and talked about whether theatre seats were worth the money. He dreaded the way his father clicked his tongue, ate cheese off a knife, asked his daughters to kiss him and the smell of his pipe.

Cecil described his father as a man of quality – a sport, kind and with a sense of humour – but was terrified of becoming like him. He felt he had to work unceasingly on himself to avoid this. 'He is my living nightmare for it strikes terror in my heart that I may become like him and in the ways that I resemble him I am aghast . . .' His rejection of his father was a litany of points of recoil. It in part explained his preoccupation with artefact, fantasy and style. He disliked the hair on his father's body, 'so profuse and uniform', his hands which he described as hairy and podgy with the fingers bending the wrong way, the fluffiness on the lobes of his ears, his rounded shoulders, his noises in the bathroom. 'I hate the incessant breathing, yawning, like a storm of gas escaping from a pipe – and I hate the sighs and grunts and groans and unlicensed cough. I hate the piled plates of double helpings.' Nor was Cecil overly interested in his brother, Reggie, born in 1905. He found no thrill in photographing either of them.

To compound Cecil's humiliation, his father then paid a Swedish friend, a Mr Schmiegelow, to hire him as a clerk in April 1926. Cecil learned to use a typewriter and to send out invoices for sacks of cement. He stuck it for a few months, did the minimum expected of him, nattered and drank tea with Miss Robertson and Mr Skinner and skived off at every opportunity. The situation was so inappropriate that it panicked him into serious focus on his true ambitions. He studied costume design at the British Museum, built up his portfolio, wrote to publishers asking for appointments to show his book jacket designs, tried for a job at the BBC reading stories, showed his photographs to the editors of *Eve* and the *Tatler*, tried to write a play which he could not finish and angled for invitations to the best parties and balls.

'Anything for the uprise', he wrote of his social aspirations. He quit Schmiegelow's office in September 1926. Word got round that his charges for 'home-made' photographs were modest, which led to a steady trickle of cash. Then, at a ball at the Hyde Park Hotel he was noticed by Allanah Harper, who was extravagantly rich, but had broken away from the debutante world and

much to her mother's disapproval, discarded her ostrich feather fan and silver kid shoes in favour of a highwayman's cape and buckles. She now made a niche for herself in the half-worlds of Chelsea and Bloomsbury, and gave me a key to that fascinating other-life for which I had been searching.

She brought Edith Sitwell to Sussex Gardens to have lunch and to be photographed by Cecil. 'Edith ate heartily of a piping hot fish soufflé which was a triumph except that it had bones in it.' When Manley (the family servant) proffered red wine with the fish she 'entolled in her bell-clear voice, "White, please"'. She recited from Gertrude Stein during dessert and spent the whole afternoon in exotic poses. She epitomised an artistic aristocrat and by posing for Cecil gave him a chance to rise above his bourgeois background. His photographs of her were a triumph and by the end of 1926 his profession was underway:

> The telephone bell rings all day. It seems that the young girls I've lately come in contact with have nothing better to do than to call me: . . . 'Take my photograph again and let me bring Tanis, Meraud, Honey and Rosamond' . . .
>
> The girls sat round in various stages of *décolletée*, as I like to take bare shoulders. With everyone in her slip, the room looked like a dormitory. (When I was photographing the du Maurier sisters, outspoken Daphne said it looked like a brothel.) . . .
>
> We had a riotous afternoon. Inez's friends kept saying they hadn't enjoyed themselves so much for ten years . . . I tried to keep my head and bring into play all the stunts and tricks I've developed.

He took most of the developing to Selfridges' photographic department, then spent hours retouching prints with pencil and paint. His pictures were like gifts. Glamorised and outrageous, they provoked shrieks of enthusiasm and gave him an income and a reason for keeping company with the upper echelons of society, the 'Bright Young Things'. His clients were the daughters and wives of fathers and husbands who graced the pages of *Debrett's*, *Who's Who* and Mrs Whish's social column in the *Daily Express*: Teresa and Zita Jungman whose stepfather was Richard Guinness; Tanis and Meraud whose mother, Mrs Benjamin Guinness, was

London's most celebrated hostess; Lady Eleanor Smith, who wrote novels and was the daughter of Lord Birkenhead; Inez Holden who wrote novels too; Lady Mary Thynne who was to marry Lord Nunburnholme; Elizabeth Ponsonby, 'always ready for a lark'; Peggy Broadbent, Cynthia Noble . . . All gave fabulous parties, had town and country houses, butlers who did not serve red wine with the fish, and fathers who did not eat cheese off knives. To be photographed by Cecil became the in-thing – as fashionable as Oxford bags, brilliantine and cocktails. Cecil and Reggie kept cards on the hall table at Sussex Gardens with IN on one side, OUT on the other. Cecil's read OUT most nights.

True elevation came with the help of Stephen Tennant. Stephen was the fifth child of Lord Glenconner and Pamela Wyndham. Inherited money on both sides made for a life of privilege and luxury. Among their properties was Wilsford Manor in Salisbury. The grounds needed the work of sixteen gardeners and the surrounding land was theirs from Stonehenge to the Avon. Lord Glenconner died in 1920 and two years later Stephen's mother married a family friend, Viscount Grey of Falloden, who owned Falloden Hall in Northumberland.

Stephen studied at the Slade, wrote poetry and prose, finger-waved his hair and sprinkled it with gold dust, was the friend of Rex Whistler, the lover of Siegfried Sassoon and the hero, Cedric, in Nancy Mitford's novel *Love in a Cold Climate*. Asked as a child by his father what he wanted to be when he grew up, Stephen replied A Great Beauty. His mother dressed him as a girl until he was eight and thought him a genius, his hectic vocabulary inspired by William Blake.

His sensitivity was acute, his understanding of literature and painting wide, his health and mental stability poor. He liked to dress up, paint, perfume and pose. At a party given by Mr Neil McEarharn he appeared as the Queen of Roumania. When he saw

Cecil's photographs they triggered a nerve. Here in black and white was the reflection of his own preoccupation with femininity, artefact, narcissism and lost identity, where a man might appear to be a woman and a woman might appear to be a doll.

Cecil met him in December 1926 at a party given by the Guinness sisters, Tanis and Meraud. He felt 'puffed with pride that he so gushed at me. He'd noticed masses of things I'd done . . .' they sat in a corner and made elaborate plans for photographs in fancy dress and balletic pose.

On 22 December, a Wednesday, Stephen, Cecil and the Guinness girls went to the Circus at Olympia. Stephen wore a black leather coat with a wide chinchilla collar and blew kisses to the world at large as he rode a papier-mâché horse on a merry-go-round. They all had rides on the switchback railway and the giant racer cars and shrieked and whooped and camped it up while hoi polloi 'stared and glared and even laughed'. Cecil, known to squirm at the slightest *faux pas* from his father, condoned outrageousness from people so rich, so aristocratic. He loathed though the exploitation of the circus performers: an elephant on a bicycle, 'little midgets' and 'malformed people', terrified lions, dogs made to jump through hoops, a tattooed woman with 'sheepish kind eyes', 'the fattest woman like a great sow', a man on a tightrope dressed as a woman. He thought it a spectacle of indecency and it made him feel sick.

The party went back to the Guinnesses' house, sang sentimental songs, played games of who was like what flower, gave imitations of 'awful people' and planned costumes for eternal photographic sessions.

Stephen wrote to Cecil of his thrills at the circus and his hope of further bliss:

I want to be photographed drowned in picturesque rags like this . . . A sham moon would be such fun! & your lighting always looks like moonlight anyway & is the loveliest lighting I've ever seen in any photographs.

A dream came true for Cecil when Stephen invited him to Wilsford for the weekend of Saturday 15 January 1927. In the morning, at Selfridges, he had his hair trimmed and his face massaged:

> Massey, the man who always does me, gave me a particularly strenuous massage and pummelled my face until he was worn out and exhausted. It was almost like a rape . . . I am very ticklish and nearly died with suppressed laughter when my chin and neck were fingered.

Clay was spread over Cecil's face to tone his skin and tighten his pores. As it set, he fantasised 'as usual' that the mask would be as beautiful as Paula Gellibrand, who was one of his favourite beauties, was married to the Marquis de Casa Maury and wore model clothes by Worth.

Cecil's luggage was smart and his underwear silk, new and expensive. He anticipated a perfect weekend. Reggie drove him to the train and he travelled down with Eleanor Brougham, erstwhile lady-in-waiting to the Queen of Spain, with Steven Runciman, a Fellow of Trinity College, whom Cecil had known and photographed at Cambridge and with Dorothy Wilde – Oscar Wilde's niece, who wrote, took cocaine and had a fraught affair in Paris with Natalie Barney.

They were met at the station and chauffeured to Wilsford. Cecil thought the place lovely, picturesque and 'obviously the home of artistic, clever people'. There were aviaries in the gardens and a profusion of exquisite, delicate flowers. They were ushered into a long oak room, where sat Stephen, his mother Lady Grey, and the Jungman sisters. The room seemed wonderful to Cecil with enormous soft chairs, hyacinths and freesias, a 'lovely untidy litter of books' and a huge wood fire.

Stephen was wearing plus fours and a jumper with a lizard skin belt. He said 'glorious things the entire time. Funny, trite, importantly exact things'. No matter that he shouted with excitement and that his voice sounded affected. Cecil was enraptured and thought this the happiest weekend of his life. He was complimented and flattered for his sophisticated, brilliant and witty eyes, for his sureness and accuracy and for his porcelain skin. They all said 'ecstatic' things about him until he felt he was 'dying of happiness'. He thought Lady Grey gracious, queenly and eloquent. They sat on the floor in front of a great log fire, burned scent in a long-handled spoon and played 'Analogies', word games and 'Interesting Questions'.

At bedtime, Stephen showed Cecil to the Celandine Room – 'all the bedrooms have equally lovely names'. Stephen 'was almost embarrassingly social . . . I am more polite and womanly social than most but Stephen is incredible. One cannot get within him at all.' He went 'mad with joy' at the sight of Cecil's dressing-gown. Tailor-made, of imitation leopard skin, it was in the style of a Russian Coachman's coat – very long with a high double-breasted waist and original coachman's buttons.

Cecil wandered around the Celandine room in 'a trance of happiness': the William Morris wallpaper of little flowers and leaves in different greens on white, the four-poster bed, hung with chintz, the vases of white hyacinths, jasmine, columbine, roses and violets, all in mid-winter, the lamps in odd corners, the wood fire, the piles of all the books he had ever wanted to read – it all gave him 'jets of delight'. He put on his flimsy, speckled pyjamas that went completely with the room. He wrote in his diary that he wanted to eat all the books and all the flowers and Stephen as well.

The next day they screened the windows in Stephen's bedroom for a photo session. Lady Grey posed precisely and took great pains to get her hands right. Cecil thought her lovely, though sometimes – with his eye for the unlovely too – he viewed her face as 'crabbed, snarled and parroty'. Stephen postured and prinked 'in a way in which in anyone else would have been disgusting'.

After elaborate preparations and endless delays Cecil took group photographs of them all dressed in extraordinary garments and lying upside down. There were 'screams of laughter' in the middle of most of the poses. He and Stephen then gave imitations of chorus girls, Cecil pretended to be Gladys Cooper and they all danced Viennese waltzes and gavottes. 'The energy and vitality of Stephen was terrific and he looked so very beautiful.'

They played more games and tried to draw the faces they thought they would like to have. Then Cecil had a bath in a lovely room with a wood fire and pots of flowers, put on his new silk underwear and dressed for dinner. The food was excellent, the champagne cool and he was sad when the visit came to an end. 'It was awful to go,' he wrote. They sat in the flower-filled sitting-room listening to 'Bye bye blackbird' on the gramophone. There was a long wait at the station, the train was full and they travelled back to London in the luggage van.

Cecil considered the weekend a 'great move' in his life. He was at last among people of his choice. He felt 'gloriously happy and thankful' that he had met Stephen and inordinately relieved that he had moved from his father's Holborn office and not continued in that 'rotten, miserable, unsuccessful, unhappy, undeveloped state'.

Stephen was ecstatic when Cecil sent him the prints of his mother:

Oh I can't tell you how *lovely* I think the big silver ones are!!!! I sit and gaze and gaze at the full-face one. I have not shown them to mummie as I shall produce one for her as a radiant Easter present.

He wrote of 'blissful afternoons of photographic egotism' and longed for more of it all. Lady Grey loved number 8 and wanted to buy the negative, and was happy for Cecil to send numbers 1, 2, 3 and 4 of her to the society pages of the papers.

Later in the year, in August, Cecil had another stint, photographing Stephen alone, who wrote of the results from Falloden Hall:

Dear Cecil

You say that I must tell you quietly and seriously what I think of the photographs. When I tell you that I am *nearly crazy* at their beauty you may be able to understand a fraction of my difficulty . . .

I think seven or eight are *quite* perfect, luscious and dizzy and melting and the bare shoulder ones are like sculpture, too beautiful for words! . . . I can't believe that ever even for *one moment* I've looked as beautiful as this but I suppose your camera is enchanted and I suppose you touch them up brilliantly. I don't suppose they are like me and perhaps that's beside the point . . .

I just go on looking at them in a dream of bliss . . . if I had the money I would order a hundred of almost all of them and send one to everyone I've ever met – how flattering are they?? I cast desperate glances at the mirror while looking at them.

Here was a sister spirit, who revered the enchantment of Cecil's camera and the brilliance of his touch-up paint and who knew the sexual impulse behind his creative eye. Stephen felt free to write to Cecil 'I arrange magnolias all day' or 'Where can I get the leopard skin which forms your ravishing dressing-gown?' or to tell him that he was making Valentines: 'I've just made one that would *ravish* you. I give a little sigh whenever I look at it and realise that a Valentine is the very core of beauty to me. Lace on lace on lace. There is a lace gate which opens.' He could ask Cecil to photograph his boyfriend, Siegfried, 'Take lovely ones. Large heads. I want one marvellous full face one and one marvellous profile looking his very best. Not the tortured scarred hermit.' Cecil gave Stephen the brilliance of his own arrested image, more flattering than any mirrored reflection, and silvery pictures of his mother and lover that he could gaze upon at will. Stephen could give to Cecil an invitation to fairy-tale society. An invitation to a world closed to Ernest Beaton and Mr Schmiegelow. Far from being left in the cold by these awesome aristocrats, Cecil was flattered, admired, accepted, adored – and paid.

As his success snowballed, he found in himself unquenchable ambition and an inordinate capacity for work. His house at Ashcombe, with the circus bedroom, was inspired by Wilsford – Edith Olivier, to whom he was introduced by Stephen, helped him find it. Parties and commissions followed from Wilsford. And then a contract with *Vogue*. And then a contract with *Vogue* in America, commissions for photo features of the Hollywood stars, articles about beauty, photographs of royalty and his infatuation with Greta Garbo.

This infatuation, too, Stephen could well understand. Together, at Wilsford, they looked at photographs of her: 'We swooned at the beauty of Garbo whom Stephen in character and personality resembles a great deal,' Cecil wrote in his diary.

7

Cecil's Years Between

'One must live for oneself. One's own life is all one has.'
Queen Christina

Fourteen years passed between Cecil's first and second meeting with Greta Garbo, years in which reality contrasted with his stylised photographs with a harshness that showed his images as a mask, a meretricious façade.

Stephen Tennant's mother, Lady Grey, died in April 1929. She had a stroke while gardening at Wilsford. Stephen, on holiday with Siegfried in Versailles, received the news by telegram. Cecil, at a dinner party in New York, heard it as a chance remark. He saw the implications of her death: 'There would be no one to look after Stephen – poor Stephen . . . poor, poor Stephen.'

'Grief', wrote Stephen to him after his mother's death, 'turns one into such a queer being.' By degrees he retreated from the dizzy, party world. He was often ill – first with tuberculosis, perhaps aggravated by the exotic birds kept by his mother in huge aviaries in the grounds of Wilsford – then by incapacitating depressions and their psychotic flip side that battered and destroyed his insecure identity. 'I feel so ill and wretched,' he wrote:

> you see now I have nobody to fuss over me and forbid me to do things so I have to do the forbidding myself as I can't face all that illness again. You can't imagine how lonely it is without my

mother as my Nannie. I am in some ways so completely desolate and in a way, luckily, I don't feel able to have fun like I used to, or to tire myself out – and think it *more* than worth it – which I used to do.

He spoke of the 'crushing tragedy' of ill-health for someone as feverishly social in temperament as himself and stalled at meeting Cecil:

Yes let's meet in Spring – somewhere . . . let's make a plan nearer the time and go to some lovely place and draw and write shall we?

And you must help me with your lovely taste in knocking this house to bits in the Spring – and we'll flood it with Borzois and start a stable, ride on the downs and live in white glass rooms confected by Syrie [Maugham] and be *Oh* so beautiful and gay.

In the twenties, Stephen was an heretical inspiration to Cecil, the dazzling outer form of an ever-tempting inner dream. Cecil was enchanted by his wealth, narcissism and way of parading femininity with a confidence as taboo to men as were Greta's trousers and Mercedes' neckties to women.

But Stephen's beauty faded. His appearance cracked, like *The Picture of Dorian Gray*. He grew fat – within twenty years he weighed twenty stone. Corroded by mental illness, he took to using cheap perfume and to applying his make-up crudely – bright blue eyeshadow, too much rouge and powder. By early middle age, what was left of his hair was dyed purplish magenta, grey pushing through from the roots. He lost his teeth and did not always wear his dentures. The golden suits and flowing coats gave way to baggy khaki shorts, dresses, ballet pumps, a clutch bag, a garden basket filled with pot pourri, bright silk scarves and huge jewels.

Cecil observed life's assault on Stephen's beauty and in time, Greta Garbo's, his mother's and his own. He abhorred such realities, turned to his work as a cosmetic, a concealment and went from success to success. 'All his thrilling life he scorned when life showed a dark wing,' Stephen said of him in 1981. Nothing obstructed his huge ambition. His talent for the 'uprise' and shrewdness as a photographer, took him into the highest echelons of established society. The Queen Mother visited him for lunch. 'For Cecil Beaton – who knows how to hitch his wagon to a star', Stephen inscribed a poem he sent him. He negotiated commissions for film, stage and costume designs, drawings for book jackets, illustrations for magazine articles, contracts for books and journalism.

At Ashcombe he recreated all he admired about Wilsford; the huge wood fires, romantic gardens, rooms with names, doves in the dovecot, extravagant hospitality with the talented, rich and gay. But when Stephen inherited Wilsford, under his uncertain stewardship, it became a travesty of what it was. The prototype turned to parody. 'I shall be very catty if your salon is prettier than mine and I shall stolidly imitate all your ideas,' he wrote to Cecil in 1930.

Stephen filled the house with silver and white baroque furniture, mirrors, and white carpets à la Syrie Maugham, kept shells and stones in the bath, painted many of the rooms pink, covered the stairs with fishnet and strewed the rooms with fans, lengths of cloth, woolly animals, pictures, books and scribblings. In the garden he kept reptiles, terrapins, cockatoos and an ibis, and pink and gold statues.

He measured his failure against Cecil's success. 'I do admire the *Drive* with which you organise your life,' he wrote to him. He painted, paid privately to publish his own poetry and for forty years struggled with the manuscript of an unfinished novel: *Lascar: A Story of the Maritime Boulevards*. His intelligence rebuked him for the chaos of his life. 'I like the unquestioning, cool intellectual detachment of Henry Reed's poetry. The refusal to be easy of approach. The temperate statement. The reserve of feeling.' To his private journal he confided

You will have to put a spurt on now Stephen if you wish seriously to make a name for yourself. You must hurry up if you really want it. Success. Never expect the world to be indulgent or easy of conquest. Work, sweat, dedication are needed for even the beginning of a career. Success is the child of audacity and hard work. There are no short cuts. If you write regularly every day the task becomes habitual.

In a foreword to a book of essays by his admired American friend, the writer Willa Cather, he wrote 'Art is not life . . . it is a method, the only one, of preserving the beauty of transient things, the wonder of youthful happiness . . .' Somewhere in the chaotic clutter of Wilsford, lay Cecil's photographs of him, forever beautiful and young.

During 1933 and '34 the Beaton family fragmented. Both Cecil's sisters married and he designed their wedding-dresses, choreographed the ceremonies, blazed the publicity. Nancy married in January 1933 at St Margaret's church in Westminster, dressed in ivory satin, ermine and pearls. The bridesmaids were linked by ropes of flowers. Cecil rivalled the bride, said the *Tatler*, in lavender grey trousers and waistcoat and a huge white satin stock made from his mother's wedding dress. The groom, Sir Hugh Smiley, of Great Oaks, Goring Heath, Oxfordshire, an officer with the Grenadier Guards, had, said Cecil, 'pale blue Hanoverian eyes and clipped speech and a brusque manner and at first it was difficult to get used to the idea of his being a member of the family'. The previous year he had been spurned by Nancy Mitford. She wrote that she liked his car and his income and thought him 'awfully nice and kind in his own way. But think of having blond and stupid children. But then one could be so *jolly well-dressed* & take lovers.' The following year Baba married Alec Hambro, of the Hambro banking family. She wore white satin and held dark red roses. Her bridesmaid wore crimson velvet and Cecil filled the church, St Mark's in North Audley Street, with pampas grass dyed red, and red poppies – 'symbols of blood and death'.

Perhaps these were for his brother Reggie, who had killed himself on 18 October 1933. Reggie went out that day at about teatime saying he was going to see friends. He left his card on the hall table turned to OUT. He died at eleven o'clock in the evening at Piccadilly Tube Station. The train service was held up for fifteen minutes and the police phoned the Beaton home at midnight. At the inquest, the train driver, George James Penton, of Egerton Road, Alperton, said that as he emerged from the tunnel he saw Flying Officer Beaton on the platform about a yard from the edge.

> He was looking straight ahead across the line. When I was a few feet from him he put his hands in front of him and dived in front of the train.

Reggie was twenty-eight and attached to Number 101 Bomber Squadron of the RAF at Andover, in Hampshire. Ernest Beaton told the Court that Reggie was worried about his eyesight and had seen a doctor, thinking he had conjunctivitis. He said Reggie was on leave for two weeks, liked the airforce, had no troubles and was in good health.

A friend of Reggie's, Mrs Margery O'Brien, told the Court he had previously blacked out when flying and that this had worried him. She said he was of a nice disposition and that she was sure he was not involved in a love affair. Captain Roland Spencer said he had seen Reggie at lunchtime at the RAF Club and had asked how he was feeling. Reggie said, 'A bit shook up.' He told him that the previous night he had been to the opening of a dance club, got home late, took 'a bunch of aspirin' to make him sleep and woke up at noon. On the way to the bathroom he had some sort of blackout.

Cecil told reporters, 'I cannot think why Reggie should have gone to the Piccadilly Tube Station.' The Coroner returned a verdict of suicide while of unsound mind and concluded that Reggie's worry over his eyesight had made him take his life. There was no alcohol in his body.

Cecil wrote in his diary that he felt sinisterly unmoved when he heard of Reggie's death, 'it leaves me so cold I am amazed'. Reggie, on the day of his death, had asked him a lot of questions before going out, but Cecil was reading a letter from Peter Watson and paid no attention. Cecil spent the afternoon riding in Richmond Park with Peter, then they went on to cocktail parties together.

Details of the family's appearance of grief imprinted on his mind. Baba, in a dressing-gown, without her make-up, her face shiny and pale, the light bright yellow, her hair fringed, telling him Reggie had been killed. His mother, dejected, weeping bitterly, chastising herself for scolding Reggie and allowing him to go out. His father (who had to identify Reggie's body) lying in bed, looking unattractive, coughing a lot, some of his false teeth out. Cecil observed every jot of surface detail, but was paralysed at centre. He did not use his observations to make psychological interpretations or to forge emotional links.

Cecil had seldom talked with Reggie or written to him. He felt they had nothing in common. Nor could he console their father though he knew Reggie had been the favoured son. Motoring back together from the funeral, 'in our black bereavement', his father took out his watch through force of habit and said, 'Now let me see what exactly is the time – how long has that taken – Oh I see, less than I had thought.' At one point he wept. Cecil drank sherry with his parents at the funeral gathering, then escaped to Ashcombe with Peter Watson and Rex Whistler.

Ernest Beaton could not come to terms with Reggie's death and became withdrawn and less able to manage his business. Etty, his wife, depressed by the tragedy and by their diminished living standards, withdrew from him. In December 1934 they moved from their house in Sussex Gardens. They relinquished their lease, sold their furniture for very little money and moved to two rented rooms in Notting Hill. 'The family has broken up,' Cecil wrote in his diary, '. . . and suddenly my parents' world has gone from beneath their feet.'

At Christmas they stayed with Cecil at Ashcombe. He found the forced jollity unbearable. Glasses were raised to absent friends. His father's inertia and habits goaded him and he had difficulty in being civil. As ever he was preoccupied by the fear of resembling him. 'I know that if I let go I should become the same.' It took constant activity, constant effort, to assert the personality manufactured as his own.

It was Ernest Beaton's last Christmas. The following April he had a stroke, was advised to give up work and died in August. His business losses claimed such capital as he had accrued and Cecil's mother would receive only £15 a month from a trust fund. Cecil, the surviving man of the family, felt responsible for her, financially and emotionally. 'We are the only two left,' she wrote to him, 'and I always worry while you are away in case of accidents or illness.'

Nor did Cecil find solace from these woes in his own affairs of the heart. His feelings for Peter Watson, by whom he felt snubbed and rejected, caused him little but humiliaton. He thought Peter more intelligent and better informed than himself and he extolled the way he bolted his food, or talked with his mouth full, or licked tomato juice from a glass. Cecil idealised his own desire: 'Physically he is maddeningly exciting to me – a huge frame sparsely covered with skin – huge knobbly hands – a broad neck and skeleton thin face – and the circles under his eyes so mysteriously deep.' His feelings were unrequited, so he did not have to test the 'maddening excitement' of desire against his own performance as a lover, or contend in an everyday sense with the reality of his lover's habits.

The affair undermined him. Many times, when he phoned Peter and asked if they might meet, Peter was too busy and made him feel embarrassed. 'It is quite easy to be busy and not to make anyone, even in my predicament, feel they have made a mistake.' He tried to explain that he needed to break free because he had made Peter into a god, that he was obsessed and miserable, always aching for Peter's presence, and always jealous.

Peter refused to involve himself in Cecil's declared feelings with their histrionic edge. 'If we cannot see ourselves as victims of others, we have to realise we are victims of ourselves,' he wrote to him. He said that love was subtler and more complicated than Cecil allowed, refused to discuss what he felt and time after time made it clear he would be relieved were Cecil to find someone else. 'Your own technique has made it uncommonly difficult for me to deal with you.'

Jealousy exacerbated Cecil's feelings of rejection. In 1933 Peter bought his man of the moment, Robert Heber-Percy, a Daimler. Cecil made a jealous fuss. Peter then sent a blank cheque to Ernest Beaton who had asked Cecil if it was on account of his blue eyes. 'Oh dear, how much nearer the point he was than he believed,' wrote Cecil in his diary. That was as close as father and son came to discussing Cecil's sexuality. Cecil used the cheque to buy a thousand pound Alvis. He brooded that his love would never be reciprocated, that his beloved 'will never be in love with me and will always fall for strumpets' and that through each and every intrigue he would be marginalised and miserable.

Lord Berners, poet, painter, composer and eccentric who lived at Faringdon House in Berkshire and was himself in love with Robert Heber-Percy, spoofed this and other intrigues in a privately published *roman-à-clef, The Girls of Radcliffe Hall*, written under the alias Adela Quebec. He set the tale in a girls' public school. Cecil was Cecily Seymours; Peter, Lizzie Johnson; Robert Heber-Percy, Millie Roberts; Oliver Messel, Olive Mason; Doris Castlerosse, Mr Dorrick the dancing master and Gerald Berners, the Headmistress, Miss Carfax. 'I do think it is perfectly monstrous that Lizzie should give Millie a car,' Berners wrote:

It is so unfair on poor Cecily, who is simply longing for a new car. Cecily is Lizzie's best friend and Lizzie has never even thought of giving her a bicycle.

Chagrined by the mockery of what he considered his deepest feelings, Cecil destroyed all copies of *The Girls of Radcliffe Hall* on which he could lay his hands.

Ill-at-ease with his sexuality, provoked by Peter and 'desperately in need of a successful love affair', he had various flings with women and men. In January 1933, as a salve to the pain of pining for Peter, he frolicked with Doris Castlerosse, who was rich, musical and fashionable. She did not get on with her husband, Valentine, a Viscount and gossip-columnist, fond of a drink, whom Beverley Nichols described as 'gross and lecherous and fundamentally dishonest'.

The affair only compounded Cecil's problems with Peter and led to conundrums of love: 'It seems so terrible,' he wrote in his diary, 'that I go to bed with "Doritzins" out of desperation when it could be so celestial with the bedfellow I love.' And how ironic it was that Peter, who did not love him, was so angered by his relationship with Doritzins whom he loathed, that he refused to see Cecil at all.

In spring in New York Cecil flirted with the dancer Tilly Losch, but found her offhand, so then had 'quite a charming romance' with the writer, Michael Duff. He liked his height and straight back, his heavy-lidded eyes, his spoilt mouth, his aristocratic nose, his charm, his lovely figure, his stutter. They drank gin and ginger ale in Cecil's rooms at the Sherry Netherland. They talked about Michael's mother, life at his family home – Vaynol, the novels he wrote and masturbation. Michael, 'sitting bolt upright like a dowager' said he always did it on train journeys, helped by the motion of the train.

Cecil thought him marvellous-looking, though lacking in 'rude chic'. He found him more attractive in tweed suits and tail coats than in pyjamas. He was put off by noticing that his back was spotty and that his nose needed blowing and felt certain he would be a bad lover. They gossiped late into the night. 'It's such fun having someone sleeping in the same room. We like the idea of dormitory life – midnight feasts and pillow fights.'

In effusive prose, Cecil continued to tell the world about Greta Garbo. He claimed his 'personal portraits' of her were based on observations made when he met her at the Gouldings'. In *The Sketch* in July 1934, he wrote of her beauty, her magnetic, gay, tragic, sensitive, intelligent personality, her biscuit-coloured hair, unlined face, skin smooth as marble, her nose 'so delicate and sensitive that she seems to be conscious of perfumes too subtle for other people to enjoy', her pearl-like teeth, incredible eyelashes, deep sense of humour and, unlike Michael Duff, her infinite chic. And then, with a twist of venom, of the sort he could level against Peter Watson, or his father, or women in general, or all whom he felt in some sense put him down, he berated her:

She is receptive to little except herself . . . She is not interested in anybody or anything in particular and naturally she has become as difficult as an invalid and completely egotistic; unused to putting herself out for anyone, she would be a trying companion, continually sighing, full of tragic regrets, without making any definite move to alter her general state of affairs.

Emotionally, Cecil, at the age of thirty, had found little for himself. Work was his consolation and area of control. By 1934 his contract with Condé Nast of *Vogue* paid him $17,000 a year and he sailed twice a year to New York on the *Queen Mary* or the SS *Aquitania*. To adorn his suite at the Waldorf Astoria, he travelled with huge trunks filled with paintings by Picasso, Derain and Matisse, bright cushions, screens, women's hats, stuffed doves, cobalt blue and red cocktail glasses and a six-foot Ficus plant. He scoured the junk shops on Third and Madison Avenues and acquired carved arabesques, gesticulating cupids, silver stucco work and bits of imitation Tiepolo ceilings. *Vogue* sent beautiful women to him and he photographed them in grottoes of flowers, against backgrounds of polka dots or in mirrored halls or baroque bowers. He photographed Natasha Paley, Helen Bennett, Gloria Swanson, Marlene Dietrich, Mona Harrison Williams, Katharine Hepburn, Mrs Patrick Campbell and all the fashion models of the moment. The papers wrote of his parties:

> Among those present were Mrs Harrison Williams, Mrs Randolph Hearst, Countess di Zoppola, Eleanor Barry, Elena Tiffany, Prince Serge Obolensky . . . the party was also a welcoming one for Jean Cocteau, French artist and author, who is passing through New York on his way around the world.

Cecil disliked being thought of principally as a photographer. Between 1936–8 he flourished as a set and costume designer, too. He designed costumes and scenery for C. B. Cochran's theatrical reviews, for Frederick Ashton's ballets *Follow the Sun* and *Apparitions*, starring Robert Helpmann and Margot Fonteyn and *Le Pavillon* for Boris Kochno at the Royal Opera House, Covent Garden.

In England in the winter of 1936 talk of King Edward VIII's love for Wallis Simpson and his anticipated abdication eclipsed the facts of economic decline, the rise of fascism and the rumblings of war. Greta Garbo, working on retakes for *Camille*, wrote to her friend Hörke Wachtmeister in Stockholm to ask if she, Greta, was forgotten now that Mrs Simpson was so interesting to everyone. 'Dear Mrs Simpson, now her quiet days are over. She'll be pursued wherever she goes.'

Cecil was invited to photograph Wallis Simpson, whom he first met in 1933 in America at an Arts Club Ball. She was introduced to him as a vague relation. Her husband, Ernest Simpson, was the brother of the aunt of Hugh Smiley, who married Cecil's sister, Nancy. Cecil, on that occasion, described Wallis as a 'brawny great cow in sapphic blue velvet' with a raucous and appalling voice.

By November 1936, when she was renowned as Edward VIII's mistress, and Cecil was invited to her house in Regent's Park to sketch and photograph her, he found her more alluring. She chatted to him about the unlikelihood of her marrying the King and of her hatred of gossip. She called him Cecil, told him to call her Wallis and offered him whisky and soda, eight different kinds of canapés and green grapes stuffed with cream cheese. He asked her if he might photograph the King and she said, 'You mustn't put any background in, he'd hate it.' The King had a bad cold, but he let Cecil do a sketch of him in profile.

These drawings and photographs were shown in an exhibition of Cecil's work at the Carroll Carstairs Gallery in New York. While this was on, Edward VIII abdicated after a reign of 325 days and announced his intention of marrying Mrs Simpson when her divorce came through. It was good publicity for Cecil and crowds thronged the gallery to see his pictures. *Vogue* then published, in January 1937, his exclusive portraits of Mrs Simpson. She was wearing necklaces of rubies and diamonds. She wrote to him from Cannes, where she had fled from publicity, to say that she liked the pictures and wanted to buy his sketches of her.

This was the making of his fame as a Court photographer. In May 1937 there followed the coronation of George VI. *Vogue* wanted photographs of Duchesses and Peeresses galore for their coronation number. Cecil photographed Lord and Lady Pembroke in coronation robes, the Duchesss of Westminster at her house in Little College Street, the Duchess of Northumberland, Mistress of the Robes to Queen Elizabeth, and the Grand Duke and Duchess of Hess.

In June he was invited to take the wedding photographs of the abdicated Edward and of Wallis Simpson, now Duke and Duchess of Windsor. He travelled to the Château de Candé at Tours, where they were to be married in a private ceremony on 3 June. Constance Spry was there, arranging mountains of flowers. So was another photographer, Mr Soper, whom Cecil ignored, thinking him a hack. Cecil took pictures of the couple in their wedding clothes on 2 June, the day before the ceremony: Wallis wore a blue dress and matching hat with feathers and the Duke a morning coat. They all lunched on the terrace. Cecil and Wallis had curried eggs and rice and kidneys and the Duke had strawberries and cream. Cecil thought the Duchess looked anxious and her face had come out in spots.

Vogue had exclusive rights over the pictures and, convinced of a lucrative scoop, Cecil hurried to their Paris office to have the pictures printed. He then flew to London fantasising about affording a new roof for the studio at Ashcombe, a new road down the valley and presents for his mother and friends. But the lesser Mr Soper pipped him to the post and syndicated a snap of the Simpsons to all the daily papers. The editor of London *Vogue* thought the picture was Cecil's and accused him of betrayal. Wounded and resentful, Cecil demanded an apology. '*Vogue*', he wrote in his diary, 'offers me little more than money and if I were a brave and courageous person I would give it up entirely and start something else.'

Neither bravery nor courage compelled him to give up *Vogue*. For the February 1938 issue some six months later he illustrated an article on New York Society by Frank Crowninshield. His doodly drawings of party life showed jazz musicians, cocktail shakers, false eyelashes and flappers. He drew a Western Union telegram and the society pages of a fictional newspaper scattered among the debris of champagne buckets, glasses and ashtrays. On the telegram he wrote: 'Party Darling Love Kike.' On the paper he wrote: 'Why??? is Mrs Selznick such a social wow – Why is Mrs Goldwyn such a wow? . . .

10.

CECIL FREQUENTLY PROPOSED MARRIAGE TO
GRETA. HER USUAL REPLY WAS 'PERHAPS' OR
'MAYBE'.

9. Cecil in bed at Ashcombe.
Self-portrait, 1931.

10. Greta as Anna Karenina.
Photo by Clarence Sinclair Bull, 1935.

11. Cecil in the costume he designed for
All the Vogue, Cambridge.
Photo by Dorothy Wilding, 1925.

12. Greta, photographed by Cecil in
her California garden, March 1948.

13.

14.

IN CODE CECIL'S PHOTOGRAPHS SHOW MERGED
IDENTITY, NARCISSISM, INSECURITY. GRETA'S
ANDROGYNOUS BEAUTY HAUNTED HIM – AND
HIS SENSE THAT SHE TOO WAS OUT OF LINE.

13. Cecil and Stephen Tennant.
Photo by Maurice Beck and Helen MacGregor, 1927.

14. Greta Garbo for *Susan Lenox*.
Photo by Clarence Sinclair Bull, 1931.

15. Cecil by Cecil, 1927.

16. Greta and Mercedes de Acosta
in Hollywood Boulevard.
Newsphoto, 1931.

Mr R. Andrew's Ball at the El Morocco brought out all the damned-kikes in town.'

Kike is a derogatory term for Jew. The El Morocco was, by the late thirties, the most famous night club in New York, frequented by the producers and moguls of Hollywood, like David Selznick, head of Selznick International Motion Pictures and Samuel Goldwyn of MGM, both of whom were Jewish. Reduced in size for publication, the lettering was legible only through a magnifying glass. An assiduous journalist spotted it when copies came out on 24 January 1938 and asked *Vogue*'s editor, Margaret Case for an explanation. Cecil was summoned. He felt scared in the taxi on the way to *Vogue*, but much more scared when he saw Margaret's face and the faces of the editors, lawyers and advertising men, gathered outside Condé Nast's office.

Condé Nast withdrew 130,000 copies of *Vogue* and Cecil gave a statement to the press:

Late this afternoon I apologised to Mr Nast for all the confusion and trouble caused by an utterly thoughtless and irresponsible aberration of my artistic temperament. Now I feel that I owe just as sincere an apology to the wide public that has been made conscious of this unfortunate lapse.

In my illustration of an article in *Vogue* there appeared some marginal lettering which was never meant to be read and which cannot be read without a magnifying glass. I regret this ill-mannered expression of my irritation and annoyance caused by some bad films I had just then seen. I know that none of my many Jewish friends will think that my silly little joke had any bearing on the standing of their great community. I am particularly distressed that my thoughtlessness and really quite meaningless indiscretion should have occurred at this time of unreasoned persecution of the Jews, which I abhor and detest just as deeply and sincerely as any other civilised human being.

On the evening of 24 January, Cecil went to the opera. A note was brought to his box by Condé Nast's butler, telling him to call at Nast's house before 10 pm. Nast fired him, paid him £3,184 compensation and told him he would not be able to work again for *Vogue*. The affair cost *Vogue* $36,000 in lost revenue.

Cecil thought the fuss unfair and felt 'reduced to a pulp' by the whole business. He did not see a connection between his own prejudice, which was snide, casual and unremarkable in the circles in which he moved, and politicised anti-semitism. His unedited diary entries were sprinkled with references to 'Jew producers' and to 'coons'. Unpenitent, in October he published another of his autobiographical books: *Cecil Beaton's New York*. In it, he wrote:

> In a city made up of so many nationalities and races, dangers lurk in everyday activities. It is difficult not to offend someone present when expressing an opinion in public. One can even reap a whirlwind (as I unfortunately discovered) by using a slang word of which one does not appreciate the full implications.

New York stores would not stock this book. The booksellers, Massey's, took one copy. The value of Cecil's photographic prints and drawings fell and he was cold-shouldered for years in film and theatre where so many directors and producers were Jews.

Without commissioned work from *Vogue*, and with his American contacts severed, Cecil travelled with friends in Europe and North Africa and resisted news and portents of war – the distribution of gas masks in Wiltshire villages, the digging of trenches in London's parks. Stephen Tennant said he liked Hitler's mysticism, the way he parted his hair and the mad stormy look in his eyes. Cecil's widowed mother gave up her London flat, moved permanently to Ashcombe and complained that Cecil left her alone too much with all the domestic matters to sort out.

In July 1939, some weeks before Germany invaded Poland, Queen Elizabeth summoned Cecil to Buckingham Palace. At first he thought the phone call was a hoax:

> But it was no joke. My pleasure and excitement were over-whelming. In choosing me to take her photographs, the Queen made a daring innovation. It is inconceivable that her predecessor would have summoned me – my work was still considered revolutionary and unconventional.

His knees shook when they met to discuss what dresses, tiaras and jewels she should wear. He found himself imitating her jerky speech and staccato expressions. He kept saying it was a great happiness for him, and he asked her to wear as much jewellery as possible. 'The Queen smiled apologetically – "The choice isn't very great you know."'

He spent more than three hours with her and photographed her in a ruby-encrusted crinoline of gold and silver, with diamonds the size of walnuts and rows of enormous pearls. He worried about the lack of definition in her face, persuaded her to put on eyeshadow and, as a memento of the honour bestowed, stole and sniffed her hand-kerchief, 'scented with tuberoses and gardenias'.

Cecil's reverence for The Queen was real. She, like Greta Garbo, was a symbol of female power, a heightened presence. Crowns, orbs, jewels and robes were the ultimate props in the dressing-up box, the trappings of superior status and a way of concealing identity behind a festooned façade. In his diary he wrote of how the presence of royalty disturbed and excited him and raised the tempo of his life 'like a wedding', and of how 'sadly let down' he felt when he left Buckingham Palace and picked up the threads of his 'more dreary existence'.

But Cecil also, with scathing misogyny, felt compelled to blow the cover, to scorn such elevated status and suggest that beneath the trappings was a ridiculous nakedness, no better than his own. Publication of his photographs of The Queen, in December 1939, coincided with that of a high camp spoof on royalty he had written, a quasi autobiography of a baroness, featuring the antics of imagined royal relatives. Called *My Royal Past* and ostensibly the autobiography of Baroness Von Bülop, née Princess Theodora Louise Alexina Ludmilla Sophie Von Eckermann-Waldstein, the book included photographs of Lord Berners in ermine and embroidered robes, Francis Rose in a dress with his moustache painted out, and Michael Duff and Frederick Ashton in tiaras, garters and decolleté gowns. 'In my garden of memories' and 'Myself and Wee Wee, a splendid little pal', read the captions to the photographs of Cecil's gay friends in regal drag.

The book satirised Cecil's own preoccupations and proclivities, as well as those of the royals whom he derided and adored:

Standing before the mirror, trying on my aunt's hats and cloaks, as young girls will do, I realised how happy those days were. Before some court function I would sit sharing a simple meal on an occasional table with my aunt, in her *peignoir*, while her jewels were being sewn on the corsage of her gown, so stiff and heavy that it would stand alone. She would eat some ham or egg dish, her hair dressed, her diadem already affixed. One evening I wittily remarked, 'You, auntie, wear your diadem as a Scotchman wears his tam-o-shanter.' Every afternoon I drove with the Grand Duchess through the parks in her carriage, and by degrees, day by day, I realised more and more that not only was my aunt imperial, but, at the same time, somehow so intensely *human*. I became my aunt's *confidante* and whenever she wished to discard the harness of royalty and make some trip incognita, I would accompany her on these innocuous little expeditions.

The trips were for sex of an unorthodox sort. Reviewers thought the book anodyne and almost funny. Peter Watson saw its cutting edge. He wrote to Cecil:

> I consider the coinciding of publication [of *My Royal Past*] with the queen's photographs perfect da-da and proof of my old contention, your implacable will to shock. It is in fact a masterstroke even to see the book with its sinister undercurrents of sex, perversions, crass stupidities and general dirt, beaming serenely from Maggs Bookshop in Berkeley Square. I admit you are the only person alive able to put such a thing across and I consider it a remarkable achievement.

Thus Cecil indulged his desire to assume the role of a woman, his fascination with royalty, his subversiveness and his social and career ambitions, all at the same time.

Such frolics went into the shade as 1939 drew to an end. 'The prospect is for a long war and the worst horrors are still unknown to us,' Cecil wrote in his diary. Londoners prepared themselves for air raids, shops were deserted and stories circulated of the German invention of an atomic bomb and of bombs 'sent by propellers from aeroplanes sixty miles away'.

Cecil said that the war was specifically designed to show up his inadequacy 'in every possible capacity'. He briefly tried voluntary jobs for which he was unsuited – food distribution and operating an early warning telephone. Then, in March 1940, he organised a pantomime, *Heil Cinderella*. Profits went to the Forces. He and Olga Lynn, who was small in height and large in girth and had been taught to sing by the Polish tenor, Jean de Reszke, were the ugly sisters, Rex Whistler painted the scenery and Michael Duff's mother, Juliet, was the Queen. The pantomime was performed in Brighton and Bournemouth and then for a week at the Fortune Theatre, Covent Garden. Cecil's costumes were 'a riot of fantasy and colour'. There were jokes about the Maginot Line and songs from musical comedies. He and Oggie Lynn quarrelled and she 'threw a temperamental scene in front of an audience', which, he said, stopped his heart.

He bought as an office base a London house in a Georgian terrace, 8 Pelham Place, South Kensington. He hired Oggie Lynn's lover, Maud Nelson, as his secretary, though she could neither type nor file, was unstable and high-handed, never dated letters and drank his gin. Most evenings he 'beetled off to the Dorchester' for wine, music and company. In the hope of being appointed an official war photographer, he took pictures of war ministers, secretaries of state, and debutantes playing with evacuated children. He sent a selection of these pictures to the art historian Kenneth Clark, who was then Controller of Home Publicity at the Ministry of Information.

While his application was considered, Cecil sailed in May 1940 to New York to take advertising photographs for Pond's Cold Cream. He 'travelled with a load of German refugees making their escape from persecution . . . How different this trip to those of the old days when there were concerts, celebrities, dances, champagne, balloons.' On deck he talked with Professor Loewi, a scientist from Graz, a Nobel prizewinner, who had been imprisoned and deprived of his possessions by the Nazis:

We sat drinking beer. Loewi talked of Garbo. But in what a way he talked of her! He has no money for the cinema, but makes one exception each time there is a Garbo film . . . Why should Garbo appeal universally – to him, to me, to millions of others? He considers that she, as with certain lyric poetry, is the condensation, the concentration of the hidden, but ever present, sadness that is in all people. For every grown-up person Garbo possesses, too, the sadness that is dormant in a child, when, robbed of its protective armour of courage against the world, it lies asleep.

Photographing the sadness of a child – three-year-old Eileen Dunne – in a hospital bed with her head bandaged because of a shrapnel splinter – almost restored Cecil to favour with *Vogue* in America. The photograph, sentimental and neither violent nor shocking, struck an acceptable note of patriotism. It was used as the cover of *Life* and as a charity poster in the States. Kenneth Clark approved Cecil's application and the Ministry of Information commissioned him to travel England, visit shipyards and munitions and aircraft factories, and provide a record of the effects of the war.

At first his wartime photographs kept to his preoccupations with artificiality, surface detail, fashion and mirror image. He showed wreckage as pattern, and bomb-damaged London as misty and surreal. He photographed a fashion model standing against a background of rubble, instead of balloons or rococo trappings. As the war went on – and he took hundreds of photographs every week – his style became more realistic and less contrived. He put aside his camp façade and moved from fantasy to documentation. 'Under a lackadaisical manner he was a determined dynamo and a stalwart patriot. His seriousness was held in reserve,' Harold Acton wrote of him. In the best of his pictures, taken of RAF fighter pilots, he harked back to his peacetime narcissism. His own mirror image is reduced to shadow and the eyes of the pilot, doomed to kill or die, meet the camera.

From tours of RAF stations he produced articles, photographs and two books – an anthology of photographs called *Air of Glory*, and *Winged Squadron*, a fictional piece about the courage of airmen, written for propaganda. With James Pope-Hennessy he collaborated on a book about blitzed London, called *History Under Fire*, showing how the city survived bombardment. Aware that the party days were over, and that the world had changed entirely, he published *Time Exposure* which showed his work from the suddenly incongruous decades of the twenties and thirties. And, ever determined to be more than a photographer and journalist, he tried to write a play.

It was about the Viceroy of India. He read passages of it aloud to the actress Coral Browne, with whom he had a secret affair in the autumn of 1941. They met in the afternoons because she was living with the impresario, Firth Shephard. Air raids provided her excuse not to return to him. (In later years Coral Browne gave contradictory accounts of Cecil's performance as a lover. To Hugo Vickers, his authorised biographer, she said he was 'very passionate and ardent'. To the actress Adrienne Corri she said that having an affair with Cecil was 'a bit like being a sailor'.)

The war, as it proceeded, changed Cecil. Though he kept distance from the battleground, and was lightweight as a war reporter, his spectator's eye became more grave. In 1942 he secured a commission from the Ministry of Information to travel to the Near East and photograph the work of the Royal Air Force and whatever was useful for propaganda or public records. 'It is a thrilling prospect and there is now a star shining brightly in front of me.'

With one Rolleiflex, which at night he wrapped in a silk handkerchief, he travelled in 1942 to Cairo, the Western Desert, Iran, Iraq, Palestine, Transjordan and Syria. He stayed in the desert, under canvas, with the servicemen and at night could hear the sound of enemy gunfire. He saw the primitive graves of German soldiers, aged about twenty when they died, and recorded the relics of battle: the carcasses of burnt-out aeroplanes half-buried in sand, overturned trucks, a litter of gasmasks and water bottles, clothing caught in wires, the boredom of men consigned to a waiting existence.

In Tobruk he photographed burned and wounded soldiers at the Sixty-second General Hospital. From being a photographer of the fashionable surface of beautiful women, he now saw different surfaces:

I could hardly believe it was human – a couple of eyes blinked out of a terrible growth of vivid blues, greens, purples, blacks and dark greens. On the head a mat of sand coloured hair . . . only the stomach remained flesh coloured and since the chest was constricted with burns and paint, the stomach had to blow itself out and in, double time, double measure.

'Do you want to take this'

But oh no! This was too much.

Instead, he photographed British Ambassadors, German prisoners, the Shah of Persia and the King of Iraq and at Damascus panicked at news of the approach of the German army, led by Rommel. He had 'walking nightmares' of being taken prisoner, scarred for life and unable to return to his former life if he survived. But survive he did and left Cairo hurriedly, with the German army ninety miles away. He returned to England via the Sudan, Lagos and Portugal.

Back home his work was praised by the Ministry of Information. He published *Near East*, a well-received book about his trip and was viewed as a patriot, a man of the establishment. He again sold his work to *Vogue*, who were now cautiously prepared to forgive his former 'thoughtless and irresponsible abberations'. And then, on 23 October 1942, he was summoned to Buckingham Palace to photograph the King and Queen and Mrs Roosevelt – whom he described in his diary as enormous and elephant-coloured. A few months later he photographed each of the royal family individually – The King, The Queen and their daughters, Elizabeth and Margaret, who reminded him of Nancy and Baba. He lunched with them all at Windsor Castle, sat next to The Queen and talked to her about nothing in particular.

The war earned him *gravitas* as a photographer and forced him to acknowledge harsh realities. His brother-in-law, Alec Hambro, was killed in active service in 1943, leaving Baba and their two young daughters. That year Cecil spent most of the time in England. He designed the sets and costumes for Shaw's *Heartbreak House*,

starring Edith Evans, and he wrote a book about British photographers.

In December the Ministry of Information sent him to the Far East
on a commission similar to the previous one. His first stop was to be
India and he was to leave right away. The Dakota in which he was to
fly to Gibraltar for the first lap of his journey crashed on take off
and caught fire. After what he called this 'false start', his Far East
tour to India and China was only relatively adventurous.

His brief from the MOI was to send propaganda reports and
photographs in praise of the Empire and the war effort. He photographed Louis Mountbatten, Admiral and Supreme Commander of
the South East Asia Command, visited eleventh-century Hindu
forts and early Mohammedan cities, stayed with the Viceroy in
Delhi who had three hundred servants, photographed the RAF
station at Peshawar, camped with British troops in jungle terrain on
the Burma front, got eaten by leeches and afflicted with dysentery,
dined at Government House in Bombay, drank rose water mixed
with hashish in Benares and hallucinated wildly, photographed Jain
temples and Calcutta students, Chinese generals, governors and
professors. The Ministry sent telegrams of rebuke for his consign-
ments of uncaptioned negatives and endless portraits of British
personalities:

> Most serious gaps in Indian series lack of typical village life scenes
> schools hospitals and social services featuring Indians.

He flew home via Aden, Cairo, Accra, Natal, Brazil, Trinidad,
Puerto Rico and New York. In all, he had travelled fifty thousand
miles and taken twenty thousand photographs. Back home, he held
exhibitions of his war pictures, wrote a book, *The Far East* and
resumed his London and New York contacts. 'Greedily I've taken
the opportunity to make money,' he wrote in his diary on 10 August
1945. He was inundated with requests for photographs and

commissions for drawings. In wartime London he had said yes to any job that brought him in three guineas. After a week in New York, at the war's end, he was making, he said, a small fortune.

It was business as usual, come war or peace. Mercedes de Acosta phoned him in New York a fortnight later and told him of the liberation of Paris. She had spent the war years in America – in California and New York. Cecil had not spoken to her for seven years and with her news the gap of the war years closed. Cecil was a sharper man in a harsher world, his photographs appropriately less fussy and more telling: 'enough of taking fashions on young models who survive just as long as their faces show no signs of character, or of elderly but rich harpies appearing as if butter would not melt in their terrible mouths'. His ambition was more ruthless, his manner more urbane. Peacetime had arrived. The next conflict was to be his affair with Greta Garbo.

8

Greta's Years Between

'I have known many men.'
Two-Faced Woman

In the fourteen years before Greta met again with Cecil, between 1932 and 1946, she reached a pinnacle of fame then closed the door on her career. In those interim years her name was linked with many men, who seemed as shadowy and insubstantial as her partners on the screen. Cast in the role of travelling companion, social escort, financial adviser, or bodyguard, they did not seem emotionally to impinge on her or to command commitment from her.

She starred after *Grand Hotel* in *Queen Christina*, which threw little light on Swedish history – the film's historical adviser called it 'entirely unSwedish' and 'utterly insulting to Swedish royalty' – but came as near as Hollywood dared to reflecting her androgyny and defiant sexuality:

> Under the most fearsome battery of close-ups ever given to a star, she remains aloof. Every inch of the Garbo countenance is exposed to the scrutiny of the audience, every eyelash and pore of the skin presented for our consideration. There is a bedroom scene which would have stripped any other actress spiritually naked. But Garbo is still her own mistress at the end of it.

In a strange, onanistic mime, which enhanced the legend of her solipsism and romantic melancholy, she moves round the room where she has just made love, touching surfaces, burying her face in the sheets and blankets, pressing her body against the bed. The director, Rouben Mamoulian, set the scene to music and told her to synchronise her movements to a metronome. John Gilbert, who was to die in 1936, wrecked by alcohol, and who had been, in life and on film, her besotted lover, watches perplexed, a voyeur like the audience. He asks her what she is doing. 'I have been memorising this room,' she says. 'In the future in my memory I shall live a great deal in this room.'

She derided Hollywood's standards and herself for bending to them. She was ashamed of Christina and would wake in the night and think with horror of it being seen in Sweden. Imagine, she said, Christina abdicating for a 'little Spaniard'. She had wanted it to seem as if she had abdicated from a boundless desire to be free. All she learned from the film, she said, was the folly of lying flat on her back on the floor when eating a bunch of grapes.

Between films, she spent months in Sweden, always amid rumours that she was through with Hollywood. She took holidays by the sea with her mother and her brother Sven and his family, rented a small apartment in Stockholm, and for much of the time stayed at Tistad castle with Hörke Wachtmeister.

The Wachtmeisters looked after her as if she was, in fact, a queen. They offered her secluded and beautiful surroundings, the protection of family and servants, the outdoor life of swimming, skiing, walking, skating and sunbathing. Her fantasy was to have a home in Sweden, a haven of her own. She urged them to look for a place for her and, if they found something financially viable, to tell her brother Sven. In California she lived in rented houses and held temporary resident's status. To Hörke Wachtmeister she described her filmstar life as prostitution. Prostitutes are never very happy, she said. But as half of what she earned went in taxes and as she intended to remain unmarried she felt obliged to keep working.

Mercedes pined when Greta spent months at a time in Sweden. 'Hollywood seemed empty to me,' she wrote in her memoir. In the summer of 1932 she began an affair with Marlene Dietrich. She went one evening with Cecil to see a performance of German dancing. She wore white trousers and a white jacket. Marlene, sitting in the row in front of them, turned and smiled at her and the next day called uninvited at her house.

Thereafter Marlene cooked meals for her and swamped her with flowers:

> sometimes twice a day, ten dozen roses or twelve dozen carnations . . . I never had enough vases and when I told Marlene this, as a hint not to send me any more flowers, instead I received a great many Lalique vases and even more flowers.

She gave them all to a hospital. And when Marlene sent dressing-gowns, scarves, pyjamas, slacks, sweaters, lamps, lamp shades 'and every known object', she 'packed them all back into their boxes and dispatched them off to Bullock's Wilshire to credit them all to Marlene's name'.

Marlene wooed with professional skill. 'Please forgive me that I cannot be with you for dinner,' she wrote on an evening when she first had to see her director, von Sternberg. She would, she said, be with Mercedes not later than 9.30 or 10 and told her to eat and go to bed and wait for her there. It was a cool affair. She had none of Greta's diffidence or vulnerability and neither Mercedes nor Cecil were in her thrall.

In the summer of 1933 she travelled in Europe, though not to her native Germany where Hitler was Chancellor. Scathing of him, she refused his personal request for her to return as the Fatherland's cinema queen. Greta was immersed in filming *Queen Christina*. Mercedes, without a job or lover, became depressed, crashed her car through careless driving and injured her face and head. Marlene paid for medical care. 'I kiss your face and your scars particularly,' she wrote on 28 July. She sent presents and photographs of herself from Vienna and, from Cap D'Antibes, records of her singing.

Mercedes was in hospital for several weeks. She then took her revolver into the hills near Santa Monica and shot at targets on trees. 'As I held the revolver in my hand, I felt again the old sense that it was a way of escape.' A concerned friend, Princess Norina Matchabelli, introduced her to a visiting guru, Sri Meher Baber, who had long black hair and a thick moustache, wore white, and sat in the Buddha position. Vowed to silence, he tapped out on an alphabet board that suicide was no answer, as it resulted in rebirth to the same problems, and that the only solution was to see God in everything.

Most of all Mercedes saw God in Greta. When separated from her she found herself able, by means she assumed were supernatural, to conjure hallucinatory images of her:

> This might be explained because my great affection for her has possibly opened a channel, on an unseen level, between us. Or it might be explained because we have known each other in a previous incarnation – perhaps even many.

In the winter of 1933, when filming on *Queen Christina* was finished, they went on holiday together in the Yosemite forest. On the second night they got lost in the dark and cold. They panicked and wandered for four hours before finding a forester's cottage. He gave them tin mugs of coffee and let them sleep on the floor by the stove until his son arrived at five in the morning and took them back to their hotel. Greta insisted on returning immediately to Beverly Hills. She said that Mercedes brought her trouble and bad luck.

In July 1934 Greta worked on *The Painted Veil*, based on a novel by Somerset Maugham. Set in a China of odd pagodas and dragons, it was a tale of adultery, punishment and revenge which cost more than a million dollars to make. She played a doctor's wife who is neglected by her husband, then enticed into an affair with a married diplomat. She called it rubbish and wrote to Hörke, on 28 July 1934, of her desire to disappear from films and to have people forget, totally, that she ever existed, so that no one would look at her as she walked down the street.

She was, though, she said, still not rich enough. That October she signed again with MGM – £275,000 for *Anna Karenina*, directed by Clarence Brown and again scripted by Salka Viertel. In it, she perfected the art Stiller had taught her of understated expression of emotion. Basil Rathbone, who played Karenin, said that by watching her he learned everything he knew about acting for the screen.

> She has the technique of economy raised to an art. She made tiny movements, minute changes of expression which I actually didn't notice at the time, but when I saw the scene on the screen I was amazed . . . When I'm rehearsing I catch myself wondering how little Garbo would do.

She had, by this time, a grandeur. The sense that she had described, in letters to friends, of living her life backwards, of never having been allowed to be young, imbued her performances with a fatalism – youth, beauty and knowledge of life combined: 'Before she has even chosen her lover, her look tells you it doesn't much matter who he is, they all go the same way home.' The New York Film Critics voted her Anna Karenina the 'best feminine performance' of 1935 and in Venice the International Motion Picture Exposition judged it the best foreign film of the year.

In May 1935 she signed contracts for two more films at $250,000 each – *Camille* and *Marie Walewska* – then fled again to Sweden. She stayed with the Wachtmeisters. In July she wrote to Salka about the scripts for both films. She feared *Camille* was too similar to *Anna Karenina* and that it would prove disastrous to do the same story again. For *Marie Walewska*, the 'Napoleon story', she had a special request. She longed, she said, to be filmed wearing trousers. She asked Salka to include a sequence with Marie Walewska dressed as a soldier going to Napoleon's tent at night. This was the old subversive androgyny that Mercedes had tried to serve. It was not a sequence that found its way into the finished film.

The same month she sent a teasing letter to Mercedes who, in California, was as ever missing her, saying that she would meet her in Stockholm 'for dinner a week from Tuesday at eight o'clock in the dining-room of the Grand Hotel'. Mercedes, equal to the challenge, wired back that she would be there, booked the hotel's royal suite, and got on a boat the same day.

> The evening was a sentimental one. We did the traditional things, ordering caviar, champagne and our favourite tunes from the orchestra . . . In that rococo room with its pink-shaded lights, its soft string orchestra and its old-world atmosphere, I felt that I was moving in a dream within a dream.

But there was no real context beyond the romantic evening and the dream within a dream. Greta found Mercedes persistent and demanding and disliked being alone in Stockholm with her. She took her to Tistad, wanting the support of the Wachtmeisters. They had a strained farewell when Mercedes left for the States. Greta told her that she must not write to her. She confided to Salka that she felt a wreck after Mercedes had gone.

She stayed with her family, and in her apartment in Stockholm at Klippgatan 6. For her mother she rented a new apartment and she wrote to Laudy L. Lawrence, head of MGM's Paris office, asking him to find work for her brother Sven. Lawrence passed the request to Louis B. Mayer on 3 December with a note:

> Sven is a nice boy but that is all. His health is very bad.

Incidentally, the entire family is in bad health, including Garbo. I believe her younger sister died from TB long ago and Sven is in bed a whole lot more than out of it. Garbo is rather seriously ill.

Mercedes heard of Greta's illness and sent a wire offering to travel to Sweden, wait with her, then accompany her back to Hollywood. Greta did not reply. On 8 December she thanked Mayer for MGM's help on Sven's behalf and told him that she had been ill since September, in bed most of the time and that possibly she would need an operation. The illness was not explained, though her symptoms were depression, weight loss and stomach pains. To Salka she wrote that she had been in bed for years. She said that though she had no lovers she supposed her troubles stemmed from wrongs done to her body in the past. Newspaper reports that her condition was critical were countered by MGM who said that she had a heavy cold. She told Mayer she wanted to do her best in *Camille* and asked for an extra month's recuperation. He sent a wire on 10 January 1936 saying that he was terribly distressed at her news and suspending all her contractual obligations until she felt better.

Before Greta returned to Hollywood the Wachtmeisters found her a nineteenth-century manor house, Hårby, in Gnesta in the province of Södermanland, which she bought for 276,000 kronor – about £14,000. It had ten rooms, a thousand acres of farmland and lakes, and was circled by an oakwood. Her brother, his family and her mother lived there for two years from 1937, but the Second World War thwarted her plans to turn the place into her home.

Work on *Camille* began on 29 July 1936. Her contract stipulated that she be paid overtime at an additional $10,000 a week or any part thereof, so MGM were anxious to keep to schedule. She was ill throughout the making of the film and her illness was exacerbated by her identification with the character she played – Marguerite Gautier, who dies of tuberculosis and love for Armand.

Greta's skeletal thinness, dry cough and febrile mood swings, the irony of her lines and the subtlety of her performance made her achievement extraordinary. The picture won the New York Film Critics Award and she was nominated for an Oscar. Years later, in an interview with *Photoplay*, George Cukor, the director, spoke of her professionalism, the control with which she conveyed sincerity and sexual intensity, and of her strange relationship to the camera:

I never told her how to play a scene . . . In her acting she was the most practical craftswoman in the studio. She could play an intimate tender scene apparently with all her concentration on the emotion of it, yet she was controlling her movement in relation to the camera and the lighting . . . she used to go to the camera and in a couple of shots capture exactly what was required of her. If, though, something went wrong and she hadn't got the scene right after the first half dozen takes, she would go to pieces. She seemed to feel that all the inspiration had evaporated and her acting then became curiously awkward and amateurish. The only thing to do was stop work and come back to it in the morning.

The key to her performance in *Camille* was her ability to suggest that she was dying of some fatal disease. When you first saw her, she had this little dry cough and she'd clear her throat. You knew something was wrong because she was such an imaginative actress. There was one scene where she had difficulty catching her breath but she was very discreet about the whole thing.

She was a very subtle actress, able with a slight gesture to be enormously suggestive. Often she was the aggressor in love-making, reaching for the man first. A love scene has to be a *scene*. Very often filmmakers don't realise that today. In *Camille* I always found the scene where she leaves the table at the party very erotic. It was so original the way she did it – that sort of hot impatience she and Armand had for each other – the way she leaned over him – her body didn't touch his, but she gave him small kisses all around the face. It was so extraordinary.

She always went through a great deal to get a scene right. I said to her once that she seemed to act a role so easily. She laughed and said that she would kill me for saying such a thing . . . She's a creature of the greatest distinction . . . She likes people but only one at a time. She hasn't a lot of vitality and too many people worry her. She was unique as an actress. A person born for the screen.

When she died in *Camille* in Robert Taylor's arms and her eyes rolled open, viewers swore they saw her soul leave her body. Adrian, who designed the costumes, hired real diamonds and emeralds because, he said, perfect beauty needs perfect jewellery. Mercedes thought the cost to Greta's health in making the film was too high and she was glad when it was in the cans.

Greta thought George Cukor extraordinarily nice, but found the work exhausting. To Hörke Wachtmeister she wrote that she was too busy for anything other than *Camille* and her health. She said that she had to work even though she felt ill. She left home at about 8 in the morning and did not get back until 8 at night. Sometimes she cried from tiredness. After her hours at the studio she had therapy, but could not tell if this helped or made her feel worse.

The sessions were with a psychologist and were for an hour and a half each time. He saw her as an interesting case of depression. She said they sat and fenced with words and kept a watchful eye on each other. She described him as a little hunchbacked man whom she was dragging down with her pessimism.

Her work regime was demanding and her application strict. She got up at six, exercised, watched her diet continually and went to bed early in the hope of sleep that eluded her. She smoked non-stop and could not kick the habit however hard she tried. Her energy was limited and only by obsessive dedication could she approximate to her own standards.

Despite what she revealed of her sexual aloofness, desire to be alone and paranoia at publicity, the press wanted romance and marriage for her. Any man, escort, friend or lover with whom she spent time was paraded as a putative spouse.

In Sweden her name was again linked with Max Gumpel. They played tennis together and he advised her on investment in Stockholm real estate. He was divorced and wealthy, so the papers described him as her 'millionaire fiancé'. 'Few people know she plans to retire soon and marry the richest man in Sweden,' wrote *Life* in 1932. She dined a few times with Prince Sigvard of Sweden, and Swedish and American papers blazed a royal romance. She went away for a few days to the Grand Canyon with Rouben Mamoulian, who directed her in *Queen Christina*. They registered in a hotel as Mary Jones and Robert Bongi of Santa Fé. The press rumoured elopement.

She lamented the folly of it all to Hörke Wachtmeister. The papers were, she said, marrying her off for the 759th time. Out of the air they contrived long pieces about how she had shot herself, married and gone to the moon. She never defended herself. But, she assured Hörke, despite what was written about her she still had no husband, no fiancé, no house, no home and still loved living on pineapples. And so, more or less, it would remain.

She met Leopold Stokowski in 1936. He was conductor of the Philadelphia Symphony Orchestra from 1914 until 1936. Hollywood then tempted him with money and he appeared in two films, *The Big Broadcast* and *One Hundred Men and a Girl* in 1936 and 1937. He asked Anita Loos to introduce him to Greta and to take her to Bullock's Wilshire and buy her some decent clothes. His own clothes were stylish. He was fifty-four, Greta was thirty-one. The press pursued them and professed to see them dancing the rumba and the 'Big Apple' at parties.

In December 1937 Stokowski's second wife Evangeline obtained a Reno divorce and custody of their two daughters, then married Prince Alexis Zalstem-Zalesky. In February 1938 Greta and Stokowski travelled in Italy and the papers wrote of their imminent marriage. They stayed at the Villa Cimbrone, owned by Lord Grimthorpe,* overlooking the Bay of Amalfi, in Ravello. Armed carabinieri guarded the place to prevent people forcing their way into the grounds. On 6 March the papers reported that Greta would marry in Turin on 15 March, that Stokowski had confirmed this with his American lawyer and that Wallace Beery, who had acted with her in *Grand Hotel*, was to be best man. 'She has been doing a lot of human things,' Hilde Marchant of the *Daily Express* in desperation at being stonewalled, wrote about Greta, 'laughing a great deal, sunbathing and learning to cook . . . She has not yet been seen in a dress. Today she wore golf trousers, thick grey woollen socks and a heavy sweater. It was the long blue trousers that gave her away.'

The Swiss housekeeper at the villa told journalists that Greta travelled with one small, battered suitcase, wore trousers and woollens, had brought no dresses nor a dressing-gown with her and brushed her teeth with salt. It was Stokowski who wore the silk shirts and used the silver hairbrushes. She said that Greta ate only salads and fruit, did exercises each morning, sunbathed nude and went to bed at 8.15 every evening.

By 17 March no marriage had occurred and Greta faced the press. 'What do you want?' she asked them, and they barraged her with questions of the sort she hated. She told them she was not engaged to be married to Leopold Stokowski or to anybody else and appealed to them to leave her alone and in particular to stop hiding in the park of the villa and intercepting her telephone conversations. She made one of her frank and soulful pleas:

---

* The second Baron Grimthorpe, who died in 1917, was reputed to be Violet Trefusis's father.

There are some who want to get married and others who don't. I have never had an impulse to go to the altar. I am a difficult person to lead. I haven't many friends and I haven't seen much of the world. My friend, Mr Stokowski, who has been very much to me, offered to take me around and see some of the beautiful things. I optimistically accepted. I was naïve enough to think I could travel without being followed and scrutinised. It is cruel to bother people who want to be left in peace. This kills beauty for me.

A few days later the couple slipped away from the villa in Ravello, sailed to Tunis on the *Citta di Palermo*, and motored south in Stokowski's grey sports car to Hammamet and southern Tunisia.

In May they went to Sweden and stayed for three months at Hårby with her mother and Sven. She felt that the place was a mess, that her brother could not properly take care of it, that her attempts to help him had failed and that she no longer knew what to do for him. She made an effort to get on with Stokowski, but was aware that their energies were different. Though it was, she said, hard to be alone, sometimes it was even more difficult to be with another person. At the end of July, Stokowski left her for America.

A couple of months later, and after nearly a year away, Greta sailed back to Hollywood and on board ship gave another interview of the sort that lose reporters their jobs. She gave no answers to questions about Stokowski. Asked if she would ever marry she said, 'There seems to be a law that governs all our actions so I never make plans.' Asked if she considered 'single blessedness' the proper state for a professional woman she replied, 'If you are blessed, you are blessed, whether you are married or single.' Asked if she would like children, she said, 'No, the world seems much too difficult. I would not want to raise a son or any children to go to war.' And asked if she had enjoyed her vacation, she replied, 'You cannot have a vacation without peace and you cannot have peace unless you are left alone.' She was not seen with Stokowski again.

MGM's plans were for her to star in her first comic role, *Ninotchka*. She wanted George Cukor to direct, but he was working on *The Women*, with Norma Shearer and Joan Crawford, so the job went to Ernst Lubitsch. She wanted either William Powell or Cary Grant as her co-star, but the part went to Melvyn Douglas, who had worked with her in *As You Desire Me*, seven years previously. His reviews had been poor.

With Lubitsch's direction, a script by Billy Wilder and Walter Reisch and photography by William Daniels, she gave a deadpan comic performance. She received $125,000 for the film – $150,000 less than for *Anna Karenina*. In it, she debunked her own legend. 'Garbo laughs', was the publicity line. Asked by one of the comic commissars, 'Do you want to be alone, Comrade?' she answers, 'No.' Lubitsch treated her with gallantry, told her how he saw each scene, then left her to find her way. He knew she could not perform on technique, but needed to feel the reality of each scene. As usual, she would not look at the rushes, but she saw a private view of the film at the studio with him. He asked her if she liked herself in it and she said she did not know. She was nominated for an Oscar for her performance, but the award went to Vivien Leigh for *Gone with the Wind*.

By September 1939, newspapers were reporting a new romance for her – with Gayelord Hauser, a dietitian, lecturer and writer on food. Mercedes introduced them. Hauser, ten years older than Garbo, lived in Beverly Hills in a house called 'Sunrise Hill', which had a swimming-pool, a badminton court and a view of Coldwater Canyon. He lived there with a man called Frey Brown, who had studied at the Chicago Institute of Fine Arts. They owned stores that sold 'natural foods', ran diet, exercise and therapy classes and advised personal clients, among whom were Adèle Astaire's mother and Lady Mendl and Mona Harrison Williams, on how to be beautiful, healthy, slim and forever young.

Hauser wrote many books, with titles like *Mirror, Mirror on the*

Wall and *Look Younger, Live Longer*, about real food, keeping fit and the foibles and gratitude of his rich and fashionable clients. He claimed that he changed Greta's eating habits. He wrote that when he first met her she was eating boiled vegetables and not much else, and that on his insistence she changed to a 'high-vitality' diet, with ham, chicken, cottage cheese and wheat germ mixed up with raw vegetables. He implied that his intervention transformed her from an anaemic insomniac into a happy and energetic extrovert.

Soon after Miss Garbo began this new way of nutrition, she accepted the leading role in the film *Ninotchka*, widely publicized with the wondrous statement 'Garbo Laughs!' Many people congratulated us both on the 'new' Garbo.

Mercedes agreed that Greta was happy while making *Ninotchka* but did not believe that this was because of the dietetic wizardry of Gayelord Hauser. She thought it came from working on comedy not tragedy and with a good script and director. The newspapers, for their part, on 15 November 1939, six days after the film's première, declared that Hauser had given Greta a diamond ring which she was wearing on 'the proper finger'. A few weeks later Gayelord and Frey Brown and Mercedes and Greta took a trip to Reno, Nevada. Mercedes said that they were both good-looking men, and delightful companions, and that the trip was a great success. They motored across the desert, picnicked on secluded beaches, went to a rodeo in Reno and 'to some kind of a gambling place which was very tame and not at all what Greta and I had hoped such a place in the "Wild West" would be'. The following year, in February 1940 the *Hollywood Reporter* revealed that the four of them were sailing to Jamaica 'to dine on pineapple, papaya and coconuts'. They cruised the Bahamas in a yacht owned by Axel Wenner-Gren, a wealthy Swedish industrialist who, as the war progressed, was thought to be a fascist. Hauser let the International News Service know that he intended to marry Greta in Florida before their holiday was over. No wedding took place, though there were no signs of rift and he continued as her escort and dietitian.

She welcomed his advice on matters that preoccupied her – food, fitness, sleep and keeping calm. Like Cecil, he had a talent for the uprise and was happy to escort her to lunch at the Colony Club and to tea with Mrs Cornelius Vanderbilt. Greta taught him to stand on his head. 'Nothing relieves the constant downward pull of the face and abdominal muscles so quickly as this upside-down position,' he wrote in *New Treasury of Secrets*.

The war trapped Greta in Hollywood and stymied her plans for retiring to Hårby. Fearing a German invasion of Sweden, she brought her mother and brother to Santa Fé, New Mexico, where she felt the climate would be good for her mother's heart. She told them not to talk about being related to her. When she stayed with them, she asked Salka to address letters to her as Occupant, 1672 Cerro Gordo Road. Her mother, in particular, felt wrong in America and wanted to go home. And Greta wrote often to Hörke Wachtmeister on the theme of her homesickness for Sweden, for the forests and lakes and for summers 'when it rains and that marvellous melancholy enfolds us'. But afraid of ships being mined or torpedoed, she would not travel by sea. Hörke sent Swedish newspapers and film journals to salve her homesickness, and quantities of Chropax earplugs, in the vain hope that she might sleep at nights.

The war broke into Garbo's acting career. She was always more revered by European than American audiences and her films made their money from foreign sales. In small-town America she was thought too mysterious, too enigmatic – not cute enough for the average man and baffling to the average woman. 'What relation had Miss America', wrote Mercedes, 'to a Viking's daughter whose soul was swept by wind and snow?'

In 1941, with Europe at war, France occupied, and Germany

having banned Hollywood's films, MGM tried to market Garbo in a film with exclusive appeal to Americans. They came up with *Two Faced Woman* in which she was to appear as an 'oomph girl', dancing the chica-choca and with her hair cut in a curly bob. The far-fetched story was of a serious-minded ski instructor who pretends to be her own glamorous and fictitious twin sister as a ruse to win back her inconsequential husband from his sophisticated girlfriend.

With George Cukor directing and Melvyn Douglas as the leading man, the hope was for a comedy comparable to *Ninotchka*. But the plot was so implausible that no wizardry, sincerity or diversion could make anything of it. In August 1941, Greta wrote to Hörke that she had no idea what the film would be like and she regretted the endless changes to the story, but that as she would rather go walking in the country than fight with the scriptwriters it would turn out their way.

The film was released in November. Anita Loos wrote to Cecil from her home at Ocean Front, Santa Monica, that it was 'a bit of a stinker through bad story and stupid supervision . . . Garbo is still with Hauser, leading a pretty dull life.' The film was denounced by the Legion of Decency as 'immoral and unChristian in its attitude to marriage and its obligations, with its impudently suggestive scenes, dialogue and situations.'

A furore of condemnation from the moral right augured badly for box office sales. It was banned in Providence, Boston, Hartford, Buffalo and St Louis. A Republican congressman introduced a bill to halt its distribution and the Catholic Interest Committee of the Knights of Columbus of Manhattan and the Bronx demanded that it be withdrawn immediately.

At pains to ameliorate the damage, MGM, at a cost of $14,000, inserted an additional telephone scene that suggested Melvyn Douglas knew all along of his wife's ploys and was merely teasing her. This expediency made Garbo look ridiculous, and rendered the plot banal to the point of idiocy. The anodyne version premièred on 31 December, three weeks after the Japanese had bombed Pearl Harbor and America had entered the war. MGM advertised it as 'a bright spot in a serious world' and blazed the slogan 'Go gay with Garbo'. Reviewers savaged it, called her performance gauche and stilted and 'as shocking as seeing your mother drunk'. They described the whole film as absurd and embarrassing.

Garbo had a history of imbuing indifferent scripts with her own special reality. In most of her roles, even those which spelled the death of art, she found some kernel of emotional truth which she buried within her to make the thing grow. This film she described as 'just nothing'. She whispered off-set to Melvyn Douglas, 'They're trying to kill me.' To Hörke she wrote that it was heartbreaking for both Salka and for herself, but that as more important things were happening in the world it seemed best to say nothing. When the film's failure became apparent, she released herself from her contract with MGM and, at the age of thirty-six, made a casual exit from the studios that was to prove permanent.

It was an inglorious swansong and she reproached herself, said Mercedes, for having taken part in the whole charade. She was humiliated by the reviews and by the fuss from the church and the women's clubs. The experience confirmed her disaffection with Hollywood and its allegiance to commerce above art. In some profound way she had sold them her self and it reduced her if they used her insensitively. She knew well that the fame that elevated her was based on transient things. Time, she wrote to Hörke, had left its mark on her face and body. When she aged or failed, her critics, she knew, would be probing and unkind. Though she did not particularly want the things money could buy, she felt she needed money for her security and protection. Talk of freezing the assets of foreigners, because of the war, made her anxious. She looked, with no great enthusiasm, for a house to buy in Beverly Hills, as a hedge against rising rents and a hostile world and reserved the right to be melancholic and alone.

She expressed a wish to assassinate Hitler, who had liked the film *Camille*. She told a New York friend of hers and Cecil's, Sam Green, that she would go to Germany to persuade Hitler to surrender and, if he refused, she would shoot him. Apart from such a fantasy, she stayed silent about the war. She had no interest in world affairs. She disliked violence – she told Cecil that she would ban it all, including boxing, were she to rule the world – but she never espoused a cause.

She declined to record a government message, for overseas transmission in Sweden, expressing America's respect for her homeland. Her diffidence, her refusal to go on tours to sell war bonds, and her association with Axel Wenner-Gren, led to rumours that she was pro-fascist. Salka Viertel talked to the press on her behalf in an effort to scotch these rumours. She explained that Greta had not been on war-bond tours because she could not face crowds. She said that Greta bought many bonds herself, gave to the Red Cross and War-Relief Funds and helped Salka in her work in rescuing anti-fascist refugees from Europe. Salka pointed out that she and Berthold were under death sentences from the Nazis, that she worked for the anti-Nazi league, and was unlikely to be the close friend of a fascist. She read out a statement ostensibly from Greta:

> I am for all the people who are oppressed and who are being treated badly. I shall always be on their side. It will be plain to everybody that this is *not* the side of the Nazis. However, I am *not* a political person. I never had any political leanings or affiliations either here or in Sweden. I nevertheless am sincerely anti-Nazi.

As a way of expressing her rejection of tyranny Greta considered making another film with MGM – *The Girl from Leningrad*, in which she was to play a Russian resistance fighter. The fee was $70,000 on agreement and a further $80,000 on completion. But when she read the script she said she found it depressing. The film was never made and her uncertain, fifty-year-long retirement continued.

The house she bought during the war years, as a refuge against the world, was at 904 Bedford Drive, Beverly Hills. It had a walled garden which she dug and planted. She walked by the shore, read, bought a few paintings by way of investment, and tried to live a life where nothing much was expected of her and she could drift through the days. To her Swedish friends she sent the usual refrain. That still nothing was happening to her, no change, no children, nothing, as ever.

She and Mercedes did not meet much during the war and Mercedes looked for love elsewhere. In 1940 she had a brief affair with Ona Munson, who the previous year had starred as Belle Watling in *Gone with the Wind*. 'I long to hold you in my arms and pour my love into you – with all my heart and soul,' Ona wrote on 26 February 1940, when parted from Mercedes. Marlene Dietrich knew of the liaison. Ona hinted at intrigue and made Mercedes jealous:

> I went to Ciro's again on Thursday night and Marlene came in with a party and once again she turned the eyes of everyone on me until I blushed to the roots of my hair. She stared continuously and I got so uncomfortable I had to leave. I must say that's the first time that sort of thing has happened to me.
>
> . . . Darling mine hurry home because I love you terribly and miss you very much.
>
> All my love to you alone – Your O.

Mercedes, in New York when she received these letters, was organising an exhibition of the clothes of her sister, Rita Lydig, for the Museum of Costume Art. Rita Lydig, who died in 1929, had been a 'legendary woman of fashion' to whom Cecil devoted a chapter in his book *The Glass of Fashion*. He wrote of her eleventh-century lace dressing-gown for which she paid $9000, her three hundred pairs of shoes, made by Yanturni who was curator of the Cluny museum, her rose-point petticoats, fezzes of unborn lamb, and umbrella of platinum with 'Rita' set in diamonds on the handle.

Mercedes, disconcerted to hear of Marlene's interest in Ona, was offered reassurance of a sort:

> . . . Darling I'm amazed at you even thinking such a thing as regards Marlene. I knew it was laid in my lap the very first night I saw her because she was so obvious and I merely mentioned it on the other two times I saw her because I thought it would amuse you not worry you. That is the last thing in the world I'd want to do. And she most certainly hasn't been on my mind, nor have I any desire to see or meet her. Just the opposite in fact. So for heaven's sake get such silly notions out of your head. I love you and you alone and am not interested in any chi chi with Marlene or anyone else and you above all people ought to know that. As I told you in the past, the only rival you have to contend with is work.
>
> . . . The papers here say that GG is back, but of course I don't know if it is true.

Mercedes claim to distinction was that Greta and Marlene had been her lovers. After reading Mercedes' memoirs, Alice B. Toklas wrote to Anita Loos, 'You can't dispose of her lightly – she has had the two most important women in the US – Greta Garbo and Marlene Dietrich.' Ona found such sexual status impressive. Like most of Hollywood she thought Garbo a great actress, 'more personable and magnetic off the screen than on. Her presence filled the room . . . and such eyelashes.'

But by the winter of 1941, her own affair with Mercedes had cooled, and she was referring to 'peculiar circumstances' that precluded their meeting. In 1942 she joined CBS as their first woman producer, and in 1950 married her third husband, the Russian artist and theatre designer, Eugène Berman, who had studied under Bonnard and Vuillard, and whose work was bought by Cecil and by Gertrude Stein.

Mercedes, during the war, edited a magazine called *Victory* for the Office of War Information in New York. She rented an apartment at 471 Park Avenue. Greta stayed for some months of each year in a suite in the Ritz tower. Mercedes could see these rooms from her own bedroom window. Though the intimacy she wanted with Greta was over, at night in the blackout they signalled to each other from their windows with lighted candles. 'Why we weren't arrested for showing lights', Mercedes wrote, 'I will never know.'

In autumn 1941 when Greta complained to Gayelord Hauser that she had nothing to wear, he took her to the dress designer, Valentina Sanina, who had a studio at the Sherry Netherland. Valentina's business affairs were managed by her husband, Georges Schlee. He was there on the day Greta first went to Valentina's and, so the legend goes, was startled by the nonchalance with which she took off her clothes in front of him for a fitting.

Whatever the preliminaries, a relationship began between them that lasted until his death in 1964. She, and Cecil, referred to him as 'the little man'. He acted as her business agent and adviser and by investing her money made her extremely wealthy. Like Stiller, he was a Russian Jew. He was five years older than she, controlling and devoted. Cecil saw him as a rival. Schlee spanned the worlds of business, showbiz and culture. He cruised on Onassis' yacht and was at Noël Coward's parties. Reserved, circumspect and authoritative, he shielded Greta from the press, made decisions on practical matters, escorted her socially and left her free from commitment to proceed as she pleased.

He and Valentina had left Russia at the time of the Bolshevik Revolution. They travelled in Greece, Italy and France and arrived in New York in 1923. Valentina was then acting with a travelling theatre company. She moved into costume design, opened a small dress shop on Madison Avenue and made dresses stitched with Russian embroidery. Mercedes' husband, Abram Poole, painted a portrait of her showing her with long golden hair that reached almost to the ground. She opened her own fashion house in 1928 and in time Irene Selznick, Gloria Swanson, Gertrude Lawrence and Katharine Hepburn were among her clients. The clothes she designed were subtle and unrestricting. Their muted colours and simple styles appealed to Greta.

She said she married Schlee for security, not love. They had no children and lived in a spacious apartment in midtown Manhattan, on East 52nd Street. At first she seemed at ease with the ménage that developed with Greta. The connection was regal and enhanced her own status. The three of them appeared at parties and restaurants. Sometimes the two women wore identical Valentina designs and played at some illusion of twinship. But then Schlee and Greta began to seem more like a couple, dining, travelling and socialising together, though it was Valentina with whom Schlee continued to live.

As for Greta, she continued her regime of living alone, of early nights and impenetrable reserve. Toward the end of the war, in December 1945, she wrote to Hörke Wachtmeister in her wry, self-deprecating way, to say that she was still just as lonely and that nothing had changed. She spent her time wondering why she did not have some wonderful person with whom she might travel the world. But she had no one. 'And so it goes.'

As her retirement from acting and her withdrawal from adulation began to seem real, newspaper reports became more cutting. She was said to wear old clothes and to hide away to attract attention, to keep imported sardines and crackers under the bed to nibble in the night, to have had 'terminal quarrels' with Salka Viertel and with the 'woman fencing champion', Mercedes de Acosta.

As the years passed, Valentina grew to detest her and refused to speak to her. Noël Coward, one September evening in the mid 1940s, wrote the diary entry: 'Drinks with Valentina, who bared her soul a little over Georges and Garbo. Poor dear I am afraid she is having a dreary time.' Mercedes believed, erroneously, that the relationship between Greta and Schlee would prove temporary and that Valentina would win him back.

9

Reunion

'Marry me.'
'What?'
Camille

Cecil and Greta met again on the afternoon of Friday 15 March 1946. The reunion took place at the home of Margaret Case, New York's society editor for *Vogue*. She lived in Park Avenue in an apartment on the fifteenth floor. Georges Schlee had found a delicatessen that again, after the war, sold Russian caviare and he and Greta had called to drink vodka and eat 'the real thing'.

Cecil was staying at the Plaza. Knowing of his passion for Greta and of his ambition to photograph her, Margaret Case invited him to meet her. As he went into the apartment he saw Greta sitting at a small, round table:

> I felt knocked back – as if someone had opened a furnace door onto me: I had almost to gasp for the next breath. The warmth of her regard, her radiance, her smile . . . I held onto the back of a chair . . .

She seemed amused to see him and offered him a biscuit spread with what she called 'kahr-vee-yeyarr'. He scrutinised her and found her changed – her face thinner, lines round her eyes, her hair no longer golden but 'cinder-mouse', her hands weatherbeaten, her ankles and legs with 'the scrawny look of a waif's or of certain poor, older people' and wearing a hat that looked as if it belonged to a tinker, and a shirt that looked as if it belonged to a highwayman.

Schlee made jokes and told funny stories. Conversation ranged from the Paris Flea Market to circus clowns, to types of underwear. Greta alluded to her previous meeting with Cecil: 'I didn't wear lipstick when you knew me before,' she said. She smoked five Old Gold cigarettes, ate caviare, drank vodka, then said she must go. 'Panic struck me,' wrote Cecil. 'Perhaps this was the end. Or would another lapse of ten years pass before we again met?'

He urged her to go out with him onto the roof garden and look at the New York skyline by night. There was an icy wind. He blurted out compliments that embarrassed her, felt the knobbles of her spine and smelled, as he was soon to tell the world, 'the new-mown-hay freshness of her cheeks, ear and hair'. Before rejoining Schlee she promised she would phone Cecil, but forbade him to phone her.

Back at the Plaza, Cecil wrote of the conquest in his diary and waited for her call. He was in rooms 249–51 – the Cecil Beaton suite. The hotel's director, Prince Serge Obolensky, a Russian aristocrat and friend of Schlee's, had commissioned him to decorate the rooms in his own style. When Cecil was in New York he stayed in them at half-price.

A fortnight went by without a word from Greta. Then she phoned one afternoon, asked him what he was doing and invited herself to tea.

She was wearing dark blue, looked pale and had been harassed by autograph-seekers. She sat beside him on the long crimson sofa and smoked her cigarettes. She told him she had caught a cold on the roof terrace, that her vertebrae were easily nudged out of line and that she preferred unpasteurised milk in her tea.

She evinced no particular interest in him and responded to all his questions with evasions. And she showed no curiosity in the photographs left lying around to impress her, nor in his startling taste in interior decorations – the chandeliers, velvet drapes, net curtains appliquéd with birds, the ornate mirrors and gold filigreed chairs. But Cecil was jubilant, for she was there, alone in his room with him and the meeting was in itself a conquest and a triumph. He felt that her presence seemed to make the room hers. He could look at her and chronicle every wrinkle in her skin and listen to the way she pronounced words with her lilting accent: luck she pronounced 'luckke', natural as 'nahr-turrell', valuable as 'vuargh-luobbhle'.

No matter that 'the whole conversation had a rather wacky, inconsequential quality', or that the gulf in attitude between them was so wide: her secretiveness, his desire to tell all, her love of simplicity, his flamboyance, her need for solitude, his incessant socialising. To be alone with her was a dream come true.

Her departure was abrupt. Cecil escorted her down to the street:

Returning to my room I wondered had she really been here? Or had I, by some extraordinary wish-fulfilment, dreamt into actuality the scene that had passed?

I looked around to see proof that my imagination had not played a trick on me. Here was the reality: the tea cup with the lipstick, the ash-tray with the Old Gold cigarette stubs and the used matches – and the cushions against which she had leant. I would have liked to ask the hotel maid not to 'tidy' the room; I did not want her to puff out the cushions, but to preserve them just as they were now, or to cast them in bronze for always.

Throughout April 1946 they met about a dozen times for lunch or tea. On their third meeting she told him that 'her bed was small and chaste' and that perhaps, now she was getting older, she should settle for some permanent companionship. This, said Cecil, gave him the opportunity for which he had been waiting. He told her that he knew they 'were made for each other' and asked her to marry him.

I had never before asked anyone to marry me, and yet to make this proposal now seemed the most natural and easy thing to do. I was not even surprised at myself.

Greta, however, appeared surprised. She accused him of being frivolous, said that he hardly knew her and should not speak so lightly of marriage. She said that he would worry about her melancholy disposition and would not like seeing her in the mornings in old men's pyjamas. Cecil replied that he, too, would be wearing old men's pyjamas. (But that was less than true. Stephen Tennant knew of the glory of Cecil's own bedroom attire – the speckled, silk pyjamas, the leopard-skin dressing-gown.)

When next they met she mentioned a fan letter, sent her by a woman, which said, 'You have the character of a man, but the body of a woman – blast it!' Perhaps the irony of a kind of synchrony escaped neither of them – that Cecil paraded the character of a kind of woman, but had the body of a man. It was he who waited anxiously for her call and prepared his rooms for her visit. It was she who visited and left as and when she pleased.

Cecil tried to bind her to plans – to see a certain play, or the El Grecos in the Hispanic museum, or to eat soft-shell crabs in a downtown restaurant. Her answers were vague and evasive. He had to make do with scrutinising her over tea in his rooms at the Plaza. He noted that she was fairminded, without prejudice, compassionate and that when she put on her hat to leave, she did not look in the mirror.

One afternoon, as she was about to leave, she said:

I don't know you from Adam (pronounced Ardhumme) and yet I was quite willing to stay here until breakfast time. That is, if you had remained with your head on the pillow beside me like a brother.

Then she asked if she might use the phone, and confirmed her arrangements for the evening with Schlee.

Cecil felt sufficiently encouraged to write to his mother and Maud Nelson at the beginning of April, telling them that he was going to marry Greta Garbo. They laughed and cried over his letter, reached for the whisky bottle and that night could not sleep. Maud Nelson replied, 'May you find all happiness and fulfilment and may the result be something everlastingly beautiful in your life and heart.' She warned him though, 'not to go on clinging when the moment arrives, if it should arrive, when you must let go', advised him not to concentrate too much on 'the marriage side of things', and intimated that she had friends who knew of Greta's 'elusiveness and secretiveness', as well as her 'greatness and nobility'.

As for Mrs Beaton, she told her son that he was wise enough to know what was best for his future. She expressed the hope that everything would work out for the best and that he would be happy, but she was more interested to know if he was earning any money. 'I am longing to know what the future will tell for you and your financial side which we can't make out in any way,' she wrote to him.

Cecil, the 'terrible homosexualist', had chronicled his longing for Peter Watson. This did not curb his ambition to marry Greta Garbo, who was 'made for the screen' and who shared his own complex relationship to the camera and to the captured image of beauty. She possessed the beauty he sought to mirror. She had shown, in his favourite film of her, *Queen Christina*, that though truly regal, she was an androgynous Queen. But she was not like his *Royal Past*, where queens were men dressed in the curtains. Nor was she like England's real Queen – very short and with 'a face that lacked definition'. For Cecil, Greta was the Queen of Queens. Were he to marry her, he would be her Duke, the commoner who conquered. Such a marriage would tantalise society and set him above it. Something of her allure might brush off on him and her androgyny free him from any need to be a conventional man. Though he professed dismay at how 'like a bushfire' the gossip about his private life spread through London, it was a bushfire that he was at pains to ignite.

Mercedes, who after the war spent a good deal of time in Paris, knew of Cecil's ambitions over Greta as he knew of hers. A friend, a Kathakali dancer, Ram Gopal, wrote to her from Bangalore in April 1946 at the time when Cecil was writing his bombshell letters to his mother:

> Wait till I see Greta someday. I certainly will let her know and make her realise that love such as yours is something nothing in this world can ever give her, even though she may be sought after by superficial friends who wouldn't turn to look at her but for her being the famous person she is.

Some seven years earlier, Cecil's friend, Gertrude Stein, had said to him: 'Your balance is what is important. The balance between fantasy and reality.' That point of balance was the hallmark of his work and left him emotionally free. Greta's solitariness and uninterest in marriage were legendary. She enjoyed Cecil's company, within the parameters she set. Cecil felt her elusiveness as an always present danger, 'as if she might at any moment fly away'. But there was also reassurance in her unavailability, for it left him free to fantasise, woo and pursue, without the problems commitment might bring.

She said that he made her laugh and she invited him to 'steppe outte' for frequent walks with her in Central Park. He crowded all his work into the mornings so that by lunchtime he could make his way to the Ritz. They walked for miles – round the reservoir and all the way from 59th to 96th Street. She seemed happy when she was out – drinking water from the public fountain, mimicking a chimpanzee in the zoo. At the Metropolitan Museum she made 'birdlike noises of delight' at the details of rabbits, butterflies and wild flowers in the Unicorn tapestries. She said of the needlework 'it's incredible that human beings can do such things,' and told him that reds, rose and dull pink were her favourite colours.

She cared more for Michelangelo's sculptures of nudes than did Cecil, who preferred adorned bodies:

> When we looked at huge over-lifesize nudes, I realised how little the human body means to me in comparison to her. She was positively ravenous in admiration of the physical perfection of some of these figures which she judged as if they were fruit or succulent sweets.

She quoted snatches of poetry by Heine and Sappho and told him she was reading the biography of a Swedish poet – a young woman named Harriet Lowenhjelm, who died of tuberculosis and thought of herself as a man. (Greta's incognito of Harriet Brown was Harriet after this poet and Brown for anonymity.) One day she asked Cecil to give her the sketch of himself by Christian Bérard. It showed him beside a drawing of a beautiful woman. He felt, by her request, that he had won a place in her life.

Often, in the role of protective escort, he accompanied her on shopping expeditions for sweaters, shoes and clothes. When strangers approached and asked for autographs, she groaned and turned away. She was quiet, unpretentious, private and could not be flattered. 'Her laughter breaks my heart,' he said. After every meeting they waved goodbye with a great display – waving their handkerchiefs until out of sight.

They spoke of shared plans, of journeys to Switzerland or to Chinatown, but her visits to him were always impulsive and curtailed. Once, instead of a walk, they went to a gymnasium and did exercises. Another time, at a beautician, they had mudpacks put on their faces. Afterwards Greta said, 'Well are we now married?' When he got back to the Plaza he phoned her at the Ritz, asked 'Is that my beloved?' and she answered 'yes.' He asked if she loved him and she repeated, yes, and he went on asking until he irritated her. One evening they went to dinner with Mona Harrison Williams and danced to the tune of 'If I Love You' from *Carousel*. Cecil sang the words all the way home.

It was a friendship that seemed easy, unpressured and even sweet, but on an afternoon in May she stepped into the snare of his ambition. She told him that she proposed going to Sweden for a holiday – her first visit since the war. She was going with Schlee. 'If only you were not such a grand and elegant photographer . . .' she said, elliptically. 'Then you'd ask me to take your passport photograph,' said Cecil.

He called it the 'crowning' of his photographic career. She arrived at the Plaza wearing a biscuit-coloured suit and a polo-necked sweater, her hair a 'lion's mane'. He took a few formal pictures for her passport, then prompted her into all sorts of poses – on a chair hugging her knees, lounging on the settee, staring out of the window, clutching a bunch of lilac and a kind of lyre. From his dressing-up box he persuaded her to wear a pierrot's ruff, a tam-o-shanter, long earrings and a mandarin suit. It was a bewildering sequence of pictures. She kept saying that she had had enough and wanted to leave. Cecil tried to appear nonchalant and knew he could use no special lighting and only limited props. Yet here, more than Stephen Tennant or the Queen of England, was his alter ego, his mirror image, his dream of beauty, posturing for him and furthering his career.

She had asked him for a passport photo because she felt unable to go to an ordinary photographer. The formal photographs of her were of no particular interest to Cecil. He preferred it when she began to perform to his camera, wearing his fancy clothes. In what she construed as the privacy of his hotel room they played a strange charade. He controlled the camera and what she wore. Grotesquely costumed, she became his buffoon.

He maintained that she pencilled a cross on the back of those contact prints which she agreed he might publish in *Vogue*. He took the pictures to Alexander Liberman, *Vogue*'s art editor, who could hardly believe his eyes. For ten years Greta had refused to be photographed and here was a scoop of pictures of her. Since the 'kikes' saga *Vogue* had been cautious and had given him fewer commissions. Cecil hoped these photographs would restore his reputation. Liberman wanted to publish one photograph of Greta, laughing, across a double-page spread. Cecil urged him to publish fourteen. They were to appear in the August issue when she was in Sweden.

On 1 June Cecil sailed for England to design, for Frederick Ashton, a ballet based on Ouïda's novel *Moths*, starring Margot Fonteyn and Robert Helpmann. At home there was an unsigned telegram from Greta bidding him good morning.

Through Schlee she heard of the proposed publication of the photographs in *Vogue*. She sent a cable warning Cecil that if more than one appeared he would not be forgiven. In July she sailed for Sweden with Schlee. She tried to hide from the crowds of spectators, photographers and journalists at the dockside. She said that she was tired, that she wanted her privacy, that she had no plans. She sent a letter to Cecil voicing her deep distress at the prospect of having costume pictures of herself published that had nothing to do with her work. She asked him to destroy them. 'I am, after all,' she said, 'a serious human being.'

Cecil sent cables, letters and flowers. He displayed remorse, but publication proceeded. His efforts at conciliation with Greta went unacknowledged. In his diary he wrote that he felt he had committed murder. He pleaded that it was a misunderstanding and he thought he had her permission, but a letter from his mother, dated September 1946, referred to his having overdone things without Greta's consent. It was the first of his betrayals and Greta's silence was his punishment.

That summer a Los Angeles management put on the London production of *Lady Windermere's Fan*. Cecil designed the costumes and sets and acted the part of the 'waspish gossip' Cecil Graham, who finds Lady Windermere's fan under a cushion in Lord Darlington's rooms. The Californian press praised him for the 'opulent magnificence' of his designs. His dresses, with lampshade skirts, puffed sleeves, 'daring' décolletage and quantities of lace, each weighed forty pounds. The Duchess of Bewick's hat had butterflies on wires all over it. Critics said that his costumes and scenery stole the show from Oscar Wilde.

Cecil's ambition to marry Greta did not eclipse his sexual interest in men. The part of Lord Windermere was played by Geoffrey Toone. Cecil wrote in his diary of how charming Toone was being to him, and how full of possibilities life was 'if one knew how to seize them'. But Geoffrey Toone pushed him away, saying that such emotional demands worried and upset him.

In Los Angeles, in August, Cecil kept phoning Greta's empty house, knowing she was in Sweden. He sent 'countless fervid letters' to the Beverly Hills address she gave him, 622 Bedford Drive. One night he walked round there only to find that it was not her house at all, but belonged to Harry Crocker, a friend who sorted her mail. She had not trusted Cecil with her real address which was 904 Bedford Drive.

In September she and Schlee returned from Sweden. At the quayside she said to reporters: 'I think being in the papers is silly – just as you think it's silly to be writing about me. Now take all your friends and go home – have coffee. Please.' Asked about her future she said, 'I have no plans, not for the movies, not for the stage, not for anything. I'm sort of drifting.' Asked if there was truth in the rumour that she would be marrying Cecil Beaton, she said, 'Well, well, well.'

After a short run in San Francisco, *Lady Windermere* transferred to Broadway. From New York Cecil kept phoning her, first at the

Ritz and then at her Beverly Hills home. He could hear the operator
being told by Greta's 'sad-voiced servant' that Miss Brown was not
at home and she did not know when she was expected back. He
arranged for an acquaintance to put a note under her door at six in
the morning and he bombarded her with letters and telegrams to
which she did not reply.

But Cecil was a persistent man and after a week or so got through.
She thought the call was from Schlee – the operator said only that
New York was calling, not that Cecil was on the line. She told him
nothing of her Swedish trip, called him Mr Beaton and said that she
had received his letters, but could not read his writing. Then, as a
tease, with an impulsiveness she loved and with the kind of challenge
which Mercedes would meet, knowing that he was two thousand
miles away, she invited him to come on over. He asked if he might
come at a later date, but she said, Only now. Cecil accused her of
enjoying making him suffer. She replied that she would not do
anything to make a human being suffer.

Such banter he took as proof that the tiff had passed and that all
was well. He called their relationship strange and violent and
intuitive 'as only happens when two people meet who are magnet-
ically drawn to one another'. No matter that she asked him not to
phone, told him her personality was too different from his, said that
there was no point to his letters and asked him not to write them. He
had captured her in his photographs and now he meant to capture
her with his curious kind of love. He, like her, was an actor. He told
her that on his first night on the Broadway stage, an unknown
admirer had sent him tuberoses. 'You'd better get off that stage,' she
said.

In November Cecil's mother crossed the Atlantic to see him in
Lady Windermere. He met her at the quayside where she stood,
dazed and wearing a dead orchid which someone had given to her in
London as a *bon voyage* token. She seemed, Cecil thought, to have
come from a different planet.

She wonders why I am always in such a hurry, why I talk so fast and become impatient. I have tried to make things agreeable for her, and friends have rallied, but I have failed in not devoting myself to her with more understanding and patience . . . It has been a baffling visit for her.

And her prospective daughter-in-law would not answer the phone to her son.

Maud Nelson was sufficiently worried by Cecil's marital prospects to light candles for him and Greta in Brompton Oratory and to pray for them both. She described her disappointment that things were not working out properly as almost greater than Cecil's. 'I confess to feeling angry and bitter that you of all people should have had such a long and painful Gethsemane,' she wrote to him in January 1947. Much of the London gossip about his proposed marriage was fuelled by her. James Pope-Hennessy wrote to him that it was ultimately dangerous for him to have 'the presence of the Oggie circle' so near to the centre of his private life. He thought Cecil should have employed an 'other class' secretary. Olga Lynn was renowned for her parties. Cecil described her as a born hostess who 'lived in a glitter of Christian names'. She and Maud lived together in a turbulent way. Maud, said Olga, was 'one of the most promising of the English *Lieder* singers, with perfect diction in both French and German'. She became Cecil's secretary when her singing career failed.

Cecil returned to England that January and persisted in phoning Greta, though on the rare occasions when he got through, she asked him to refrain from calling and revealed nothing of herself or of her plans. He was inured to unreciprocated passion and undeterred by her coolness. He wrote letters to her almost daily, to which she seldom replied. Knowing that she would destroy them, he kept carbon copies, which he stored in a tin box, so that posterity, at least, might learn of his pursuit of love.

Nor was unrequited love all that he had to contend with. To compound his problems post-war Britain had elected a Labour government and the Empire was falling apart:

Each month brings further humiliations: these are our last days in Burma; we have left Cairo and lost India. Mr Atlee's gang has brought disaster in practically all forms upon us . . . Under the auspices of Mr Emmanuel Shinwell the coal supply has almost completely given out; gas flickers weakly – even hospitals are without hot water. Edith Olivier and other elderly ladies have not been permitted to switch on their electric blankets and the death rate from pneumonia has rocketed.

Worse for Cecil than the loss of India, after the war he lost his tenancy of Ashcombe. Since 1930 he had turned the place from a derelict farmhouse into a legendary home. The tennis court, gardens, glasshouses and studios were all created by him. In autumn 1945, the landlord, Hugh Borley, wanted the place back. Acrimonious letters from solicitors accused Cecil of contravening the terms of his lease by keeping domestic pets and made him liable for dilapidations totalling £1000.

He searched for a new home and in June 1947 bought Reddish, a Wren house in the village of Broadchalke, eight miles south-west of Salisbury. He paid £10,000 for it. On first view he thought it rambling and bleak, but when he went back with his mother and Maud, his spirits lifted. Mrs Beaton approved:

Her heart went out to the house of warm lilac-coloured brick and she loved the way it lay with the garden rising to a paddock, the long vistas of lawn sheltered by a double row of limes and elms, with the kitchen-garden enclosed with a typical Wiltshire wall of chalk topped with thatch roof . . . Two adjoining thatched cottages, surprisingly like Ann Hathaway's with their own gardens, were also part of the property. My mother saw the possibilities of making the terrace, with its southern aspect and old-fashioned roses growing over a balustrade, into a sheltered spot for outdoor lunch or tea.

Cecil worked hard to convert the house to his taste. He would wake in the night and make notes about enlarging the hall, covering the beams and putting in new windows. He thought it a real house, the 'abode of an adult person . . . not a fantasy, makeshift presence like Ashcombe'.

But the abode of this adult person needed a mistress as well as a master. With his mother ensconced there, in an effort to make the ménage complete, he wrote fervid letters to Greta inviting her to 'come and build your nest here at Reddish House'. He informed her that he had never wanted to devote himself to any one woman before, that she had the lion's share in all his plans, that one day all obstacles between them would be overcome and that he was a very genuine person if permitted so to be.

In the summer of 1947 Greta was travelling in Europe with Schlee, whom Cecil referred to as 'the Russian sturgeon' and 'the second-rate dressmaker's assistant'. She stayed with Schlee in his villa, Le Roc, at Cap d'Ail on the French Riviera. In mid-August she sent a large box of chocolates to Cecil at his house in Pelham Place. Cecil saw the gift as a love tryst: 'Your present to me has come like manna from heaven and I know you are as understanding and true as I have always believed you to be,' he replied.

Two weeks later she arrived with Schlee in London. As she left the *Queen Mary*, she gave reporters her usual brush off. She said that she had hoped to get off the ship unobserved. 'I cannot understand,' she said, 'why people cannot understand a perfectly natural and genuine desire I have to be left alone.' Cecil, tantalised, saw in the newspapers photographs of her going in and out of Claridges wearing a huge white hat. One evening, in room 124, she let the bath overflow. Afraid the water would drip to the room below, she spent an age mopping up with towels and her bath sponge. She then moved to room 239.

Cecil implored her to call him and one day she left a message with Maud, saying that she would visit. Cecil cancelled engagements, adorned Pelham Place with flowers, resisted eating fish for fear of making the place smell and thought that every car door that slammed, presaged her arrival. But she did not show up, and he received a message from her that she had been delayed. 'Delayed,' wrote Cecil to her, 'I suppose Heloïse and Abelard were delayed.'

His only certainty was work and he was never so besotted as to let that slip. In the early months of 1947 – from March on – he concurrently designed the costumes for two films directed by Alexander Korda: *An Ideal Husband* and another version of *Anna Karenina*, starring Vivien Leigh. Karinska's daughter, Madame Paulette, made Vivien Leigh's dresses and hats from Cecil's sketches. In May there was a heatwave while, on set, props men nailed icicles to windows and laid carpets of snow on the ground. Vivien Leigh complained that her gloves were too small, her corsets too tight and that Cecil's photographs of her were hateful. Korda kept disappearing to Hollywood to fight some lawsuit. Each day Cecil was at Shepperton Studios at dawn and seldom left before nine at night.

IO

Consummation

*'I have imagined happiness, but happiness
you cannot imagine, happiness you must feel.'*
Queen Christina

In October 1947 Cecil again went to New York, booked in at the
Plaza and

> telephoned immediately to the Ritz Tower – to the person who
> has occupied my mind for the last two years. 'Miss Brown
> don't answer.' Why is she hiding from me again? I am in
> despair. How to get through the day? Are my hopes dashed?
> Will I never see her again? Next day I telephone Wickersham
> 2–5000; my heart is pounding while I wait to be put through to
> her room.

Greta spoke. She had sinus trouble. She was surprised they had
not seen each other for a year-and-a-half and would visit him some
time soon, but not at weekends, which she reserved for Schlee. Cecil
cryptically told her he had a lot of things for her. He meant unposted
letters about his burning love.

On Monday 3 November she phoned and asked if she might call
round that afternoon at three. Cecil pencilled a red cross in his diary.
He photographed Gertrude Lawrence in the morning, then went
back to the Plaza and prepared his rooms – flowers, Old Gold
cigarettes, bowls of fruit, books lying open with careful noncha-

lance, the best of his photographs casually displayed. He wore his second-best suit, felt sick and kept going to the lavatory.

She was fifteen minutes late. When she rang the bell, he kept her waiting, in an effort not to appear as eager as he felt. She rang again.

Only a thin slice of wooden door now separated us . . . Now I would open and know my fate . . . I had rehearsed all sorts of welcome: 'My, my, my!' or 'Well, well, well!' or 'At last after all this time – what a long time it has been!' or 'What a charming surprise!'

I teetered towards the door: with a sweep I opened it . . . my heart withstood the impact: I still survived. She was wearing a black peaked hat and a falling dark coat: her mouth was very red, her face peakier than I had remembered, the nose more pointed. Her body had become a shred – there was hardly any flesh on it. Bowing formally, my reflexes caused me to exclaim: 'What a charming surprise!'

'Surprise?' she said. She kept the conversation light, chatted of how she liked hunting in the junk shops on Third and Fourth Avenue, of her anxiety when the bath overflowed at Claridges and how amused she had been when with Schlee she met Michael Duff in the south of France. She did not look at any of Cecil's photographs or refer to her past. He asked about her emotional and spiritual experiences since last they met and she brushed such questions aside. He asked what she wanted most from life, 'It would be foolish to tell you,' she said, 'and I am not as foolish as all that.' But Cecil was triumphant, for she was again sitting on his settee, smoking her cigarettes. 'So you're massaging my back again, are you?' she said, as he resumed his wooing ways.

When it got dark, she drew the mustard-coloured velvet curtains. 'I was completely surprised at what was happening,' wrote Cecil in his diary that night:

It took me some time to recover my bafflement . . . we were suddenly together again in unexplained, unexpected and inevitable intimacy . . . I was hardly able to bridge the gap so quickly and unexpectedly. I had to throw my mind back to the times at Reddish House when in my wildest dreams I had invented the scenes that were now taking place.

They arranged to meet for dinner the next evening. He was late back from a cocktail party and she was waiting outside his door wearing a sou'wester hat and looking 'almost simian with untidy hair and large, smudged, red mouth'. Her hands were gnarled because, in California, she had sanded then painted all the windows of her house. Life, she said, was made up of work or unimportant details and there was no particular difference. She gave him the impression of having been lonely while travelling in Europe with Schlee, 'the little man'. Schlee made all the arrangements and she paid her share of bills at the end.

There followed a lacuna and Miss Brown did not answer when Cecil phoned. Ill with a cold, she stayed away for a week, saying that he muddled her. On 11 November when she reappeared in the afternoon, he found her pallor 'excessively, touchingly, wonderfully beautiful'. A friend, Mrs Sanson from Santa Barbara, in a fur coat and a smart back-tilted hat – 'the last sort of woman one would expect to be a friend of Greta's', picked her up from Cecil's rooms. Greta introduced Cecil as her fiancé, threw cushions at him, then went off with Mrs Sanson on a shopping spree.

Cecil noted in his diary her every trivial remark, their every meeting, phone conversation and walk in the park. His documentation of her was unknown to her and of the kind she had learned to dread: a record that insisted on unrelenting self-consciousness. Forbidden again to photograph her, he made notes about her in a similar snapshot way – though he purported to be wooing her. One day, out of the blue, she asked, You don't write about people do you? Cecil professed shock, ducked the question and protested indignation that she could even imagine that he would do anything that hurt her. 'I love you so much,' he said, 'I only want to do the things that will make you love me more.'

In the cold of New York's winter, they resumed their walks in Central Park. On Friday 14 November they arranged to meet by the archway to the zoo. Cecil's nose went mauve as he waited and to get warm he wandered into the monkey house. It was smelly in there and not his favoured way of passing an afternoon. But when Greta arrived wearing a Pilgrim Fathers hat with a large black bag slung over her shoulder, he felt she was 'unlike the rest of humanity' and utterly romantic. Passers-by, as ever, asked to take photographs of her, or asked for her autograph. As ever, she ignored them or refused.

She agreed to have tea at the Plaza, but would not be seen going into the hotel with Cecil. He went on ahead, told his secretary to leave, lit some candles and set the scene. Greta bought biscuits, then tried to slip in via the back stairs. Serge Obolensky saw her, and she panicked at the thought of his telling Schlee.

After tea she said:

Don't ask questions. Don't scrutinise. She kept looking at her watch. 'Isn't it awful to be with someone who is always following the clock, who is so strict and won't let you ask questions or scrutinise.' Suddenly, as if it were the most ordinary question in the world, she stretched out her arm towards the other room and asked with disarming and natural frankness, 'Do you want to go to bed?'

Sometimes photographs are more like people than people themselves . . . This afternoon there were many flashes of her in the Pilgrim hat as she was in *Queen Christina* and later in the half light she was the living embodiment of her 'stills'. Later she said 'La nuit tombe' and outside there was only artificial light.

He had so confused reality with its image that Greta Garbo in bed was more a photograph than flesh. He had become the camera and turned reality into illusion. His observations were like snapshots but now he was in the frame with her. And the images that flashed on his inner eye were from the film when she dresses as a man.

He wrote that she exuded 'ambiguous sex attraction, half boy, half woman'. He said that she taught him about making love so that he realised how much time he had hitherto wasted and how little he knew of the procedure before meeting her. But he was, he felt, being 'used for his body' – which made a change, for he was more used to pining for unavailable sex. She told him that 'she did not like anything rough or staccato', visited when she pleased, left early and always gave priority to Schlee.

Cecil told his friend Mona Harrison Williams that he was in love with Greta. She advised him to play hard to get and to give the same treatment as he received. Women, she said, were far less nice than men. He should endeavour to provoke Greta by his coolness and if the rejection game worked, to keep at it without mercy.

For four days he resisted phoning. Then, when he did, he intimated that Mona and certain men were sexually interested in him and that he was 'stepping out in both directions'. He felt that his tactics of jealous manipulation and simulated indifference roused her interest in him. When she suggested calling round, he told her it was too rainy. She said she would call anyway, and arrived dishevelled, wearing woollen scarves and a waistcoat and an overcoat that was too short.

On Thanksgiving Day, 27 November, he sent a vase of white orchids and a love letter, then left, without telling her, for Boston for the weekend. She rang while he was away, called to see him on the Monday and seemed jealous, he thought, behind the bantering, or at least inquisitive. She again drew the velvet curtains and, said Cecil, 'we talked of many intimate things that it is difficult to talk about, but managed to achieve a happy understanding and mutual enjoyment.'

Their usual tryst was in the afternoons, she never stayed the night and kept away for days on end. He rationalised her relationship with Schlee as a drab necessity that she had to go through with. She told Cecil he draped himself too much, that when phoning he should not posture with his hand on his hip and that, as she wanted to make a man out of him, she supposed she would have to propose to him. On 1 December he wrote in his diary that it had been a pleasant evening for them both, 'but less ecstatic for me for I had to hold onto myself to prevent myself from being devoured.'

The following afternoon they walked in the park. He wanted to kiss her by the reservoir but she was worried about being seen. 'Are you eaten up with passion?' she asked. In the Metropolitan Museum she told him of the paintings she had bought as investment and which she kept in her California home – a Rouault, a Renoir, a blue period Picasso of 'a horrible-looking woman'. She said she never looked at them.

One afternoon they watched the televised wedding of Princess Elizabeth to the Duke of Edinburgh. One evening they went to see *The Winslow Boy* which had been a success in London and was now on Broadway. 'Throughout the play she stared at me' Cecil wrote in his diary – which made him reflect on how he similarly used to stare at Peter and on how annoyed Peter then became.

Cecil believed that marriage was in sight:

One day I might get her worked up sufficiently to rush off to a registrar. For myself I am not only willing, but desperate, and confident that we could have the infinite joy of making a new and successful life together.

He did not expand on what he might do, sufficiently to work her up and rush her off, nor what the context of their life together might be.

She told Cecil that she adored him, loved him and was in love with him, but she was laughing as she said it. Years later she referred to their time together as 'fooling around'.

On 8 December, they went to the theatre, then to a cabaret at a night club called The Blue Angel and to Hamburger Heaven, but she left when bothered by a drunk man who asked for her autograph. They walked back to the Ritz and she invited Cecil in, saying she would give him a couple of apples.

So Cecil found himself, for the first time, in the 'sacred precincts' of her rooms at the Ritz – in the forbidden Suite 26c. He made a mental inventory of letters addressed to Harriet Brown, twin beds with candlewick covers, hats, bills, receipts, magazines. She would not turn on the main lights so he 'peered into the gloaming'. In her kitchenette she prepared a meal of Swedish bread, ham, cheese, unsalted butter and beer. They talked of the passing of time, kissed 'for the thousandth time' and at three in the morning Cecil walked home alone, pondering on how the situation 'could be consolidated into something definite and binding'.

The answer was that it could not. She had no intention of being bound to any arrangement and all her promises were vague. She maintained her air of secrecy, indulged her mild paranoia, kept her eye on her watch and was anxious that no one – and particularly not Schlee – should know of these meetings with Cecil. When Obolensky again saw her going up the back stairs of the Plaza she said, 'Well I do have the rottenest luck. I bet the little man will see me next, and then my goose will be cooked.'

Cecil gleaned the scant biographical facts which the world already knew: that in her family there had never been any interest in the things she liked, that Mauritz Stiller had been the great influence in her life, that Hollywood frightened and disappointed her. Their outings together were companionable – Christmas shopping at Macy's then to a bookshop with a Swedish gift department, full, Cecil thought, of hideous things. Sometimes they lunched at a little Brazilian restaurant and shared a bottle of Chilean wine.

Walking back to his hotel through a snowstorm, she told him she remembered little of their first meeting in Hollywood all those years ago, apart from his soft white leather jacket. Cecil was glad they had deferred their relationship until he was more 'experienced' a lover. She said she had left it late to be married, but a Frenchman had told her that he liked his women, 'like a salad, *un peu fatigué*'.

Cecil believed that he and Greta were enjoying themselves in an uninhibited, unshy way. 'With each meeting we seem to know a little more of one another – or at any rate I of Greta.' When he persisted with his fantasy of marriage she embellished it:

'You would say, "Run and get the spray will you dear – I see those roses are beginning to get the blight." Eventually I'd get so tired of fagging after you that I'd say: "Jehovah come here!" and a little negro boy would do all the running about.'

When he said that he would like them to have a child together she replied that if they did, she would behead it. All she would seriously say was that she liked him, and that whenever she said goodbye she wanted to see him again.

Once, he met her by chance in the street, her mink coat tied with string to stop it flapping open. Another afternoon she phoned in tears, saying she was ill. When he went to meet her she was drunk, confused and crying. Often she seemed forlorn, vulnerable, anxious about the traffic, or about being attacked.

He thought that she missed acting, but that she was conscious of 'all the things that weren't there before' in her face. He thought she would feel humiliated to see herself reflected as imperfect, with the world staring at her. She was, she said, still discussing the possibility of playing George Sand (Cecil warmed to the idea of her wearing velvet trousers and smoking a cigar). She would also like to play St Francis of Assisi and Dorian Gray. '*Travesti*', wrote Cecil

> has obviously titillated her and, since early days, she has enjoyed wearing the more romantic of men's apparel in her films. Ventriloquists' dolls and pierrots possess an ambiguity that delights her sense of the perverse. This is, no doubt, the reason why stories have circulated about her having odd tendencies.

He had odd tendencies too. He had enjoyed wearing the more romantic of women's apparel without the pretext of films. For them both, costume and the camera were ingenious masks behind which to reveal sexuality, while half hiding what could not be openly shown. The conundrum of 'half boy, half woman' called for a particular sort of disguise. The informed viewer might raise the mask and see the true face behind it. Both Greta and Cecil concealed and revealed in their work, while keeping social proprieties and protecting themselves. Cecil's fashion models were *his* ventriloquist's dolls.

Her attitude to lesbianism, he called 'unsympathetic and recoiling'. As for homosexuality in men, 'she insists that it should never be made obvious that a man possesses instinct which might offend the more "normal" population.' He confided to her the details of his effeminacy as a child: how he wore his school cap like the ladies who modelled in the *Sketch* and *Play Pictorial*, his passionate interest in women's fashion and love of make-up. He said how his father had wanted him to be a cricketer, like himself and had punished him for painting his face. He told her of his 'first stirrings of love' at Harrow, and the lack of all sex at Cambridge and he showed her the photographs of himself in women's clothes from his Cambridge days. She said they were 'too much' and that it must be terrible for parents, who wanted their offspring to lead conventional lives, to find them turning out so oddly. She asked if he was demonstrative to his mother, and when he said that he was not, remarked: 'Parents make it so difficult for us.' As for herself, she had had a troublesome, difficult time when young, which taught her much about life. She had been a tomboy, the ringleader of a gang and had preferred toy soldiers to dolls.

Cecil thought her impervious to people who behaved badly toward her. She advised him to be calmer, more generous and not so critical and outspoken. 'I admit', he wrote, 'that I am incapable of analysis and am not the deepest of wells. I am grateful to Greta that, with her guidance, I am able to scratch a little beneath the surface to look for the meaning of things.' He felt that all barriers of reserve seemed to be down between them and he could see no obstacle to their living the rest of their lives together, it was both easy and indicated. 'No it's not easy,' said Greta.

You have not had a difficult life as I have. It's easy for you to be gay and happy. Occasionally you may have been sad, when someone has not loved you as much as you loved them. But life has been difficult for me. I am a sad person . . . a misfit in life.

Cecil perceived obstacles to their marriage as coming from problems within her personality not his own. He hoped that were she to live with him in England and work in films for a European audience, she would feel more at home. He discussed, with Alexander Korda, the idea of her starring as Elizabeth of Austria in a film of Jean Cocteau's *The Eagle Has Two Heads*, with sets and costumes designed by himself. Greta seemed enthusiastic and twice saw Korda with Schlee, but the plan came to nothing.

She was wooed regularly to return to work. In December Tennessee Williams talked to her about starring in a screenplay of his, *The Pink Bedroom*, directed by George Cukor:

To my surprise the fabulous lady received me alone in her apartment at the Ritz Tower.

We sat in the parlor drinking schnapps. I got a big high and I began to tell her the story of *The Pink Bedroom*. There was something about her curious and androgynous beauty that inspired me out of my characteristic timidity. I told her the story and she kept whispering, 'Wonderful', leaning toward me with a look of entrancement in her eyes. I thought to myself, She will do it, she'll return to the screen! After an hour, when I had finished telling the scenario, she still said, 'Wonderful!' But then she sighed and leaned back on her sofa. 'Yes, it's wonderful, but not for me. Give it to Joan Crawford.'

He also hoped she would play Blanche du Bois in the film version of *A Streetcar Named Desire*, but she told Cecil she could not identify with a character who told lies and 'saw things round corners'. She said that though the effects of the brutality she experienced in childhood would always be with her, her character was honest, clearcut, lucid and masculine. She did not elucidate on what this brutality was.

But in a none too clearcut piece of theatre, she said to Cecil, on 20 December, that she was going to see the stage version of *Streetcar* with Schlee and that 'if the devil's in me I'll come right over afterwards and spend the night'. The devil was not in her, and she arrived at the Plaza the next morning, a Sunday. They were lovers in their way and then, with her hair tied with yellow ribbon, they shared a bath. 'We laughed a lot and I felt very happy,' wrote Cecil.

Lest he should deceive himself too deeply that such behaviour might presage marriage and old men's pyjamas, she told him of a man who contacted her about a house to sell. She visited him, they looked at the downstairs rooms and the garden, then she thought to herself Why not, and asked if there was a beautiful view from his bedroom. She did not see him again.

On Christmas Day she and Cecil lunched with Mercedes at her Park Avenue apartment. 'Have you room for an extra lost soul?'

Greta asked her on Christmas Eve. Mercedes wanted to know who the lost soul was. 'You'll know soon enough as long as you've got an extra plate,' said Greta. Cecil called at the Ritz Tower at noon. Greta's room was full of packages and 'slowly dying flowers'. She had been up since seven, wrapping her presents. While waiting, Cecil idly opened the kitchenette door. She admonished him violently, saying she hated curiosity and disliked it intensely when people did not mind their own business. He felt 'utterly crushed' and took time to calm down.

Mercedes was ill-at-ease and not in the least pleased to see Cecil. She had asked him point blank if he was having an affair with Greta. Cecil told Greta of the question. She thought it vulgar of Mercedes to ask. Mercedes kept referring to her own intimacy with Greta – their holiday in the desert, 'that time when you wouldn't let me buy that coffee pot . . . that pink vase you liked so much.' Greta, Cecil said, 'smacked her down', and disassociated herself from all claims. A Mr Everley arrived, a 'rather pathetic chorus boy sissy' and the atmosphere was unpleasant and strange. Greta called Cecil 'Mr Beaton', but when he called Everley or Mercedes 'darling', she said to him under her breath, 'Don't you dare ever call anyone darling but me.'

With a tea towel tied round her middle she cooked ham and eggs, distributed her presents, bossed Mercedes around and sprawled on the sofa singing 'Nobody knows the troubles I've seen but Jesus'. She left promptly at three to meet Schlee. Cecil accompanied her some of the way, but when they neared Schlee's apartment she walked ahead alone.

It snowed heavily on Boxing Day. Cecil invited Greta, Schlee and a dozen select guests for drinks at the Plaza. The atmosphere was again one of rivalry and tension, another triangle of discord. Schlee 'emanated a troubled, electric atmosphere' and would not look Cecil in the eye. When offered a drink he said he would just have a sip to show there was no ill feeling. Cecil tried to kiss Greta goodbye while Schlee was putting on his snow boots. 'A look of terror came over her face' and she said, 'Oh don't be so foolish.'

And so the pattern of the affair became defined. Walks in the park, sex in the afternoons, kissing, massaging of vertebrae and waving goodbye. She never went beyond frivolity, or allowed any marginal trespass into her private world. She never confided her feelings about Schlee, who continued to live with his wife. Cecil chose to deceive himself about the profundity of what she offered to him. She seemed to want refuge in his superficiality, to have him as her lover because he need not be taken seriously as a lover. He wrote of the smallest exchange between them in embellished prose. It was the verbal equivalent of his photos, an extravagant façadism, an adornment to conceal a void.

As for their lovemaking, it had its restraints and disturbed no one taking tea in adjacent hotel rooms. He related to her how he had been woken by 'the most agonising sounds' from a woman in the next room at the Plaza. He realised that she was 'in the throes of love-making and that the cries, so heartbreaking to hear, were part of her enjoyment. Ecstasy is revolting,' he said, 'if it comes to this.' Greta said the man must be a brute.

On New Year's Eve of 1948 they went to separate events. Cecil was invited to a large party at Mona Harrison Williams. Greta had arranged to spend the evening with Schlee. At 10.30, toward the end of the formal dinner, the butler told Cecil, 'It's Mr Thompson on the line.' This was the tactic used by 'Mr Toscar' to summon Mercedes, on their second meeting, from lunch with Pola Negri. Cecil left Mona's party without saying goodbye to anyone, took a taxi down Park Avenue to the Ritz and thought himself the luckiest man alive to be keeping this tryst with the one person in the world he wanted to see.

'Our embrace was tender. We did not have enough arms to entwine round each other's shoulders and waists.' Greta had quarrelled with Schlee. She said she had been very cruel to him, that he was the best friend she had ever had, and was devoted to her, but she could not bear to be tied down. She and Cecil walked back to the Plaza and drank 1840 whisky, given to him by Margaret Case. Cecil gave a toast to their own marriage. Greta seemed diffident. He implored her not to leave him or to make him unhappy. He was, however, drunk. The whisky was on top of champagne and brandy at Mona's. He caught sight of his reflection in the mirror:

> I was appalled by the swollen, bloated face that confronted me, lips all smudged with rouge and eyes bunged up. I said how is it possible for you to like anyone who looks as awful as I do? She made a kind reply and I clasped her again.

She told him she would soon be travelling to California to sell her Beverly Hills' house. She intimated that he might visit her there.

At midnight they looked from the window as motorists sounded their horns and pedestrians cheered. Then they walked to the Ritz Tower. Greta wandered around her apartment in knickers, white socks and Cecil's hat. When he was back at the Plaza she phoned to say she had read in the papers that New York marriages are undermined by drink.

For the most part Cecil rationalised her relationship with Schlee as a stale obligation. In February 1948, coming out of the cinema one afternoon, they met Schlee by chance. Greta was pleased to see him and arranged to meet him in five minutes' time. He was easily intimate with her and took no notice of Cecil beyond shaking hands. Cecil had a cold moment of truth, felt marginalised, desperate and as if he wanted to destroy whatever there was between himself and Greta.

One evening he followed her to the opening night of *Mr Roberts*, a Broadway play 'about sex-starved sailors in the Pacific'. She sat with Schlee in the front row. Cecil got a ticket, 'at the thirteenth hour', in the third row, then played a furtive game of staring at her throughout the play. She wore a black skull cap and medieval hood and he thought he had never seen her looking more beautiful. In their afternoons at the Plaza he had seen her with bedraggled hair and in old clothes. Now she was like a perfect celluloid image and he was the voyeur. 'Occasionally we indulged in a dangerous game of staring full-face at one another.' He thought the 'vibrations' he was sending out must be felt by everyone in the theatre. Certainly they were felt by Schlee. When Schlee turned and looked, Cecil hid his face.

It was a strange game, Cecil so intent on meeting Greta's gaze, so assiduous at avoiding Schlee's. He did not intend to provoke Schlee. The face he wanted reflected back to himself was Greta's, not Schlee's. In his photographs of women he implied a viewer, gazing at a mirrored gaze. In this gazing game, a slight diversion at a third-rate play, he was both camera and mirror, Greta the perfect reflected face. He stole illicit images of her. The game was the essence of his preoccupation with image. Garbo was again more like a picture than herself, turned into image by his photographer's eye.

At one in the morning Greta phoned him at the Plaza. Schlee had complained and Cecil must not now make arrangements to visit her in California. Cecil argued that Schlee had another life too, and had no right to monopolise her. Greta said she would explain the situation the next day.

Over tea in the Palm Court, she told him that Schlee heartily disliked the nuances and atmosphere of what was going on. He had devoted himself to Greta for four years and did not want a rival. He had told Margaret Case he regretted letting Greta meet Cecil again and could harm him if he wished. Greta said that she did not want to force the issue, but repeated that Cecil should not visit her in Hollywood. Cecil asked what was to prevent him going on legitimate business, to discuss plans for designing a film for Hitchcock. She 'gave an asiatic wink' and said that if that was the case, she could not prevent it.

There was no moral dimension to Cecil's pursuit of Greta. His

18.

CECIL WAS A ROMANTIC ROYALIST BUT HE SPOOFED
THE MONARCHY TOO. *QUEEN CHRISTINA* WAS
SCRIPTED FOR GRETA AT HER OWN REQUEST.

17. Her Majesty Queen Elizabeth at
Buckingham Palace.
Photo by Cecil Beaton, 1939.

18. Greta Garbo as Queen Christina.
Photo by Clarence Sinclair Bull, 1933.

19. Cecil with feathered fan.
Photo by Dorothy Wilding, 1925.

20. Baroness Von Bulop 'In Pensive Mood'
(alias Cecil's friend Antonio Gandarillas).
Photographed by Cecil for My Royal Past, *1939.*

20.

22.

GRETA LIKED 'FOOLING AROUND' WITH CECIL BUT
AT HEART SHE KEPT HER DISTANCE. 'HE TALKS TO
NEWSPAPERS,' SHE SAID.

21. Greta and Cecil in London.
Newsphoto, 1951.

22. Cecil's 'passport photograph' of Greta,
May 1946.

23. Self-portrait with camera, 1951.

24. Greta and Cecil cruising the Greek islands,
July 1965.

sympathy for Mercedes left him too, in his ambition to be centre stage. On 6 February Greta took him, uninvited, to lunch with Mercedes who became 'addle-pated, tactless and silly' in Greta's presence and unable to prepare lunch. Greta told her to sit down and got the lunch herself – crusty bread, butter, red wine and hardboiled eggs with chives. Five days later Mercedes asked Cecil to have dinner with her alone. He was apprehensive that she would ask embarrassing questions about his 'intentions' toward Greta. Greta told him to look her straight in the face and say, 'I don't know what you're talking about.'

But in fact Mercedes talked of her concern for Greta, of the paucity of Greta's life without work, her days spent aimlessly walking, her lack of friends, the way she took orders from 'the little man', the unsuitability of Gayelord Hauser and Stokowski. Mercedes said, with or without conviction, that she wished Cecil would marry Greta.

What was enacted was a teasing, insecure dance where Cecil, Schlee and Mercedes moved to partner Greta, who spent time with them all, but not too much. She kept no photographs of them, no letters from them, 'no relics involving any human beings'. Cecil recorded in his diary an evening in February when they all jostled for position. He was with Greta in her rooms at the Ritz:

the telephone bell went through us like a pistol shot. It was my rival. He was sorry, but he would have to take his wife to a first night tonight. I too was going to the first night with my friend, Leonora Corbett. 'Wouldn't you like to come and sit with me while I have my supper at Mercedes's?' this was Greta's preliminary step in a concerted attempt to make me break my theatre date with Leonora. I laughed. 'You know it would be impossible to chuck at this late hour. Imagine Leonora's fury!'

However, on my way to collect Leonora I did go to see Greta and Mercedes and found them both in a very giggly mood, indulging in cross-banter and *double-entendres*. By now Greta, by every device possible, was trying to force me to stay and have dinner with them in order to be late for Leonora. She pretended that she had never seen me before in a dinner jacket – that she did not know I had this, or liked that. She kept winking at me, and indulging in a pantomime of our being comparative strangers.

I left for Leonora and the theatre. During the first act I thought perhaps Greta would now be feeling lonely back in her hotel rooms, so in the first interval I would telephone. It took some time to find a call box and when I did it was occupied. Why the hell was the occupant in there so long? I nearly banged on the closed door. At last the occupant came out. It was my rival. He had obviously just been telephoning Greta. We made polite conversation about the play and praised the impeccable charm of Gertie Lawrence. Then I went into the kiosk and, roaring with laughter, put in my nickel. Then more laughter as I explained to her that I had followed 'the little man' into the box. She was in good spirits and, after certain badinage, thanked me for my sweet thought in calling. I wondered if she had said the same to 'the little man'? But realizing that he hurries to the telephone on every occasion . . . and that he has probably done this for years, gives me an indication of how dreadfully devoted he must be; he is something serious to have to contend with.

Woo as they would, there was no getting closer for any of them.

Cecil flew to California on 3 March, ostensibly for a work trip. He was to stay twelve days, with *Vogue* paying all expenses. He viewed the visit as a chance to consolidate his position with Greta, free from the rivalry of Schlee or Mercedes. But within two days Mercedes wired Greta to say she too was coming to California. 'That would make for complications,' Cecil wrote in his diary, 'as Mercedes could be very proprietary.'

As for Greta's feelings about Cecil's trip, she was pleased to have him around, not least from fear of being too much alone in her house, which had recently been burgled. She was his occasional lover, but she spent a good deal of time putting manure on the oleanders in her garden and hiking in the mountains. She made few concessions to his stay and asked him to leave early in the evening, so that she might go to bed at 7.30 pm.

On arrival, Cecil booked in at the Beverly Hills Hotel. The following morning he dressed in a lightweight suit and felt very spruce. He breakfasted on orange juice and bacon and eggs, then waited by the hotel bus stop for Greta to pick him up in the car. She drove up wearing old trousers and a jersey, told him to jump in and said, 'So you've come all this way to see your girlfriend.'

Her maid, 'the dragon', had the day off. Greta was diffident about her house and did not want Cecil peering at things. When he got through the front door he 'gathered her into a series of long embraces'. She asked him 'if he really wanted to' so early in the morning, then he followed her through the sitting-room and up the circular stairs to the pale blue, pale grey and burgundy coloured bedroom.

By simulating indifference he managed to see the house – her bookshelves, her cupboards with tennis racquets and old mackintoshes, her paintings – two Renoirs, a Modigliani, a Rouault and, in the sitting-room, a Bonnard still-life of a jug of poppies. Most of the rooms were empty. So this was where the 'Divina' lived, he noted in his diary. Had it been any woman less than the Divina, he would have found the regime then offered to him intolerable. They saw virtually no one – she was edgy even about the intrusiveness of her maid. They sunbathed, then for lunch had matzos, salad and milk. In the afternoon she lent him corduroy trousers, several sweaters and a brown anorak, drove him to Santa Monica and for miles they walked along the shoreline – climbing over breakwaters and rocks, and 'running after seagulls and pelicans'. She was extremely fit, Cecil observed, from all her daily exercises – 'in Olympic trim'.

They saw a bird with a broken wing being pecked by gulls, and lovers being spied on by a voyeur. Greta scraped the tar off Cecil's shoes, pretended to be a tough guy making some sexual proposition to him, then said 'I can't think quite what to do for dinner – whether to take you out to a little Italian place and look into your eyes, or whether to give you something at home.' She gave him something at home – lamb chops with the fat cut off and steamed vegetables, which they ate on the sofa, under the Bonnard poppies. And then, 'still quite early according to most people's timetable', she said goodnight. Cecil spent the evening at his hotel writing his diary account of the day, of how happy they had been in their 'fervour' in the grey and burgundy bedroom – 'something very violent had overtaken us both'.

Greta's gardening project throughout his stay was to spread manure over all the flowerbeds – she got up early to do this. She made frequent trips to the market to buy more sacks of it. She did strenuous exercise routines and sunbathed. Lunch was always salad. Their hikes, which lasted for hours, were either by the coast or into the mountains and they went on them even when it rained, for she liked walking in the rain. Supper was griddled lamb chops and steamed vegetables and only occasionally veal.

She would not let Cecil draw her and reluctantly let him take a few photographs. 'These were done under protest and she did not look well. Her hair suddenly became fluffy and messy and she looked unlike herself, rather vulgar and middle-aged.' Cecil, who noted every capillary and pore, found his affections altered according to how he felt she looked.

In the market one morning while she dithered about buying some stainless-steel kitchen utensils, they by chance met the actress Constance Collier with her 'redoubtable Man-Friday' Phillis Wilbourn. Greta crept up on Constance and kissed her and there followed a teasing sexual banter: Constance asked, 'Why don't you two settle down?' 'In reply Greta ruined my reputation by saying:

"But you don't think he's that sort of a man, do you?" Phillis led the laughter.' They then met Constance and Charlie Chaplin for supper and Greta did imitations of Cecil and Michael Duff in tight suits, spluttering about the British Empire.

One afternoon Cecil booked a viewing room at MGM and together they watched her in *Anna Karenina*. She told him about Russian life and how the snow scenes were done with feathers. As they left, the projectionist, seeing it was Garbo, tottered and almost fell. Back at Greta's home Cecil talked of his relationship with Peter Watson. He thought she seemed jealous, as if she sensed an ambivalence from Cecil toward her. She asked if he loved her and her apparent jealousy and insecurity proved the prelude to their best sexual encounter. After it, she said 'that I had never before made love to her as I did tonight. I felt very happy and pleased with myself and great satisfaction for my prowess as a lover.' Though in public he was her camp, gay friend, in bed she vied with the man he loved.

Cecil's visit was not unmitigated bliss. He caught a cold and sore throat from the contrast in climate to New York. There were days when Greta was tired and wanted to be alone, or simply did not want to see him. For *Vogue* he took desultory photographs of Beverly Hills beauties, work that seemed to him to mirror a 'vulgar and relentless' world. Korda sent a telegram confirming that there was no chance of making the film *The Eagle Has Two Heads*. So Cecil saw his chances of making a film with Greta, or even of persuading her to visit England, recede. And he saw too, in some half-defined way, that this love affair was for her no more than idle diversion. 'I realised that there was nothing concrete about our future: I had no hold over her.' She said that attachment was a dangerous responsibility, intimated, yet again, that she did not consider him a serious person and implied, in a tired way, that though she was not in love with Schlee, this did not imply that she was in love with Cecil. 'You see how difficult and neurotic I am,' she said to him. 'I'm impossible to get along with.'

She became brown from lying in the sun, her arms ached from digging in the garden and she seemed content to walk by the shore or in the mountains, eat a simple supper and go early to bed. Her lovemaking with Cecil was no more than frivolity and contained no coded promises of commitment, no intention of a shared life. He had visited the sequestered refuge of her home and noted everything he had seen there, but was offered none of it for himself.

Toward the end of his stay he reflected that he had done nothing for months but feed his obsession with her and he felt the need for his own work. On the day of his departure, he took her a huge armful of flowers – ranunculi, stocks, gardenias, roses, orchids, hyacinths and freesias. He cried when he said goodbye, waved to her elaborately from the taxi, listened as the driver boasted of how he had once been heavyweight boxing champion of the world, then made a diary entry of his feelings and his tears.

11

Disaffection

'My soul is tired. Oh the asphalt makes my legs so tired.'
Greta to Cecil, 1952

On his journey home to Reddish House Cecil wrote to Greta thanking her for the salad lunches 'shared with the blue birds', the walks by the Pacific Ocean and in the mountains, the trips to the market and to the seed shop. He had lived with her, he said, 'outside of clock time and in another sphere of happiness'.

> It was wonderful for me to feel so close and attached and I felt we got to know one another much better. You can rely on me always to feel for you an increasing devotion and affection. Thank you. Thank you.

In response, Greta sent a one-word telegram to the ship – 'Cecil' and he made what he would of that.

In reality few people had less capacity to thrive outside of clock time than Cecil. He had little attraction to a karmic state of being. Long hikes in the hills and a return to a house with unused rooms, no visitors and scarce possessions was not particularly his definition of the good life. His interest was in admiring flowers and land-scaping a garden, not in digging it and spreading it with manure. Nor did Greta have a strong tie to her house. She had bought it as an investment, as a refuge from the studios and the world. In 1951 she put it on the market and moved to New York, seeking the anonymity of the city.

Cecil returned to England ambitious to continue as a photographer and stage designer, to become a playwright – he began a play about Gainsborough's daughters – and to make Reddish House and its grounds into an estate comparable to Ashcombe. He continued with the fantasy that Greta would join him there as Mrs Beaton. He wrote to her two or three times a week 'in order to keep myself green in the memory of my friend. I loved writing to her, for it brought her closer to me.'

He addressed her as Dear Sir or Madam, Dear Boy, or his Dear Young Man. From time to time Greta replied, wishing him well, telling him of her uncertain plans and calling him her darling Beatie, or Beatie Boy. She said she was alone in the filthy air of Manhattan. More often than not she had a cold which she could not shake off. She thought she got so many colds because of her tonsils. She was frightened by the bouts of illness Schlee endured. She said that she had messed up her life, described herself as fighting it out with her troubled soul and trusted that, with the will of the Lord, they might meet again soon.

Pending the arrival of Greta Garbo, Cecil's mother and Maud Nelson were at Reddish, managing his affairs in his absence. They divided their time between there and Pelham Place. He had tried to tell Greta about them but she had stopped him, saying, 'That's enough of that. I see perfectly that you are hag-ridden.' Both women had become a problem. His mother embroidered cushion covers, made rugs and read library books, but she had no friends, was quarrelsome with Cecil, tippled from the drinks' cabinet, thought of the place as hers and complained of his guests eating the rations. He wrote to Greta about one of their many flare-ups:

the rocket went off, ignited by the fact that my mother has been much too close, on top of me, and has come to feel my country house is hers. I hate to make my mother unhappy and these unpleasantnesses are so degrading to the soul; but I must be allowed my own life. I am now middle-aged and temperamental and cannot be treated as a naughty child. *Assez.*

Maud Nelson, though company for Cecil's mother and a mediator in the rows, did not, over the years, improve as a secretary. She failed to catalogue his photographs and designs and was given to taking a great many of his clients into her 'strictest confidence'. She described herself as highly strung, highly sensitive and highly intelligent, and she was allergic to pollen and dust. By spring 1948 she had decided that Greta was not the right person for Cecil to marry. 'I would love you to marry someone not younger than thirty or older than thirty-four so that you could raise these little Reddishes for Reddish,' she wrote to him.

Cecil returned home from Greta to debts. His tax demands for 1946 and 1947 were steep. He owed £6,100 to the Inland Revenue and had only £3,000 in his bank account. Maud was stern:

Well you can't have your cake and eat it and you have bought Reddish and furnished it etc. You have earned a large income and therefore you have large taxes to pay *like everyone else. There is no way round it* and you are far more generously treated by the Inspector of Taxes than most other people are. Practically half your household and entertaining expenses – and God *help me* what I put down to these expenses is no one's business – are allowed you. In other words, the State pays for half your pleasures in life.

Well according to your horoscope you are having good financial times ahead and I can't worry myself ill as I did last winter. I am just going to trust in your star and in your play and if it is a great success and you want to devote the rest of your life to writing, then after this year you may have to make Reddish your home and give up Pelham Place in some way that we make money on it – which would not be very difficult. Very few people can afford to run two places nowadays unless they are living on their capital *as most people are* since it was officially announced only 200 people in the country have £5,000 a year to spend after taxation is paid – so that gives one to think.

Maud's problematic health and private life meant that she needed a good deal of time off. A particularly bad asthma attack at the time of the move to Reddish House was followed by a car crash which cracked her skull and broke her nose. She told Cecil that she loved him deeply, but that she was not *in love* with him, or else she would be jealous of Greta. Her relationship with Olga Lynn became strained and she spent time calming down with Brigitte, who gave her *Peace of Soul* by Fulton Sheen to read, with chapters on 'Sex and the Love of God' and 'The Philosophy of Anxiety, Fear and Death'. Brigitte often prayed for Maud, which Maud found a 'wonderful, glowing, invincible thing'. Cecil began to wish that he could rid himself of Maud, who had been with him since 1940. The emotional realities of Reddish were not as he would have them.

Peter Watson visited in 1949. Cecil had seen very little of him for four years, but after three days with him felt 'all the same emotions' and his departure left a void. He persisted in hoping that Greta would fill that void and that Reddish House would be their marital home.

He set about creating a paradisiacal setting. He created a winter garden – it had a white marble and black diamond floor, a Chinese chandelier and cane furniture. He bought antiques from Mr Percy Bates and other Salisbury dealers, hung the library and master bedroom with Charles II wallpapers and turned the five acres of grounds into a showpiece garden. His herbaceous borders were filled with lilies, delphiniums and hollyhocks, there were red geraniums in tubs by the garage wall, apples in the orchard, roses galore and his lawn was the best in the West Country.

Greta, for her part, moved with customary indifference in 1949 into a four-roomed furnished apartment in Hampshire House on Central Park South in New York and resisted invitations to return to the screen. To offers of leading roles in *The Paradine Case* and *I Remember Mama*, she sent a telegram to MGM, 'No murderesses, no mamas'. Her relationship with Schlee, who continued to live with Valentina, was constant if colourless. He went with her to talk to various producers but she expressed no regrets when the projects foundered. In the summer of 1949 they travelled together to Italy to discuss with Walter Wanger plans for a film based on Balzac's *La Duchesse de Langeais*. It was called *Lover and Friend* and was to co-star James Mason. The Italian press besieged her. 'If I'd had a gun I swear I'd shoot them,' she told Cecil. The papers printed pictures of her wearing a wide straw hat, dark glasses and sandals – pictures which she hated. Press photographs conveyed a literal reality without the code of art and within their candid frame she was less than divine. She stayed in her hotel and went out only twice – to a gallery and a church. The film company could not raise sufficient cash and wanted her to 'smile at rich Italians' who might back the project – which she refused to do. Newspaper reports said the backers pulled out after she asked £120,000 as her fee.

Cecil met her in Paris when she was on her way home with Schlee from this fiasco. He professed to be staggered by her beauty but she demurred. 'I still have eyes to see, and I know how I look,' she said. She was now forty-five. But she admitted that tests for the new film, her first for ten years, had pleased her and that her eyes had a depth not conveyed in earlier pictures.

Cecil was pleased that she seemed bored with Schlee. He felt it was because of Schlee that arrangements for the film had foundered. 'He is an amateur in the movie world yet seemed to think he could take them all on at their own game,' he wrote in his diary. The three of them went for a day to Chantilly, to Cecil's friend, Diana Cooper. Her husband, Duff Cooper had been British Ambassador in Paris from 1944 to 1947 and the French government let them continue renting a house at Chantilly. Cecil tried to be casual to Greta and to defer to Schlee, 'to keep his ego titillated', but scrutinised him with 'steely glares of hatred' when safe to do so. He tried to induce Greta to leave Schlee and go with him to England, which she declined to do.

> But on the way home from a walk to the chateau of Chantilly she whispered, 'Won't you take me to Montmartre tonight?' But I knew she was only saying this because she knew I was going to the theatre with my little Greek friend Lilia Ralli.

It was an endless tease, a flirtatious game. It began to seem like another of those Hollywood scripts she wanted to forget where the men were like moths, circling around light. In *Camille* Robert Taylor says, 'No one has ever loved you as I love you,' to which Garbo replies, 'That may be true, but what can I do about it?' During a rare interview in the fifties, asked about love, she said 'I cannot talk about these things because I know nothing of them, nothing.' But she admitted to difficulty in buying well-fitting shoes.

She referred to Hollywood as a distant place. In 1951 she took American citizenship, but more to secure her financial investments, than as an act of allegiance to her adopted country. It became an automatic reflex for her to shield her face from the cameras with her hand, put a handkerchief to her mouth to conceal the lines of age, and to draw the curtains against the prospect of strangers.

As she grew older, she indulged none of the usual Hollywood cosmetic against ageing – of face lifts, dyed hair and the excessive application of paint. Her hair turned grey, she wore easy, well-cut clothes, avoided the company of actors, and told Cecil she wished she had been a writer or a painter so that her work might have been more separate from her self. To Cecil her life seemed empty, and her retreat inwards like the waste of endless opportunities for glory.

'How sad a thing for an artist to abandon his art,' Tennessee Williams said of her. 'I think it's much sadder than death.' To Salka she confided that though she planned in her mind to do things, she always procrastinated and always postponed, and then tomorrow it was the same story.

But her fans were faithful. In 1954, fifteen years after its first showing, there were queues in New York to see her in *Camille*. The novelist Jean Rhys, seeing the film that year in London, wrote to her daughter:

> I went to see a revival of La Dame aux Camelias with Greta Garbo. She is so lovely, really she haunts one. She makes everyone else meaningless and rather vulgar.

A season of her films on Italian television led to a seventy-five per cent drop in cinema audiences. Ingmar Bergman, David Lean, Luchino Visconti all wanted her to star in the films they directed. Somehow she never quite said yes. She stayed aloof, summered with the discreet rich on the French Riviera, wintered in Sweden and made no reference to her past.

By contrast, Cecil filled his life with work. In 1949 he published a book about his fifteen years at Ashcombe. In 1950 he designed *The Second Mrs Tanqueray* at the Haymarket Theatre, Liszt's ballet *Apparitions* directed by Frederick Ashton and starring Margot Fonteyn for Sadler's Wells, a production by Laurence Olivier of *The School for Scandal*, a Jean Anouilh play *Cry of the Peacock*, *Swan Lake* with Karinska for the New York City Ballet and a Benjamin Britten ballet *Les Illuminations* which opened at the City Centre in New York in March.

As for photography, he did lucrative advertising shots and there were the usual commissions from brides, actors, society personalities and members of the Royal Family. He took pictures of the Duke and Duchess of Windsor, the Duchess of Kent, Princess

Margaret on her nineteenth birthday, Prince Charles, when a month old, with his mother – she ordered forty-eight prints at two guineas a go – and the newly-born Princess Anne.

At the beginning of 1950, again as a commission from Serge Obolensky, he decorated an apartment on the thirty-seventh floor of the Sherry Netherland Hotel. The suite was at the top of the turret of the building and had views of the East River and the Hudson, Fifth Avenue and Central Park. It was the same arrangement as at the Plaza and Cecil hired it at a fifty-per-cent discount with twenty-five per cent off in the restaurant, whenever he was in New York.

While working on the decorations he saw Greta. She was still negotiating over the *Duchesse de Langeais* film. She told him of her worries about camera angles and what she would look like on screen, if the project were to happen. A Hungarian skin specialist called Laszlo attended to a rash on her chin and an 'exercise man' called Kounovsky supervised her callisthenics. One day she had felt so depressed and low that she wept in front of her doctor.

He said: Go ahead, it'll do you good; cry away! What is the matter? Tell me a few things about yourself. What is your private life? Have you got a boy friend or a girl friend? The latter question gave her such a surprise that she stopped weeping. Next time she went to the doctor she asked: Did you think I am a lesbian? He said, I meant any sort of friend: you're too much alone.

At a Russian restaurant, on Cecil's last evening in New York, Greta and he ate shashlik, drank vodka and joked about their marriage. To his constant proposals her usual reply was, 'I probably will.' She admitted, obliquely, to problems with Schlee, his bouts of illness and his need for nursing. Cecil chose to believe that she was thinking of making a life for herself in England, at Reddish House with him. Back at Hampshire House, she talked to him later on the phone, then said, 'Shall we do our trick of waving to each other?' It was a similar trick to the one she had played with Mercedes with lighted candles in the blackout. From the turret window of the Sherry Netherland, Cecil waved a bedsheet. From Hampshire House Greta moved a lamp back and forth outside her window. Thus, like ships that pass in the night, they sent their signals of caution, friendliness and separate journeys.

Cecil regarded photography as less than art and stage and set design as ephemeral. He worked for pleasure but also to escape a sense of nihilism. The talents he would like to have matched, which to him epitomised glamour and style, were those of Greta Garbo and Noël Coward. For much of 1949 and 1950 he struggled to write *The Gainsborough Girls*, in the hope of creating a play that would withstand the test of time. Gainsborough had again and again painted double portraits of his daughters, Mary and Margaret. An early painting showed them hand in hand chasing the same butterfly. In later years they pursued the same man, who married the elder daughter, though not for long. The sisters then lived together until old age.

Cecil's play reflected his fascination with sisterhood and merged female identity. His producer friend Hal Burton warned him though that as a piece of theatre it lacked dramatic form, sharp dialogue or narrative flow. But Cecil's ambitions for it were high. He worked with more dedication on this than on any other project. Its failure became a point of awakening as painful in implication as the dawning truth about his relationship with Greta.

It first opened in July 1951 at the Theatre Royal, Brighton. Greta was in Capri, on holiday with Schlee who was ill. She hoped the play would be 'a raving success'. At the dress rehearsal Cecil knew he was not faced with a raving success:

By the end of the evening the anticlimax was appalling: the play had never come to life. The few people in the audience made no comment. Joyce Grenfell appeared like a lightning-struck sheep and added not one word. My agent looked even more like a ruined pudding than usual; he merely cleared his throat. Mrs Myers, the wife of the American producer, when asked if she would like a sandwich, said: 'I would like a taxi.' A strange chemical reaction took place in me; suddenly I was robbed of all hope. But perhaps the dress rehearsal disaster was a good sign: it was said to be. Next day I worked non-stop in the theatre on set, costumes and script changes; but the cast was not sure enough of their lines to be given the cuts I now suggested.

But I didn't realize how much cutting was necessary until the audience was there – a terrifying first-night crowd of London friends and critics. A steel-like curtain of defiance seemed to go up between them and the play. The first act went without laughs. Later things warmed up, but never were the laughs as I had hoped for . . . At the party afterwards my friends tried to give me the impression that the evening had been a success.

I was awake very early next morning . . . with no exception the reviews were bad. 'Trite dialogue.' . . . 'Heavy disappointment. Enchanting to look at.'

For two weeks I had had a feeling of sickness in my stomach, but now I was aghast. I felt as miserable as one only does when one falls unhappily in love. My mother and Baba were in the next bedroom. I had to wake them with the news that the reviews were bad. I felt more queasy than ever. It was like telling them of a family death – they did not know how to comfort me. What was there to do? Try and swallow the cold breakfast.

I got out the script again, for the thousandth time, and I started to make cuts so that, by the next evening, the changes would be made . . . Under great duress I worked in my hideous hotel room, and managed to find a typist to take down a new scene. It was rehearsed and put into being: but none of it was fun any more. The critics had written failure over my play, and I couldn't get rid of this horrible feeling; I turned even against my scenery and costumes.

Cecil's dreams of greatness as an artist faded away that night. He confided to Greta his disappointment that all his hard work had come to nothing, described his life as empty and lonely and said that he wanted a six-month holiday and to get married and make radical changes to his life.

Mercedes, now living in Paris, told Cecil that she thought it was too late now for him to marry Greta. And at home he feared that life had become centred around his mother. He professed to love her dearly, and always returned from the States with presents for her – a Balmain shawl, a teapot from Chinatown, chocolates, nylons, a bottle of pink champagne – but often the tension between them was appalling. He became nervous and unstable when he saw too much of her. Her health was deteriorating, she broke her wrist, drank too much, had respiratory problems.

Nor did Maud improve. He told Greta that he felt 'hemmed-in' by her. She had had a mastectomy and chemotherapy and all manner of emotional problems. After a row with Cecil she told Olga Lynn, Brigitte and Mrs Beaton that she intended to resign. Cecil accepted the idea with alacrity. 'I think you must agree that you are not really strong enough physically to cope with the exigencies of so taxing a task master as myself,' he wrote. He did not want to part on bad terms, although he carped at 'certain aspects' of her technique as secretary.

Maud replied:

It frankly amazes me that you should accept my resignation so easily – personally I think it is very foolish of you . . . No secretary is perfect. The things you have against me (notes not in notebooks, files not up to date, your theatrical designs not catalogued, etc.) have not caused much mischief . . . Olga warned you right at the beginning that I was not strong, but you still insisted on having me.

She pointed out that she had been doing the job for the past ten and a half years, that it was due to her financial acumen that he had been able to save £8,000 and buy Reddish, and that she tried to help when he had rows with his mother. Cecil capitulated and she kept the job for a while.

Into this strange and discordant ménage, Greta Garbo arrived in October 1951. The previous month she told Cecil she was on the edge of breakdown and that Schlee, too, was ill. Her uncertain plans were ten days in Paris and then, if Cecil still wanted her to come and visit, it might, at last, perhaps, be so.

So on the night of 15 October, the local village publican, Len Gould, drove Cecil to Southampton docks to meet Greta's ship. Cecil took the ferry out to the ocean liner *Liberté* which was en route from Cherbourg to New York. Greta and Schlee were waiting in the ship's restaurant:

> They did not smile on seeing me: it was as if I was coming to make the final transaction of a business deal. The general atmosphere was so grim and overladen with tension that I wondered if, at any minute, one of them would suddenly inform me of a change of plan. Without allowing time for such an opportunity, and with an impatience that was quite ruthless, I snatched my friend by the arm and guided her down the gangway into the waiting dinghy. It was with the greatest feeling of relief and happiness – too good yet to be true – that I looked back to see the golden illuminated liner receding into the distance.

He took her to his house where he could guard her, observe her and allow no one else too near. In his diary he wrote of her undergoing a transformation, coming to life, blossoming, becoming her true self, 'taking to Wiltshire ways as if this was where she belonged', losing her inhibitions and becoming totally relaxed.

Soon she was on the best of terms with the vicar, the butcher and the gardener. George and Lily Bundy the general storekeepers, and farmer Herbert Bundy and his pig-keeping wife Olive, were also trusted with her friendship.

It did not seem anomalous to him for the great communicator of sexual intensity to find her level with Wiltshire pig-keepers. Nor did it occur to him that she might simply be taking a holiday. He believed they were living together as man and wife. 'When I asked her if she thought she would ever marry me she said she probably would.'

Days at Reddish followed a pattern. In the mornings Cecil worked on his ill-fated Gainsborough play. The management had lost money on the initial run, and hoped he would breathe life into the script so that they might recoup their investment. His friend Hal Burton each morning helped him with rewrites. At midday, Cecil joined Greta who, 'dew-covered and ecstatic, would return from her favourite walk on the downs where the height of her joy was to scratch the backs of a posse of Bundy pigs in their pen'. He then spent 'every other moment of the day' looking after her, protecting her and seeing that all went well. They browsed in antique shops, visited neighbours, went to Bath, Eton and Oxford, visited the stately homes of Wilton, Longford, Crichel and Cranborne.

There were drawbacks to the idyll though, one of which was Mother.

It was not surprising that my mother should become upset that her son who remained, at middle age, unmarried, and whom she had come to rely upon to look after her for the rest of her life, now appeared as if he might be making plans to make a painful change. She was resentful. My mother has never been one to hide her feelings; when she met Greta for the first time her welcome was far from warm. Greta took no time to notice this. A 'situation' arose that made things extremely difficult. I was exasperated. How was it that one couldn't expect support and help from one's nearest, if not – at this moment – one's dearest?

Mrs Beaton made the placatory gesture of giving Greta a bunch of lilies of the valley, but referred to her, behind her back as 'that woman' and took to spending a good deal of time at Pelham Place when Greta was at Reddish and at Reddish when Greta was at Pelham Place. Greta told Cecil that were his mother to quiz her about their marital intentions, she would say, 'No, we are just two bachelors.' If, however, said Greta, she and Cecil were to decide that marriage was a good thing, they would just do it and present his mother with a *fait accompli*.

Maud Nelson's reaction to Greta was of jealousy and Peter Watson's, when he met her, was of amusement at what was going on. Cecil wanted Peter to meet Greta. It was, he wrote in his diary, the first time he 'had fallen in love seriously since meeting Peter'. He thought Greta was rather jealous of Peter and Peter not jealous in the least of her.

Despite all equivocation, Cecil treated his bachelor friend as his intended wife. His mother's seventy-ninth birthday was celebrated with a family dinner party.

Everyone else was at ease and treating Greta as if she were already one of them; there was much joking and laughter. But on this occasion it was Greta who disappointed; she made no effort to put on at full voltage her powers of fascination. Even in appearance she seemed drab.

Cecil ascribed her reticence to 'her extraordinary intuitive faculties' – a desire not to outshine his sisters and mother. He did not interpret it as a desire to be elsewhere than in the bosom of the Beaton family. For his part, he felt so fraught and found the evening so charged that he thought he might rush out and shoot himself. In a later diary he confessed that he found the whole autumn visit long and emotional and that it reduced him to 'a jellied pulp'.

Greta reserved full voltage of her powers of fascination for other spirits of whom Clarissa Churchill was one. 'Who can resist the fascination of Greta when the allure is turned on and it was certainly turned on for Clarissa's benefit,' Cecil wrote. Clarissa, who looked rather like Greta, was, he said, a most romantic character. Before she married Anthony Eden, and conformed to the ways of a Prime Minister's wife, she had worked for *Vogue* and as an assistant to Alexander Korda, worn leather jerkins and trousers, and had been a good friend of Cecil's and of others in his circle: the historian, James Pope-Hennessy, known for his fine mind and dangerous gay liaisons, and Gerald Berners, who had spoofed Cecil in *The Girls of Radcliffe Hall* and who wrote operas with libretti by Gertrude Stein. Cecil thought Clarissa and Anthony Eden were very much in love, but was sure that in the end Clarissa would be back in her cottage 'and that this will have been a remarkable phase in her life'.

James Pope-Hennessy was so taken by Greta that he did no work for five weeks:

She has the most inexplicable powers of fascination which she uses freely on all and sundry; but whether it is deliberate or not nobody knows . . . she is only explicable as a mythological figure . . . she is the Troll King's daughter from *Peer Gynt* – some strange remote being from a haunted forest who has got loose in modern life. And then it gradually dawns on one that she is entirely uneducated, interested in theosophy, dieting and all other cranky subjects, has conversation so dull that you could scream . . . Cecil Beaton guarded her like an eagle, and nobody was ever allowed alone with her.

Journalists were another threat to Cecil's hegemony. He tried to chase away the tweed-suited men from the *Salisbury Times* and *Western Gazette* who hovered outside and the dark-suited men from Fleet Street who came down to interview Miss Garbo and to ask if it was in order to congratulate Mr Beaton. A large black car stayed parked in the village for days and flashlights popped as Cecil escorted Greta over the hills past Mr Bundy's pigs.

Stephen Tennant met her twice. She visited Wilsford and he exuded over her petal-like fingers and melancholy eyes. She admired his new Venetian blind. In a reciprocal visit, he took the scientist Julian Huxley to Reddish. Huxley answered her questions about the courtship of the praying mantis and how she devours her mate.

In London Cecil took her to the Changing of the Guard at Buckingham Palace which fascinated her and on a tour of the sites of his infancy, which did not. 'It was not because Greta showed any curiosity in my beginnings – rather in spite of the lack' that he showed her his school, his birthplace in Hampstead and so on. She seemed surprised at his enthusiasm, for she evinced no interest in his past, nor in anything else that he was doing.

One morning another reality sneaked into Cecil's dream. He went into her room:

> She was serious: she had had a letter from 'the little man'. 'He's very clever,' was all she said; but later she admitted that he wrote: 'There's nothing left now but to announce your good news.' However the question of marriage did not seem to become any more positive than before. Whenever I brought up the subject Greta would cast it aside or make a joke of it. None the less I was not unhappy – in fact the reverse. The fact is that we got along so well together.

Cecil hoped that they would spend Christmas with Michael Duff at Vaynol, his family home in Wales, at the foot of Mount Snowdon. There, Duff lived, Cecil said, 'in pre-First World War comfort and cosiness'. But in November, Greta chose to go to Paris to buy a cashmere sweater and a pair of brogues. Cecil went too. They stayed at the Crillon, the weather was bad and he was fractious at being stuck in a hotel with little to do but tour the shops and museums and eat in restaurants. He thought such a life 'pointless and stultifying' and wanted her to return to England with him. She refused.

In Paris they saw Mercedes who, short of money, was living in a small flat at 8 Avenue de Breteuil with the last of her lovers, Poppy Kirk, who worked for Schiaparelli. Mercedes, in her mid-fifties, was caught one last time in a tense and insecure relationship. Poppy Kirk was jealous of Greta's presence. 'The way she and Greta fought at your flat. Thank God that is all over now . . .' Ram Gopal wrote to Mercedes a few years later, when Poppy had gone and Mercedes was alone.

Mercedes took Greta and Cecil to see Alice B. Toklas at rue Christine – named after Queen Christina of Sweden who lived in Paris after she abdicated in 1654. Since Gertrude Stein's death in 1946, Alice had stayed on alone in their apartment with their giant poodle, Basket. She wrote of the visit to an American friend, Carl Van Vechten:

> The other day in the bus there was someone wearing the most beautiful canary yellow gloves – she looked familiar – she came over to sit next to me and say – You don't remember I am Mercedes de Acosta. She has become so very bourgeois-looking and comfortably middle aged. She said she would come to see me. A few nights ago she rang up and said she and Cecil and Greta Garbo had rung the doorbell several times the night before but no one had answered (Basket and I really need a stronger bell) and could they come that evening which they did – Cecil very

tousled, exhausted and worshipful – she [Garbo] a bit shy – quite Vassarish – unpretentious but very criminal. She asked me with simplicity and frankness – Did you know Monsieur Vollard [Ambroise Vollard, the art dealer who sold works by Cézanne and Matisse to Gertrude Stein] was he a fascinating person – a great charmeur – was he seductive. She was disappointed like a young girl who dreams of an assignation. Do explain her to me. She was not mysterious but I hadn't the answer. The French papers say they [Greta and Cecil] are to marry – but she doesn't look as if she would do anything as crassly innocent as that. *Expliquez moi* as Pablo [Picasso] used to say to Baby [Gertrude Stein].

But there was no easy explanation. And then, after a couple of weeks, in her impulsive restless way, Greta decided to fly back to New York.

Cecil pleaded with her to stay, but she would not. Mercedes saw her off from Orly airport on 15 December. Cecil travelled alone to Vaynol for the Christmas holidays, exhausted to the point of tears. From Manhattan, 'Harriet' sent a thank-you letter with fond regards to Clarissa Churchill, James Pope-Hennessy and all at Broadchalke and Pelham Place. She asked Cecil to bring red paper, with which she might make lampshades, when next he was over.

Early in 1952 he sailed to New York with a commission to design the sets and costumes for Truman Capote's play *The Grass Harp*. His first call, when he arrived, was to Greta at Hampshire House. The operator said, 'Miss Garbo don't answer.' He tried later, left a message with her maid, then phoned again the next day. 'Miss Garbo don't answer.' He could not believe it. 'This is the old treatment.' After further days of silence, he received a pink azalea and ferns in a pot with a note from 'Harriet' addressed to 'Dear Dear Beatie'. She said that for several reasons which she could not go into, she was not going to call him for a while. She welcomed him back to New York and trusted that as he was such a busy person time would fly until they met again.

A week later she phoned and said she felt bad, that she had a cold and that Schlee was going into hospital. She had no vitality and was depressed. When she felt better and things were clearer they could meet for lunch together. 'A lunch together!' wrote Cecil in his diary. 'After we had been three months together as man and wife.'

Time passed without a word from her. He sent a cushion embroidered with 'Enjoy yourself it's later than you think.' Michael Duff arrived from England and she agreed to lunch with the two of them. Cecil contrived to put Michael off and see her alone. They chose the Colony. She wore a grey beret with a diamond pin and came straight from Laszlo who had massaged her face and creamed her skin. Cecil saw traces of face cream round her eyes. She drank aquavite, Cecil drank whisky sour. After a couple of drinks he asked for an explanation as to why she had refused to see him.

'Oh I couldn't tell you now, I'm tipsy.'

'Well I don't think I could return home as I shall be doing soon and tell my friends that I hadn't seen you at all. Besides, I feel that I deserve some explanation. It seemed to me that we were both very happy with each other in Europe. We didn't have any cloud on our horizon.'

'I have a completely clear conscience about the way I have behaved to you. I've never pretended to be anything I'm not.'

'I've given you my complete confidence and unless you have some good reason I feel that the fact that you would not speak to me on the telephone and gave the operator instructions "She don't answer" was very shoddy behaviour.'

'I dare say I'm a very bad-mannered wretch.'

'Not only that but you must be a very unhappy person.'

'I am.'

'You must have such a bad conscience. It must make you feel very bad that you have behaved so badly to me.'

'It does, and yet I felt that you wouldn't mind very much.'

'You thought I wouldn't say I'd jump out of the window.'

'If you said it I wouldn't believe it.'

'Actually I'm not the sort to bring my life to an end. I have interests. I have my work, friends and activities, but you have the power to hurt me very deeply. And I've been very hurt. Do you like hurting people and making them suffer?'

'No, but I can't think you would suffer so very much.'

'Why? Is it not rather peculiar after all our intimacy and mutual devotion that you should abruptly bring everything to a halt?'

'I don't think you loved me very much by the time we left one another in Paris.'

'Admittedly I wasn't as happy with you in Paris as in the country in England, but that's because I loathe the café society way of life. It seems so pointless. But you really think I didn't love you?'

'I don't think you've ever really loved me.'

'Then what have I been doing for the past five years – using up my emotions, my tenderest feelings?'

'Oh I dare say you've enjoyed fooling around. It's been quite a change.'

They both became drunk and confessional. She told him that she could not face the pace he set and that he was always dashing around. She wanted to be quiet and relaxed. She was going through the menopause and felt rather low. She asked his forgiveness for a tiredness she could not help. Had she created herself, she said, she would have been running around as much as Cecil. 'Would we have been busy!' And then in a placatory way, she said that he was looking very pretty and had lost weight. But Cecil was offended and gave no reciprocal compliment.

They met again – to drink martinis with Truman Capote, but she drifted away early to meet Schlee. Cecil noted it all in his diary. It was difficult to sustain the pretence that she would marry him – but without that pretence his emotional reality was bleak. It was difficult to accept that Reddish House was for him and his mother and Maud Nelson, but not for Greta Garbo. It was difficult to accept that the parrying about marriage had all been a game.

He was so mesmerised by her sincerity and profundity that he forgot her acting skills. Her genius, after all, was for the moving picture, not for life. She had told so many men she loved them and by so doing reduced her audience to tears. She was an illusionist, who knew how to invoke the semblance of happiness, under-standing and love. But the reality of her life with Cecil belonged to hotel rooms and snatched afternoons. She thought him pretty and amusing but if they met for lunch or tea it was according to her whim or impulse and Schlee was her more constant companion and friend.

Thousands in thrall to Garbo the star, in thrall to her beauty, aspired to be, in some sense, with her. Cecil got closer than most, through tenacity, determination and verve. But the closeness was illusory, like a scene in a film. The game of maybe I'll marry you, turned into a tease. The mystery woman tantalised but did not fulfil. The mirror that she showed him, that he thought reflected depth of feeling, in fact shone back to him the world that he knew and would like to have left – the world of lightweight feeling, and casual sex, a preoccupation with surface and nothing much beneath.

And so he began to write of steeling himself against her beauty, for he knew that the emotional terrain behind that amazing face was out of reach to him. But he could not relinquish his fantasy, now fed for twenty years, for that would leave him with a difficult reality – that he was growing old, that no one loved him and that he was, perhaps, unlovable. He began to hate Schlee and to describe him as a 'little jerk', a 'sinister little Road Company Rasputin'.

Mercedes, banished by Greta for being too exigent a friend, pumped Cecil for news. In November 1952 he wrote to her in Paris from the Sherry Netherland and berated Schlee. He told her that Greta now talked in 'ungrammatical Schleeisms – a mixture of Slav, Brooklynese and Baby Talk'. Greta complained, he said, of being unable to get rid of an interminable cold. The real trouble was that she could not get rid of an interminable bore. She had wasted her life on Schlee, – 'a dreadful bathos for a noble creature'.

He implied that her eloquence had faded. But strangers knew this was not so. The actress, Judith Malina, saw her in Manhattan the month before:

In a small Madison Avenue shop Julian and I buy white chocolates. A beautiful woman enters and in a heavy European voice asks the shopkeeper if they have come yet.

The shopkeeper asks, 'What?'

'The apricots.'

Her voice emotes around the word. She says it simply. I knew it was Garbo.

'Oh your glazed apricots. No, not yet.'

'How is your cold?'

'Better.'

'Ah, mine's still here.'

She brought her hand up to her throat and moved out of the shop.

I learn this from Garbo's performance: to be fully present in the present, to desire the temporal (for what else is a glazed apricot?), and to smile as intensely at the shopkeeper as at Armand.

Cecil flew to New York in December. He met Greta for lunch at the Colony a week before Christmas. She saw him from the other side of the street. She was wearing a beret and a long Russian coat and from the kerb bleated Beat Beat like a strange bird.

They argued about her negativism and about making something of your life rather than using catch phrases like *c'est la vie*.

Hauser had telephoned her. You're not still wandering the streets he asked her. Haven't you taken a house and haven't you done anything about anything? No. She laughed at her inability. But it is no laughing matter. Ten years ago she was so beautiful.

After lunch they shopped for Christmas presents. At Lily Dache's hat shop Greta tried on all sorts of fantastic hats. 'It was like a private pageant for me,' wrote Cecil. He chose a little diamanté crown and told her she would look lovely in it. She said, 'Yes, this should be good,' as she put it on. Then she added, 'Or it would have been a long time ago.' She looked at herself in the mirror and said, 'I used to be so pretty.'

On Christmas Day she called on him at the Sherry Netherland. He heard her arrive on the landing of the thirty-seventh floor, came out of his suite and 'full of seasonal glee' flung wide his arms and said, 'Why Merry Christmas to ye.' She stood with her basket of presents, looked dazed, then said, 'Now you cut that right out.'

Back home in January 1953, Cecil's mother looked ill and old. She got caught in London in one of the worst ever pea-soup fogs. (Many of the prize cattle being shown at the Smithfield Fair died that day of respiratory failure, noted Cecil in his diary.) His mother was taken to hospital, given oxygen and then taken back to Reddish House by ambulance.

And Maud Nelson had become more of a problem than he could bear. He took to walking the streets of South Kensington to avoid going to Pelham Place when she was there. She sold a Picasso drawing of his for £200, ate a salmon he had bought for his mother, suffered from 'nervous strain' and was having problems with a woman called Jennifer. 'I have come to the conclusion', Cecil wrote to her on 15 May 1953, 'that for the benefit of us both it would be much wiser to consider that your services as my private secretary are at an end.' She left in fury accusing him of having dismissed her, without notice, after fourteen-and-a-half years of loyal and devoted service to him, his affairs and his family.

In October Cecil heard from Mercedes that Greta had bought an apartment in the same building as Georges and Valentina Schlee. Called the Campanile, the block, built in 1927 and with a Venetian-Gothic façade, was at the far east end of 52nd Street in mid-town Manhattan, in a cul-de-sac away from the noise of the city. Her fifth-floor apartment, in which she was to live for the rest of her life, looked out over the river. There was the sun, clear light and in summer a breath of air. Somewhere the river flowed to the open sea. A concierge fielded unwanted callers, Schlee was upstairs to protect her and New Yorkers came to respect her strange if brutal solitude. It was safer and more anonymous than a large house in Beverly Hills and it was a long way from Wiltshire.

Assiduously, she began to decorate and search for paintings, furniture and ornaments. Cecil hated the place when he saw it, both for what it was and all that it implied. He loathed her taste and the fact of her having her own home so close to Schlee and so far from him. There could be no deeper attack on his long held fantasy than to see her creating a home which had nothing to do with him. He railed in his diary. The apartment should, he said, 'express someone completely unconventional with wonderful simplicity and an understanding of quality and restraint.' He called it a 'horrible mess', a 'hopeless muddle', a 'hotch potch of colours that clash'.

The walls are of a piggy beige, the curtains have pink in them, the cushions are every colour of squashed strawberry, dirty crimson, to dirty rose. Some chairs are upholstered in striped rose and buff. There is a horrible Savonnerie pink carpet on the floor and even her wonderful paintings, the Renoirs, Bonnards, Rouaults,

Soutines and Modiglianis, do not come to her rescue.

It is a hopeless muddle . . . When she asked me my advice about her bedroom with its lavender walls, with completely appalling Italian woodcarving on the walls, put in by her, I said, How can we get rid of that? It was difficult to know what to keep. I discovered that by dying the carpet very dark grenadine colour, the walls came to life and she could successfully employ the dirty, many pink striped material that she wanted for the curtains.

But she never realises that one thing reacts on another and she never remains firm about anything for more than a couple of days. Later, I heard her discuss the possibility of having a flowered Aubusson on the floor in her front room. Everywhere are flowered pots with lamps, pink, dirty pinky rose and red.

The only thing he liked was the large, plain wood table that had belonged to Mauritz Stiller.

He saw that nothing of his visual style had impinged on her, but that she was influenced by Schlee's taste ('signed pieces of auction room furniture and brothel lamps') and the French Rothschilds who decorated with formal grandeur and investment antiques. Pink was her favourite colour and she liked wood panelling, eighteenth-century French furniture, floral motifs on porcelain, furniture and fabrics, Savonnerie carpets and ormolu lamps. She disliked black and white, hard contrasts and flamboyance.

Cecil used theatrical effect in his interior decorating, Greta chose intimacy, warmth and bourgeois elegance. There was no particular sense of activity in the rooms of her apartment. She bought paintings and decorations that amused her: a faience figure of a frog, a Russian porcelain group of children at play, Ming jars moulded with flowers, a pair of Chinese glazed figures of hippopotamuses, a Persian pottery figure of a horse, an Italian wood figure of a reveller.

To fill the bookshelves, she went to the New York antiquarian bookseller, J. N. Bartfield, and bought limited editions, bound in moroccan leather and tooled in gold. By the yard, she bought the works, which she made no claim to read, of Shelley, Ruskin, Hawthorne, Fielding, Tolstoy, Thackeray, Schiller and Pepys. And she began to assemble a large collection of paintings, acquired if, individually, they touched a chord. She bought heads and landscapes by Alexej von Jawlensky, flowers by Louis Valtat, a picture of a woman looking out at the sea – *The Pink Hat* by David Levine. Her favourite painting, *Woman with Parasol*, was by Robert Delaunay. She designed her own bed out of panelling, carved with flowers, taken from a Swedish armoire. In the sixties she designed a series of rugs, in bright colours, of birds in flight, then supervised their weaving at the manufacturer's.

Her apartment was one of the most expensive in New York. It was a far cry from Blekinge Street, on the wrong side of Stockholm and the deprivations of her childhood. It was also a far cry from Cecil's dream of making her his bride.

Late in 1954 Cecil visited Greta and sat on a sofa, 'in the pink brothel lights of the hideous lampshades', drinking vodka martinis and eating slivers of gruyère cheese. He talked to her of the importance of family ties, 'how the bond of relationship held one to reality'. To compound his unease, Schlee rang down a couple of times. And then came a mortal blow: in reference to his *Scrapbook*, published some twenty-five years previously, in which he wrote of Greta, 'Her hair is biscuit-coloured and of the finest spun silk and clean and sweetly smelling as a baby's after its bath,' she said to him that he was a flippant person and therefore could not understand her.

Cecil felt 'roused to fury'. He exploded with pent-up anger and disappointment, told her not to interrupt him, said it was outrageous of her to judge him, a man of fifty, by what he had written so many years ago. He said that he had succeeded in life through seriousness and determination of character, that he had had to fight to assert himself in life, that he had developed late and been erratic when young. He told her that he had always protected her and been loyal, discreet, devoted. He said that it was she who had hurt him with her silences, that it was she who had gone into his bedroom in March 1947, 'pulled the curtain cords and turned down the bed'. He said that he 'fulfilled what was expected' of him sexually, but as for his feelings, they had not been flippant.

She tried to kiss him and calm him down. When he turned away she gave their running gag, 'Don't you want to come and live in this apartment when we're married?' Cecil looked 'with horror' at the pink lampshades, the evidence of Schlee's taste, and said that he did not. At his suite at the Sherry Netherland he paced 'like a lion', 'fuming with fury'. When he returned to London he vented his anger in a letter, alluding to what he considered the futility of her life, her unfairness, her lack of trust in him and her selfishness.

> Alas! By harping back to the fact that I, among a thousand other writers, saw fit to print something about you over twenty years ago and that this somehow has more importance to you than anything I have done or felt for you in the years since we got to know one another – it was a cruel revelation.
>
> . . . I hope I shall hear that you are soon feeling much better and that you are able to take up some interest . . . possibly working in a hospital or doing any little job for other people that will also have the benefit of taking you 'out of yourself'. If this sounds impertinent it is because I feel that only those who haven't your future interest at heart could encourage you to continue to lead the listless and ingrained sort of life you do in New York. Only your real friends are willing to risk causing you displeasure by urging you to adopt a more charitable attitude towards life.

Behind its absurdity and waspish rebuke his letter spoke of failed dreams and emotional investment that had come to nothing. It spoke too of the fact that she had eluded him and that the terms would always be hers.

'A person is always the same,' Greta said when she accused him of flippancy. Her suggestion was that if, twenty-five years previously, he would idly print things about her, then he was not to be trusted, for he might well do so again. She was right.

12

Separation

'Last night you told me that you love me.'
'O did I? Well that was last night. Today I'm very busy.'
Mata Hari

Though at heart an emptiness of feeling afflicted Cecil, he kept the surface show. His name appeared regularly in lists of best-dressed men: *The Tailor and Cutter*'s first eleven, the *Tatler*'s top ten. Eileen Hose, his new secretary, who had formerly worked for General Sir Frederick Pile, Director-General of the Ministry of Works, was a paragon of efficiency and discretion. She was all that Cecil could want of a secretary. Maud Nelson, however, was sent to Holloway in 1957 for attacking with a broken bottle a woman to whom she was attracted.

In 1956 and 1958, Cecil stunned Broadway then London with his sets and costumes for *My Fair Lady*. It was called the finest musical comedy ever and Cecil's designs, particularly for the Ascot scene, were hailed by reviewers as magical, breathtaking and brilliant. The body of his work swelled by the day. He was awarded an Oscar for his costume designs for the film *Gigi* in 1958. He photographed debutantes galore, The Queen enthroned, Maria Callas and Marilyn Monroe. With a tenacity equalled only by his courtship of Greta, he went on working at his hopeless play, *The Gainsborough Girls*. He employed a ghost writer, Waldemar Hansen, to edit and doctor his candid, revelatory, hurriedly written diaries – kept since his student days – into publishable prose. With the paradoxical humility that lay beneath much of what he did, at the age of fifty he enrolled at the Slade School of Art, determined, late in the day, to improve his draughtsmanship and to learn to use oils.

Despite the awards, praise, unstinting hard work and astonishing output, he was haunted by the sense that his work was inconsequential and would not survive him: 'I feel this to be true, to the exaggerated extent that if I don't keep going with continuous new efforts I will be forgotten, even from one year to another.' By constant striving, constant production, he tried to fill a vacuum. He thought that after his death his diary would be published with a 'certain posthumous interest', but that then the 'ripples of his existence would subside' and all his labours would have been in vain.

He kept the outward parade, but a coldness at centre, which chilled him at the time of the suicide of his brother Reggie, was again there when Peter Watson died, aged forty-eight, on 3 May 1956. Uncertainty surrounded the circumstances of his death and there was vague talk of drugs, suicide and even murder. He had, Cecil wrote of him, 'indulged in every vice except women':

> he wore awful mackintoshes – his hair, once sexily lotioned, was on end – gone the elegant clothes and motor cars. He had become thinner and more gaunt and of a bad colour . . . I would watch him as he talked and he would look like a ruffled old chicken, his complexion yellow; he had become very sloppy about shaving and generally had a few cuts around the face. But however awful he looked, he had a quality of beauty.

The day he died, Peter Watson drove from the country to the London flat of a lover, Norman Fowler, then took a bath and drowned in it. Police broke the lock of the bathroom door to find his body under water. Fowler (who three years later drowned in a hotel swimming-pool in Jamaica) was taken to hospital with shock. The coroner returned a verdict of accidental death on Peter.

Cecil, when he heard the news, 'let out a moan that was like a bull in agony, a great volume of grief'. Surveying his face in the mirror, he saw it as contorted, swollen and mauve and what was left of his hair untidy and white. He noted the tears that 'coursed down with the same intensity' as when he had been young and felt that he was grieving for the 'love of his life'. To Greta he wrote of Peter, with a spike that might have made her wonder about her own place in his estimation, 'No one has really made quite such an impression on me . . . The void is utter.'

At the funeral he felt 'strangely unmoved'. He observed that the coffin was not of Peter's taste and the red brick chapel and the service of a style Peter would have despised. He timed the whole affair – it took a quarter of an hour – as twenty-three years previously Ernest Beaton had timed Reginald's funeral. In his diary that night he wrote of his regret that the relationship had never developed into the love affair for which he had yearned.

The following month in New York, he resolved to keep distance from Greta. 'I was more determined to protect myself than ever,' he wrote. He hoped to stay with friends, but to dampen the fantasy of true love, which he felt was harming him. When he phoned her she said that after their last meeting she had not expected to hear from him again.

One evening he suggested they dine at the Colony with Mercedes. She agreed and all went well. She wore a polo-necked jersey, her hair was untidy and Cecil thought she looked like a 'wild, ragged but beautiful gypsy'. She enjoyed the evening, said it was a success and in the taxi home took Cecil's face in her hand and squeezed it tight. He put his tongue through her fingers. 'The gesture was repeated.'

He tried not to misconstrue such gestures and see them as the bonds of love. Instead, he wrote in his diary of his disaffection, of her self-absorption, boring conversation, lack of sympathy at Peter's death, or curiosity about his new secretary, or interest in his mother's health. But with any chance remark or tease she cut through his defences against her. 'I do love you,' she told him, 'and I think you're a flop. You should have taken me by the scruff of the neck and made an honest boy of me. I think you would have been the Salvation Army.' He took this as proof of her wish that she had married him. Maybe it was not too late after all. 'Maybe life held new possibilities now the stars seemed to be under such good aspect.' He asked her to stay again with him at Reddish House later in the year and she said that maybe she would, but that there again, maybe she would not. Her plans were as ever uncertain. She did not know if she would go to Paris in the autumn or with Schlee to the south of France.

That summer of 1956 she travelled to Europe with Schlee, who then returned to New York alone. Cecil visited her in Paris on 20 September, at her suite at the Crillon hotel. She made no preparations for his visit. She was in her sitting-room with Cécile de Rothschild, 'surrounded by half-dead flowers and fruit and looking pretty battered'. She wore a frown plaster. He thought her face looked wrinkled and her hair untidy. 'She has absolutely no vanity about being seen like a gypsy.'

She offered no gossip, divulged no news of her trip and was troubled by a cough. They went to supper and to the theatre and on prolonged shopping expeditions for things that could not be found. Her shoulders were too broad to wear ready-made clothes and none of the hats was right. 'I was once', she told Cecil, 'famous for a hat. Oh I loved that hat. It had a string under the chin. But I had to give up wearing it because people recognised the hat and knew it was me underneath.' They went to galleries and exhibitions, lunched at the Méditerranée, and spent long afternoons 'antiquing'. In the rue Bonaparte a Greek student summoned courage to approach her after following her for half an hour. His voice shook as he asked her to mark a cross, a line, anything, in his notebook. She refused.

She still conveyed a sense of deprivation, a need for a simple kind of love. On an afternoon when they went for family tea at the house of Cécile's cousin, Liliane, at 23 Avenue de Marigny, one of the Rothschild children played with Greta's hair. 'That child is not like the outside world which judges me by my hair,' she said.

Like a child she was exigent in her needs. She agreed to go with Cecil to England and he set aside the month of October to escort and entertain her. The night before they were to leave Paris, no taxi could be found to take them to their restaurant. 'I should have stayed in and packed,' she said. 'I can't go to England tomorrow, I'll be too tired. That's why it's so necessary to have Mademoiselle Cécile. She *always* has a car and chauffeur.'

Lunch the next day was unsuccessful, too – 'Why did I ever choose ratatouille,' she said – and the exodus from the hotel was fraught. Passers-by watched as her luggage was put into the car. Cecil's cases were in the way. They arrived too early at the airport and walked for half an hour round tulip and gladioli fields to avoid photographers. Cecil admitted to his private diary that he enjoyed the attention of the press and the focus on Greta's mystery and allure of which he felt he had become a part.

He smuggled her into London unobserved, but she stayed at Claridges and not with him at Pelham Place. Alone in his house, he looked at himself in the glass in his narcissistic way: 'my deep set eyes told of my exhaustion,' he wrote in his diary.

Next day she phoned and made some kind of flippant sexual proposition:

She is like a man in many ways. She telephoned to say, I thought we might try a little experiment this evening at 6.30. But she spoke in French and it was difficult to understand at first what she meant. But soon I discovered, although I pretended not to. She was embarrassed and a certain *pudeur* on my part made me resent her frankness and straightforwardness – something that I should have respected.

She allowed him only a little time alone with her, though he escorted her tirelessly, protected her from journalists, stayed at her beck and call. On 17 October he took her to visit Clarissa and Anthony Eden at 10 Downing Street. They drank iced vodka and Eden questioned Greta about her film career and Sweden. Outside, a press photographer who was waiting for the arrival of the President of Costa Rica, snapped Greta and Cecil as they left. Cecil's phone rang until two in the morning.

The following evening Greta dined at Pelham Place. Cécile de Rothschild and Hal Burton were there too. Halfway through the meal the doorbell began to ring. Photographers peered through the windows. Cecil asked them to move away but they stayed. Greta said, 'The boys do too much talking. Maybe it's normal. They do talk. I don't. Perhaps I'm not normal. But I shouldn't perhaps see so much of Mr Beaton for a few days.' Cecil turned off all the lights and crept about in the dark. Hal Burton called a taxi and as Cécile and Greta dashed into it Cecil watched the flashlights 'like a storm of atomic explosions'.

None the less, she stayed with him at Reddish. He was again affected by her way of taking the moment and making it hers: 'When she is settled on a sofa, with cigarettes by her side, she gives you the impression that nothing in life exists outside the present moment,' he wrote in his diary.

They went for long walks, visited Salisbury Cathedral and Ashcombe, turned down invitations to Chequers and watched the Bolshoi Ballet on television. She made 'ribald jokes' as they watched. Many of the jokes were sexual and directed against Cecil, 'but they were unvenomous and done with great charm'.

He approved of her friendship with Cécile, though he thought that like himself, like Mercedes, like Schlee, Cécile wanted to claim Greta and make her give up her independence to her. Born into the French branch of the Rothschild family she was widely read, cultured and an imaginative collector of paintings.

Cecil wrote to Mercedes, who had moved into a new flat on East 68th Street, and with whom Greta was seldom in contact, about the visit:

She has gone off to Oxford today in the company of Cécile de R. whom I think is a very good companion for her – a person of complete integrity and lack of vulgarity – a person who has quality and knows values – certainly an improvement on all that cheap Russian baby talk and 2nd Avenue junk shop level – and she has nothing to do but make things easier for Greta, who needs more and more someone to protect her.

What an extraordinary person she is! Really the great enchantress of our time.

Mercedes' friend, Ram Gopal, in London for a while, asked her to intervene on his behalf and write to Cecil so that he might meet Greta:

I only wish you were here to arrange this meeting, but since the Elusive One is here, staying with Beaton, I thought that maybe – as you had always said before – that Mr Beaton – who has become as regal as the Queen of England – as elusive as Garbo and as prissy as the fussiest Edwardian – said upon your suggestion that he would condescend to arrange for Ram to have the great honour and privilege of meeting Miss Garbo, he might do this. So do give him my telephone number and address . . . But if there is any trouble, or if she wants to be left alone allowing Beaton to wear her cloak of mystery, please do not bother.

No meeting took place.

And then, after a few days, the Elusive One decided to go back to Paris with Cécile and then on to America. Cecil voiced all his disappointments again. He had hoped she would stay in the country for a long time and had even hoped that they would marry. He had set aside time exclusively for her. She recently blamed him for not taking her by the scruff of the neck and marrying her. How, he asked, could he prevent her from making another mistake. 'O, I always make mistakes,' she said. She appeared to prevaricate and played their teasing game. She took the matches out of a box, one by one, 'as a lover pulls at the petals of a daisy'. 'She leaves, she doesn't leave, she leaves, she doesn't leave.' 'With a gay laugh of triumph' she took the last match from the box and said, 'She leaves.' She left the next day.

It was like a scene from one of her films. Cecil protested that he wished to make her less of a tease and more of a wife. On 28 October he wrote again to Mercedes saying how Greta's glimpse of life in the country had seemed to give her just what she needed and how sad it was that she was flying back to 'that dreary Schlee ridden routine.'

At heart it was hard for Cecil to delude himself that she wanted a great deal from him. And perhaps at heart it was hard to delude himself that, in reality, he wanted much from her. He took stock of himself and of the failure of his relationships with Peter Watson and with Greta. It began to seem important to him that if he could not marry her, then he should marry someone else. He felt that he did not want to grow old alone 'bothering if the Louis Seize was out of place', and he thought he would like to father a child, 'to have someone other than myself to consider'. And so he decided to find a wife of a straightforward sort and get married in a conventional way.

Mother was another reason for him to want domestic change. 'It is a very sad situation for we love one another – there is a great link after fifty-four years together and yet?' She had taken to tippling too much before lunch and dinner. Two martinis on an empty stomach left her speech slurred and her breathing heavy. Cecil spoke to Dr Gottfried about it, who said it had been going on a long time and was common in old people when they had few pleasures left. After a particularly irksome dinner party, in May 1958, when she had seemed rather grandly drunk, Cecil chastised her, went up to London with the cellar key and left her a letter suggesting she break herself of the habit of drinking more than was good for her.

Offended, she went to stay with one of her daughters, leaving a note saying his letter was rude. She said if she could find a small flat she would move out of his way. She reminded him that she was eighty-five and had only a few years or months left, that he should be more considerate, that she loved him and was proud of him and 'I find there is no gin in the decanter so I've sent out and paid for a bottle. I hope there is some left for you.'

'The tears gushed down my cheeks,' Cecil wrote in his diary. 'I didn't know I could weep so copiously. I wept for the appalling sadness of life, the loneliness of old age, the rushing by of life . . .'

Diana Cooper tried to help find him a wife. She suggested June Osborn, who was young, widowed, aristocratic and had a son, Christopher. June, said Diana, was amusing and good and would look after Cecil's mother.

Thus Cecil, throughout 1958 and 1959, pondered marriage, sent June postcards and flowers, painted her portrait and put her through various social tests – such as dinner with Lucian Freud and Francis Bacon – most of which she passed. He liked her bright blue eyes, her kindness and her wit. He did not, however, particularly desire her, disliked her aristocratic self-assurance and voice, feared that she might be too nice to him and thought her less than chic. As he wanted a wife who would adorn Reddish, he hoped 'she will let me take a hand in dressing her according to my taste'.

Apart from such minor incompatibilities, his packed work schedule, the fear that she might find he 'was less of a person than a career' and the unilateral nature of his decision, he thought the idea of marriage had many advantages. In the winter of 1958, in New York designing Noël Coward's *Look After Lulu*, he lunched with Greta and dropped the bombshell of his proposed betrothal. She looked at him quizzically, said, 'Well, well, so you've got a girl have you?' then threatened to come right over to cut her head off. Cecil extolled June's virtues: she was good, brave, noble, attractive, adorable, he would be terrifically lucky if ever she would marry him, and there was but one problem. 'You don't love her,' said Greta. Cecil conceded that was true.

Back home, all was not well. His mother was suffering from dementia. Each time Cecil returned from trips abroad, he found her iller and older. She had lost her short-term memory, asked him incessant repetitive questions, did not know the day of the week and had become untidy, restless and large. She took to wandering out on the landing and scaring unsuspecting visitors. The former cook, Mrs Talbot, nursed her, but the discrepancy between Cecil's fantasy of his mother, his root illusion of the loveliness of women, and this reality was hard to bear. 'She who used to be so elegant has become an old harridan,' he wrote in his diary in autumn 1959.

She refused her medicine, bolted her food, neglected her appearance and drank the gin. She slapped Mrs Talbot on the behind, fed the pug dog with liver and kidneys which made its skin itch and its breath smell so that it was impossible to have it in the car, and at night roamed the house. Cecil heard the floorboards creaking, as he tried to work at some Greek designs. Annoyed beyond sympathy, he ordered her to bed. 'Don't you dare come out again. You'll fall and break your leg.'

In winter 1959, 'with appalling business-like ferocity and determination' he asked June Osborn to marry him. She looked terrified and shocked, then said, 'O no, Sissil, I *don't* think it would be a good idea, not for us . . . I *don't* think it would work.' Cecil blurted out truths – about 'a great queer streak which might make things very difficult', his hopeless love for Peter Watson, his obsession with Greta, his horror at the thought of completely changing his way of life, his self-centredness and age.

When she left to meet her son, Cecil felt elated, for although she had quite clearly said no, he had, quite clearly, put the question. Never good at understanding emotional realities, he felt that he had chosen a rare and remarkable person and that 'no' might well mean 'yes'. He smoked a cigar, sent her lilac and freesias, then went to the National Gallery to look at Italian Renaissance paintings.

On Christmas Day he phoned and alluded to their tryst. She wrote to him that day with kindness, truthfulness and clarity and in words that it would be difficult to misconstrue. She told him that she had 'recovered from the shock and stared the problem coldly in the face'. She said that she was touched and flattered, but that she really believed it would not work, that the kind of feeling that they had for each other was not the sort on which to base a marriage, that their lives crossed only at the silly, social level, that they had scarcely talked alone together and that the 'queer streak which she loved in him as a friend', if he were a husband would torment him and her. She told him that her pathological untidiness would dement him, that she really did not like socialising all that much, and that marriage for people of independent dispositions like his was so very difficult that it should only be embarked upon if one could not live properly without that very person. 'Could it be', she asked him, 'that you might feel a tiny sense of relief at what I say?'

Perhaps having been married I know more about its pitfalls than you do and I don't want to seem like an old bitch in the manger when I say I am not sure if it is the right thing for you. You are a very complete person and when your Mama does die Reddish will be gayer and happier and fuller of people you love – when you are not too busy – and I hope I will be there often because you will want our friendship to go on and grow, won't you?

But still Cecil did not interpret her refusal as rejection. This, he hoped, unlike any possible marriage to Greta, would prove to be, with the passing of time, 'solid, real and lasting'. Most days he talked on the phone to her, if only for a few minutes, and he believed that she loved him. In his diary he wrote, with cool formality, of how for many years he had hoped that Greta would marry him.

> I knew in my heart that it would not be a success in the far future, yet I would have willingly taken the chance. Now at last I have shed this image from my life and June's face has taken the place of Greta's in my subconscious image of the one I love.

In May 1960 Antony Armstrong-Jones married Princess Margaret. Cecil lay awake at night wishing with envy that he was the spouse. 'Nothing as momentous as this would ever happen in my life . . . All my excitements and interests paled in comparison.' He called it a 'Cinderella-in-reverse' story. Here was a commoner marrying a Princess. Only by marrying Greta would he have had an equal fairy-tale to tell. There was a double irony to the royal marriage. Armstrong-Jones, a photographer like himself, was the nephew of Oliver Messel, Cecil's rival for Peter Watson's love. And Cecil, destined ever to be the image-maker, never the groom, was commissioned to take the royal wedding photos of Princess Margaret and Armstrong-Jones.

In an effort to be if not a sort of Cinderella, then at least a married man, he pursued June. He proposed again in the autumn of 1960 before leaving for America. He felt rushed, for he was late for the airport, and his mother kept wandering in. 'Have you thought any more about our being spliced?' he asked June. She found the conversation upsetting, saw him as shy and naïve and sent him a letter in New York about her deep instinctual feeling that it would not work and apologising for her dusty answers. 'You see dearest if I can't say yes, what else can I say but no, for I've had a long time to think.'

And so his faint chance of being a conventional chap – a husband and father with a good, kind wife – faded. It had never been his world – unequivocal, straightforward feelings, commitment and requited love. He was as much a stranger to it as was Greta, and something of their rootlessness began to parallel. But she had come to terms with it and acknowledged it as her lot. And her restless magic had its way and her charisma did not fade. At the end of 1960, when she was fifty-six, a young English playwright, Kenneth Jupp, met her in the Manhattan apartment of the actor, Zachary Scott:

I turned and there she was. Polo-necked sweater, brown jacket. No make-up . . . looking as if she'd left her bicycle in the street. A firm handshake and a polite nod before she was whisked away.

They talked an hour later when they both had wandered from the crowd to look at paintings in other rooms. Jupp was in New York for the first time with a play he had written about gypsies:

with that wonderful smile which totally transformed her appear-ance, she said, 'I have always considered myself a gypsy' . . .
  She had the ability to concentrate totally on what you were saying as if nothing else in the world mattered. All that existed was you and what you were telling her. And I believe that somewhere in that area lies the whole secret of her greatness as a screen actress: the ability to exclude everything but the moment, to exist only for right now, before the camera or before whoever had captured her interest.

She was a law to herself and did not follow the usual rules of obligation to family or to friends. Mercedes, short of money, by 1960 lived alone in a small flat in Paris with a Siamese cat called Linda – a gift from Poppy Kirk. In autumn she published her memoir, *Here Lies the Heart*, with its recollections of her halcyon days with Greta and of her rebound affair with Marlene. Greta visited while she was working on the book, but they did not discuss it. She wanted nothing written about her, and that was all she had to say. Marlene, on the other hand, annotated the galleys. Of Mercedes' recollections of Cecil, Marlene wrote: 'Many people don't know who Cecil Beaton is . . . Let him remain anonymous. It is better for the mood of the piece.' The book, when it was published, received critical reviews for its uncertain style. Greta made no mention of it and according to Cecil did not read it. But thereafter she cut Mercedes out of her life and spurned all her attempts to return to favour. Cecil commiserated with Mercedes, tried to repair the rift, and divulged to her such news of Greta as he had. They became like sisters in their shared rejection. 'I do wish you would try not to be hurt by Greta's ruthlessness,' he wrote to her. 'But if one suffers, then there is no point in trying to be offhand. Luckily I am not able to be hurt by her anymore and this too is very sad.'

He offered cool praise to Mercedes for *Here Lies the Heart*, and in October 1960 wrote to tell her that Greta was in London with Guilaroff, who had been her hairdresser at MGM. A most unsuitable companion, Cecil called him, *'pas sortable'*. He derided him in his diary, the repository of his spleen. 'Guilaroff, pathetic, out of his depth in life, a neuter, is the only sort of person left to Greta.' Only someone like Guilaroff, he wrote, would be willing to be treated like a lapdog by 'this great star of yesterday', this woman 'who never levels' and escort her on her abortive shopping trips while waiting for 'today's star' to recover from illness, so that he could go back and dress her hair.

But someone like Cecil was more than willing to put up with this great star of yesterday, pleased when Guilaroff's flat in Shepherd's Market proved small and uncomfortable and when she agreed to pay a brief visit to Reddish. He met her at Salisbury station. She was wearing ski clothes and a 'terrible pixie woollen hat that children wear in the Tyrol. Hair marron colour, long and fringed.' They walked on the Downs, had tea, listened to comic records, dined with Michael Duff and his mother, Juliet. All were disarmed by her. But she exasperated Cecil by disassociating herself from him and calling him Mr Beaton in front of mutual friends. He thought it a 'sad example of her not wishing to commit herself. She will own up to no friend.'

Back at Reddish there were kisses in the warm drawing-room and then they went to their separate rooms. 'Oh I'm such a sad little man,' Greta said to him. 'I've been out of life for so long.' The next day they drove to see Salisbury Cathedral again. She was 'thrilled to be back within its precincts', Cecil said. She liked its grandeur, the spire, the medieval knights, the Elizabethan tombs. She admired the sarcophagi of husband and wife lying side by side, kissed the cheek of the female figure and wondered what the couple had been like in life. 'Did they love one another very much?' she asked.

She was more interested in that entombed marriage than her own. Cecil drove back to Reddish for lunch and soon it was time to take the train to London. He could not resist asking her to stay longer, to return next weekend, to live with him at Reddish.

'You need to breathe fresh air and feel the tread of grass beneath your feet,' he told her.

'I know,' she said.

'You made a great mistake in not marrying me ten years ago. It would have been your last opportunity not to go on repeating your mistakes. As it is you know they are mistakes and you go on making them.'

'I know,' she said.

He dropped her at Shepherd's Market. He watched 'this dark, eccentric figure doddering towards her lodgings'. He said the sight was pathetic. He said it cracked his heart. That evening, she returned, with Guilaroff, for supper at Pelham Place. Hal Burton was there. Cecil was spiky and jealous. Greta taunted him for his severe look and for not being at all as he used to be.

The evening was soon over. In the hall, the sudden pantomime of saluting Goodnight Mr Beaton, seemed as forced as the old family jokes when I was an embarrassed child. Greta caught the look in my eye and Hal caught it too.

Hal Burton told Cecil it was inevitable that the scales should one day fall from his eyes and that when they did there should be resentment. He said that Greta was always pretending, that it had all been a game and that she would never have committed herself. The implication was that Cecil had not been pretending, but had always been sincere.

To compound his sense of loss – of beauty, of style and of life itself, in 1961, with his friends Don Bachardy and Christopher Isherwood, he paid a visit to Stephen Tennant at Wilsford Manor: 'Stephen was lying like a porpoise in one of the many bedrooms he occupies.' He looked ghastly, fat and painted, a bang of dyed hair over his forehead, greasy hair brushed forward from the crown of his head, his fingernails dirty, giggling, 'O what fun this is.'

The room was a chaos of diaries, books, photographs, papers, drawings by Tchelitchew, make-up and beauty preparations, Mexican jewellery, old silver bracelets and turquoise rings. Stephen threw things off a sofa and into a corner of the room for his guests to sit down. He was wearing tight shorts and was troubled by a stomach upset. He lay on the bed and talked of Life, the dedication of the artist, Isherwood's prose and his own correspondence with Willa Cather.

He showed them the proposed cover for his novel, *Lascar*, which he had been writing for the past twenty years, his drawings of 'wicked' sailors and his paintings of rocks bound with chains and lapped by blue waves. 'Can you think of anything more perfect than chains binding rocks to the sea?' Every five minutes he left them to go to the lavatory. His manservant, wearing white gloves, served them tea in the rose room – 'another bedroom in which some appalling, rose-sprigged wallpaper had been plastered in panels among magenta tin foil and gold embossed papers'. On the bed was an envelope with 'the Rose Room' written in magenta ink. On another piece of paper was written, 'The Curtain is Rising'.

It was all so different from 'those blissful afternoons of photographic egotism' and from that perfect weekend, more than thirty years before, when Cecil had wandered round the Celandine room in 'a trance of happiness', knowing that he had made a great move in his life. They walked to see Stephen's new lily pond and 'the horror of the garden he has created' – iron herons, wire archways, pink statues, birds in cages, snakes in the grass. By the pond, Cecil took 'one terrible photograph' of Stephen who said 'Yes, show my legs please,' as he posed like a pixie. 'Come, nestle close. Come, Don, let's all be photographed together so that I shall know you have really been to Wilsford.'

In 1961 Cecil published the first volume of his edited diaries, which expunged all mention of homosexuality. It was called *The Wandering Years*. In it was his description of his first meeting with Greta at the Gouldings' house in 1932 when he had worn his white sharkskin shorts and she had kissed the yellow rose. Stephen wrote to him:

Cecil dear

I'm feasting on your Diaries . . .

Reading your description of Greta Garbo in Hollywood – How very like me she is in some ways. The same great Drop Curtains of Melancholy, the same childish, sweet, irresponsible gaiety and magic, self-enchanted charm and elusiveness. Brio. She is very like me Cecil in many ways. You have said this to me.

Mercedes, seriously ill, underwent brain surgery. Her troubles were exacerbated by lack of money. She sold her Spanish diamond bracelet and remaining relics of better times and then, in September, wrote to William McCarthy, curator of the Rosenbach Museum in

Philadelphia, about a price for her letters from the women she had loved. She had no money to pay the rent and bills. She asked for a ten-year seal to be put on the letters, after the death of the sender:

> I can't get over the feeling that one should never give away or show letters which at the time have meant much to one and are so very personal.
>
> And yet I would not have the heart or the courage to have burned these letters. I mean of course Eva's, Greta's and Marlene's, who were loves. So it seemed a god-sent moment when you took them. I only hope, as the years go on and you are no longer there, that they will be *respected* and *protected* from the eyes of vulgar people.

She would not let him read Greta's letters: 'You see they mean a lot to me and I just could not take it to sit there and to have someone just carelessly reading them.' She argued hard about a fair price. 'I do think $5,000 too little when we include G's things. My lawyer told me today that he himself would give me $5,000 for this material alone if I would consider selling it to him, which I will not do. I need this money quite desperately.'

Her illness was protracted and painful and she became dependent on the kindness of neighbours and friends in bringing her food. Cecil phoned Greta on 17 October 1961 when he was in New York: 'Well, well, she said. I was wondering where Beat would be. Have you come over to propose to me again?' He told her that Mercedes was mortally ill and would soon die. He said she must at least send a postcard and that she would have a 'terrific conscience' when Mercedes was gone. Greta was 'deeply, deeply, upset but would never relax her judgement'.

So Cecil faced, or half-faced, the contrast between the illusions of his youth and the realities of life and time. But though disappointment etched its way into his face, he sustained success, wore wide-brimmed hats, pink suits and flowing scarves and was at all the important private views.

Amusing and defended, he used frankness like a veneer. Probed in a television interview, *Face to Face*, in February 1962, he said with deceptive insouciance that he was still looking for the rainbow's end. Adept at deflecting searching questions, he appeared entirely at ease. Asked why he wore a hat, he took off his fedora with a flourish, said, 'I don't like to exhibit myself quite bald you know,' and pretended to show what he was at pains to conceal. Reviewers praised the steel fist beneath the velvet glove.

At Reddish, his mother got worse and worse. She made little sense in what she said and talked as if her husband was still alive. Cecil began to think that medicine was prolonging her life officiously. He was haunted by the groans from her room. At night she was locked in her room to stop her wandering and falling and he heard the door handle rattling.

Her death in February 1962 came as a relief and a depression. He took tranquillisers to get through the ordeal of the funeral: 'The tears I dropped over the freesias and violets by her side were like hot tropical raindrops,' he wrote in his diary.

Reddish House seemed large and quiet. Lack of relationship began to reproach him:

I have my first intimation of what the loneliness of old age can be . . . The bookcases are full yet there doesn't seem just the book for the mood – a telephone call to a friend is unanswered, the east wind discourages a walk on the downs and it is too late to call on a neighbour . . . Tasks are found . . .

That I have not inspired real love in anyone is the awful realisation I must face. I wasn't able to inspire enough feeling in Peter and certainly Greta only superficially was intrigued. June is interested, but not enough to marry me and others have merely been phenomena of the flesh.

Greta's retreat from the world seemed total. She said that she did not feel very well, and saw practically nobody and found it difficult to decide anything. To Mimi Pollak she wrote in 1963 that she still lived on carrots, had nothing of interest to tell and no plans to move anywhere unless, she said, she could find someone who would change her completely which would not be easy.

June, after a few years, married Jeremy Hutchinson, a barrister. He was the son of St John and Mary Hutchinson, who were linked to the Bloomsbury Group. He had previously been married to the actress Peggy Ashcroft. June wrote to Cecil, 'We have been secretly in love for a long time, marriage never seemed a possibility but now they have decided to divorce I must say I am very very happy.' Unable to tell Cecil face to face because of the terrible awkwardness that descended on them over intimate matters, she hoped they would continue as friends. 'Dear, dear Cecil, you have been so angelic to me always – please never stop.'

Looking at his own reflection in a triplicate mirror at the tailor, in 1963, Cecil saw turkey wattles under his chin, a balding pate and an elderly man. He pined for travel, love affairs and the lost time of being young. In London there was a season of Garbo's films. When he watched *Anna Christie* and *A Woman of Affairs*, he found them strange and hallucinatory. He realised how superb an actress she was – 'violent, big in contrasts. Nothing small in the way she got her effects.' He was impressed by her humanity, her understanding of human frailty and the way she combined humour and tragedy. Though time had brought him fame and disappointment, there on celluloid was the perfect face, the proponent of love, the clairvoyant gaze, never to be degraded or etched away.

13

Betrayal

'Love? I don't think I know what it is.'
Camille

Georges Schlee died in Paris on Saturday 3 October 1964 at the age of sixty-five. He and Greta had planned to fly back to New York the following day. They had spent their usual summer holiday in the villa at Cap d'Ail and in Paris stayed at the Crillon. On the evening of his death they dined with Cécile de Rothschild and left her at 11.30, Greta to go to bed, Schlee to walk a little. He had a heart attack and the proprietor of a bistro phoned Greta. She scarcely understood the call and gave the man Cécile's number. Schlee died in the ambulance on the way to hospital.

Cécile took over. Greta hid from journalists, then flew back alone to New York – a press photograph showed her bedraggled and shielding her face. Cécile contacted Valentina who arrived in Paris on 5 October and took Schlee's body to New York the following day. The funeral service, at the Universal Funeral Chapel on East 52nd Street and Lexington Avenue, was Russian Orthodox. There were eighty-five mourners but Greta was not among them.

Valentina, to whom Schlee left everything in his will, continued to live in the same mansion block as Greta on 52nd Street, but was at pains to avoid getting into the elevator with her, or to cross paths. After Schlee's death she never spoke to her again. She arranged for ritual exorcisms of her New York apartment and of the villa at Cap d'Ail to expunge all trace of her. Greta passed no comment. It was rumoured that she might have married Schlee as late as 1962, had Valentina granted him a divorce.

At Christmas 1964, Cecil sent Greta words of commiseration and she replied with a telegram: 'Love and thanks. G. G.' Cecil was by then entrenched in a new affair of the heart. He had spent most of 1963 in Hollywood, on what he described in his diary as 'the greatest creative experience that anyone working in the theatre can enjoy'. This was designing the sets and costumes of the film of *My Fair Lady*. It was a commission that earned him two Oscars and a great deal of money. The film was directed by George Cukor, scripted by Alan Jay Lerner and starred Rex Harrison and Audrey Hepburn.

The schedule was exacting, Cecil's relationship with Cukor fraught with jealousy and dislike (they ended up not speaking), and Hollywood social life, in Cecil's view, empty and vulgar. As an escape from the studios, he flew to San Francisco for the weekend of 23 March. On the Saturday night he went to The Toolbox, a gay club full of men in jeans and leather jackets, where the atmosphere was 'quite frighteningly tough'. Propped up at the bar was 'a tall Scandinavian boy'. They talked until the bar closed, then drove back in Kin's Volkswagen to his apartment in Stockton Street. The place was untidy and dirty, there were dried grasses on the window-sill, eight daffodils in a black pot and 'everywhere evidence of little money but pure taste', said Cecil.

Kin was twenty-nine years younger than Cecil, an Olympic fencing champion and a student of art history at the University of California. He had not seen *My Fair Lady*, nor heard of Cecil Beaton. He talked of literature and art, listened to Schubert and Bach and was, thought Cecil, the 'perfect antidote to all that I have to suffer in Hollywood'. They spent time together at Kin's apartment, or at the Bel Air hotel, where Cecil was staying, in Beverly Hills. At weekends they walked and camped in the Yosemite Valley and the hills of California. Cecil thought his new friend 'golden, athletic and pure', 'a 6ft 4 Adonis', 'ceaselessly beautiful', and 'a rare sight and of all time . . . In every light, in movement or static pose, in sport or sleep, he is a continuous delight to the eye.'

He 'felt terribly grateful to God for having brought about this quite miraculous happening at a late stage in my life', enjoyed the anonymity of their times together and the unfamiliar sense of intimacy, and took numerous photographs of Kin. Though Californians might stare at this '6ft 4 Adonis with someone who is old enough but not the sort of person to be his grandfather', wonder at Cecil's foppish suits, hats and neckscarves, and see a stereotype in the way he picked up the restaurant bill, Cecil hoped that the relationship would survive his return to England and fill the void at Reddish House left by his mother's death. In the more forthright climate of the sixties, he hoped to live with a man not as a 'felon and an outcast'.

The following June, Kin gave up his San Francisco apartment, sold his furniture, enrolled for a two-year course at the Courtauld Institute in London and flew in to Heathrow on a student flight from Montreal. Cecil was there to meet him at the airport. 'I felt an electric current run through me when suddenly the sign told me that the student flight had landed at 19.27,' he wrote. He drove Kin to Pelham Place, considered he had brought to his home, if not Greta Garbo, then the original Apollo Belvedere and recorded in his diary 'As an adornment to my house and my life he is the most prized possession and of the greatest value to me.'

Together they toured Britain, west to Devon, north to Scotland and east to Norfolk. They visited cathedrals and the country houses of Kedleston, Haddon, Chatsworth, Hardwick, Marchmont, Lambton and Houghton, and Cecil's mother's birthplace at Temple Sowerby in Westmorland where 'tears were close', wrote Cecil. Then they took a long trip to Europe – to Munich, Florence, Siena, Bologna, Padua, Venice, Rome and on to Athens, Cyprus, Turkey.

For a time it seemed that all might be well. Kin's presence did not impede Cecil's work. Cecil designed *La Traviata* for the Metropolitan Opera House, published *Cecil Beaton's Fair Lady* and the second volume of his edited diaries, *The Years Between*, photographed Chanel, Jean Shrimpton, Picasso and various royals, had lunch with the Queen Mother and was elected a Fellow of the Royal Photographic Society. After seven months of living with Kin and nearly two years of knowing him, he felt that there was between them a happy atmosphere of trust and contentment. He wrote in his diary that he felt proud at behaving well toward another human being.

And yet, at heart, something was wrong. There were times when he wondered if he had been over-ambitious in bringing Kin into his English life, times when the Adonis seemed 'rough and ready, hearty and unhousetrained', left bread crusts on the floor, asked too many questions, was altogether human and not at all like the Apollo Belvedere. There were times, too, when Cecil felt old and unenthusiastic and in need of rest.

But the greater strain was Kin's, and at Reddish on a Monday morning in June 1965, after a year in England, he asked Cecil if they might have 'a little talk'. Cecil, in bed with a cold, listened with sinking heart as Kin told him that he felt stuck in England and uncomfortable at being kept by Cecil, that he had written to California University about a teaching job and to his family and a friend called Ed to say that he was coming home. Cecil's friends had, he said, been kind and friendly but he had no connection with any of them. 'They're so busy being clever and pleased with themselves but they don't give a damn about me . . . I listen to the talk and don't participate and no one wants me to.' He found the rain and the smallness of England depressing and when he shut his eyes he saw the hills around San Francisco and the Californian sunlight and longed to be there.

Cecil again confronted the implications of rejection:

I saw my life suddenly so unfulfilled with all the inadequate makeshift friends, the activities and affairs that mean nothing. I saw all the things that I would be missing: Kin's playing Schubert or Bach, his schoolboy, gangling, loping into the room, his untidiness, the high quality of the books in his room, our sharing every situation, analysing every friend and event, the good companionship on motor tours.

As usual, he chronicled the outward trappings of his woe. 'I became in the extremes of grief,' he wrote. 'I wept so much that breathing became difficult. My whole frame shook in an orgasm of misery. I moaned.'

Behind the display, reassuring proof to himself that he could, perhaps, feel, were cool facts: he would live with no one, the experiment had failed, intimacy had eluded him and his time would again be filled with work and social engagements that sparkled but failed to illuminate or to fulfil.

A month later, early on a morning in July, Kin left Pelham Place with all his possessions in two bags. He shook hands awkwardly with Cecil who, in his pyjamas, stood at the front door and watched the taxi drive away. Cecil went back to bed for an hour feeling 'desperately sad'. Never one to grieve for long, he then travelled that same day to Athens to meet Greta and Cécile de Rothschild for a cruise of the Greek islands in Cécile's yacht, the *Sieta*.

The yacht was harboured in the bay at Vouliagmeni. For the first time in two years he saw Greta. She was sitting on deck with her back to the quay, her hair, which had become quite grey, tied with a rubber band into a small pigtail. 'The surprised profile turned to reveal a big smile. It was almost the same and yet, no, the two intervening years since we last met have created havoc.' 'Can it be Beatie?' she said. 'My Beat!' He blurted out the news of Kin's departure that morning after a year together, how much he would miss him and how unhappy he felt. 'One whole year, my, my!' she said, and that was the only mention of the matter throughout the trip.

She had been some weeks with Cécile on the yacht. They had sailed from Italy and Sardinia and she wanted no more than a carefree holiday, swimming, sunbathing and talking of nothing in particular. She would not discuss Schlee's death, nor how she managed without him in New York. As ever she dreamed of being left in peace. She still refused to justify, to those who thought she should act, teach, or improve her mind, quite how she spent her days: 'I lie in my bed looking at the wallpaper,' was one of her replies. New Yorkers still accepted her solitariness and let her be. She walked for an hour or two each day. Truman Capote said that muffled in her clothes, as she walked the Avenues, she looked like one of the old ladies that delivered Western Union telegrams. Newspapers reported sightings of her – on Cécile's or on Onassis' yacht, in the South of France, at Klosters in Switzerland with Salka Viertel. Cecil was riled and irritated that, as ever, she refused to divulge her news or to evince interest in his. It confirmed to him that friendship, of any meaningful sort, was not on offer to him.

At first, affected by the sea air and the sun, he slept most of the day as well as the night. It was a release from the hard work of the summer and from Kin's rejection. But as the days merged and the yacht moved from perfect bay to perfect bay, he scrutinised Greta with critical resentment – as if in some way she was to blame for the predicament in which he found himself, and as if the loss of beauty he perceived in her was a moral lack, an inability on her part to be an art object, a perverse persistence in being human:

In this cruel harsh sunlight on board one sees every crinkle and crevice in the most cruel way. I have hawklike watched her in all lights, without mascara even.

She was vulnerable at being seen without eye make-up and only if Cecil saw her swimming in the early morning, or if she had gone to bed early and came to complain about the noise, could he subject her to this 'severe test'.

Sitting beside her on deck, he chronicled his criticisms of her in his 124th journal, the wrinkles round her eyes, the lines on her upper lip, the wizened skin on her arms. He criticised her ungrammatical English which he saw as a result of being solitary for so many years, her refusal to talk about her family, friends or career, her uninterest in topics to do with either of the last world wars, or in films, plays or books. He wrote of how she lay beside him restless and bored. He gave written vent to his spleen. He did not reflect that something of the malice of his writing might communicate itself to her. For she knew quite well that she had aged harshly. You do, in America, she said. She knew, too, that she had made her living from looking young and unspoilt, but felt that too many filmstars tried to perpetuate that image for far too long. And she knew the price of being solitary and apart.

The two other guests on the cruise were Princess Jeanne-Marie de Broglie, head of Christie's in Paris and an Austrian actor, Friedrich Ledebur, but Cecil doubted that Greta had remembered their names. He described the atmosphere on the yacht as changing and strange.

> On the surface – and because we are all civilised human beings, the atmosphere is light and sportive. Emotions under control. But I find that I am not the only one to sense the vibrations of rancour, jealousy and criticism that exist beneath the surface.

The vibrations were only vaguely explained. There was an evening when Greta wept for no apparent reason. Jeanne de Broglie asked Cecil why. Was it, she wondered, because she had interrupted Greta's complaint that there were no chicken legs in the supper dish? Cecil said no, he did not think it was that. Rather, he thought, that sometimes the conversations in French were too much for her, or perhaps the second whisky had gone to her head, or maybe she was missing Georges Schlee. Anyway, he said, she was apt to cry on occasion when overtaken by her mood of the moment.

'Rancour, jealousy and criticism' largely came from him. He perceived Cécile as besotted with Greta and resented the intimacy between them. Cécile told him that people had always tried to take from Greta, not give to her and that it was Greta's childish side that should be encouraged. She was tireless in trying to please her on the holiday. She was enchanted by her, and untroubled by her petulance and demands. She told Cecil of her own relief, at the time of Schlee's death, that she had gone to Paris a day earlier than anticipated and had thus been able to help Greta. Cecil thought that from that day on she filled the role of Schlee in Greta's life, 'Schlee and Mercedes combined'. He felt that she had become like Mercedes and received the same treatment and he described her as like a kid hypnotised by a snake. He wrote of the enormous cost of the cruise and of how Cécile phoned for her chauffeur and maid to meet Greta from the boat.

But the main point of his rancour was that now there was nothing from Greta for him. 'No one is as critical as I am . . . just because, having loved her so much, it is a nightmare for me to see what faults her negativeness and selfishness have brought.' He was reduced to sitting beside The Divine Garbo and writing spiteful things about her in his journal. When she went on shore with the others to buy honeycakes he 'stubbornly stayed put' in his cabin to finish his volume of Proust. At lunch he insisted on conversation that he knew would discomfit her:

I was determined that the meal should not go without topics to be discussed and so worked hard in spite of interruptions from Cécile and Greta. We talked of movies of today. Greta silent. She did not know that Jeanne Moreau had made a film of Mata Hari. She had never heard of Antonioni, Fellini, Richardson or the like. She remained stubbornly silent while the pros and cons of Dietrich were discussed. She took no part in an explanation of expressionist painting . . . One sees that those endless days and evenings doing nothing have resulted in negation. She has never let any new reflection or impression come into her head for more than a moment in the last twenty years.

But he, who let endless new impressions into his head in a constant whirl, had acquired only limited wisdom from them and no particular happiness. And he might have reflected that his reasons for wishing to talk to Greta of Jeanne Moreau as Mata Hari, or of the pros and cons of Dietrich, were less than generous to her, and that her silence came from seeing all too well the game he was endeavouring to play.

But his disaffection was equivocal. As much as ever he was affected by images of her. He watched her clasp her hands as she hoped that the sea was not too cold for bathing. He glimpsed her through her cabin window, wrapped in her bath towel, showing part of her breasts, her hair hanging wet, her 'eyes fantastically deep set and tragic'. 'Whatever she does is touched with a sort of genius,' he wrote. And in the evening on Skiathos, as sunlight spread over the sky and sea, he watched, perturbed, as she became as beautiful as her legend. He thought how she could be photographed to appear as beautiful as ever on film, conceded that her air of mysteriousness still disturbed, and that in some magical way, in her pink shirt and pink and white striped trousers, she seemed like part of the evening light.

But he had made up his mind to betray her, though he knew the moral turpitude of what he planned to do. The first two volumes of his edited diaries had been published to keen interest and generous critical praise. 'There's no point in the whole thing unless I'm frank,' he told the *New York Herald Tribune* in October 1965, three months after this Greek cruise, 'It's going to be harder in the next volume as I get closer to today.'

That volume was to be *The Happy Years*, which spanned 1944–8 and detailed his relationship with Greta at its core. Though in all his published diaries his frankness was selective, though they were revised, ghosted and edited and, like his life, concerned themselves with the surface show, contained little about his sexual escapades and few of his waspish observations, and in any real sense denied his homosexuality, or the iciness of his ambition, or his terror of decay, or his reasons for depicting people as ornaments, even so, the revelations of his love affair with Greta would be bound to cause a stir.

He made a half-hearted plan to warn her. In November 1967 he saw her at Cécile's New York apartment. She had been out Christmas shopping and was waiting for him to arrive. 'Her cheeks were flushed a shiny pink. She had on a thick pixie hat and her shoes were old and worn out.' He thought she looked beautiful because she was so completely natural.

They chatted together in a friendly way. Later he phoned and left a message with her maid. He wanted to ask her to lunch with him alone to speak to her about *The Happy Years*. She did not phone back and he did not care.

So he went ahead and signed the contract with Weidenfeld and Nicolson in January 1968 and received an advance of £1,000. To ease his guilt he railed in his unpublished diaries against her, condemned her for her selfishness, ruthlessness, elusiveness and inability to love. 'Let her stew in her own loneliness,' he wrote. He berated her for making no gesture of conciliation to Mercedes – who died that year after a decade of poverty and illness – and opined that she would give no generous help to him were he to need it.

Perhaps I am just manufacturing a situation wherein I would feel it possible to go ahead and be damned. But the years are slipping by and the situation will remain essentially the same until either of us are dead.

His rationalisations did not keep away anxiety and guilt. He briefly recalled the manuscript from Weidenfeld and struggled with his conscience.

My heartsearching about publishing and being damned have continued for a very long while . . . Then I wondered, What am I waiting for, my own death or Greta's? . . . Then I decided, since the following volume was nearing completion, that I would go ahead.

As a weak disclaimer he included a preface note in the published book:

If I have offended any friends I hope they will believe that it was far from my wish to do so. Least of all have I wanted to cause any pain to the woman who occupied my thoughts (and the bulk of my diary entries) in the years just after the war.

In November 1971, in advance of publication, *McCalls* published extracts about his relationship with Greta. There were articles in most of the American and London newspapers – in *Newsweek*, the *Daily Mail*, *The Times*. 'This is something I expected would have to be faced,' Cecil wrote. He opened the *Telegraph*, saw a photograph of Greta and himself and his stomach turned to water. He had wanted the world to know he had been Greta Garbo's lover, the way a mountaineer might want the world to know that he or she has scaled the highest peak. But now he hoped the world's interest would fade and the whole matter go away. He asked Eileen Hose to ward off any unpleasant phone calls and not show him the press coverage. His diary became a confessional, written from a desire to be freed from guilt and to be forgiven. 'The awful feelings of guilt and anxiety continue to dog me. I have headaches and feel very rotten.' At night he kept waking and thinking of some further detail in his diary as published in *McCalls* that would offend Greta or a great number of friends.

While he suffered with his conscience a formal letter arrived from Buckingham Palace offering him a knighthood. At first he did not tell anyone of the honour for fear that it would be rescinded, 'owing to pre-publication scandal'. He longed to hear that Greta had dismissed his betrayal from her mind as merely 'another example of how badly human beings behave to one another'. To compound his distress Anita Loos sent him a copy of a trashy novel that purported to be a *roman à clef* about Garbo. The critics assumed it to be about her, though it was, said Cecil, 'utterly against the spirit of everything she believed'. It described her pulling an orange about with long pointed nails and had a preface by 'GG'. He wondered if Greta would sue.

On the morning when news of his knighthood was made public, Eileen came in 'bearing branches of laurels and wreathed in smiles'. The phone rang all day and there were cables from Malta, Hong Kong, Melbourne and Florida. But there was no word from Greta, who had no reason to consider him a gentleman, let alone a Knight. 'Sir is a romantic title,' wrote Cecil. 'It is much easier on the tongue than Duke or Earl.'

For the investiture at Buckingham Palace on 3 February 1972, he wore a grey tail coat and trousers, a black silk hat, and lilies of the valley in his buttonhole. He told The Queen he never thought that taking a photograph of her as a little girl, in a pink taffeta dress, would lead to this honour. He felt that he deserved the accolade, 'not for my talent, but for character, tenacity, energy and wide-reaching efforts'. He thought that he had 'done it alone', and was sad that neither his mother nor Aunt Jessie was alive to share the tribute.

But a strange nemesis afflicted him and blighted this honour. Awake or asleep, Garbo's face began to haunt him. The image that he had so pursued now disturbed his subconscious mind. A sculpture that he was making in the grounds at Reddish seemed to turn into her and become the 'embodiment' of his troubles. A painting of a female head that he was working on in the studio reflected back her face to him and became 'part of the general malaise'.

He was anxious to the point of illness with headaches, muscle tension and depression. He fainted and bruised his head and knee when he fell. He fought off colds and flu and his body ached. To try to recuperate he went alone to the mountains in Switzerland but the same hallucinatory images pursued him. When he had walked in the day and then lay tired on his bed he saw vividly, as if in coloured snapshots, odd faces, 'a young boy with tiger's eyes, an old, wizened, tarted-up blonde'. And then an image of Greta, very young and beautiful with a red smiling mouth and wearing a fur coat. 'I asked her if she would ever forgive me. She laughed and said I had given her such a bad time. Then immediately I woke up and said, But dreams go by opposites . . .'

They were disconcerting images for a man who was near to old age. Greta, equal to the boy with the tiger's eyes, and the obstruction of the wizened old tart. Cecil felt so disturbed that he curtailed the holiday and left that day, wanting familiar surroundings and his own home.

At first, but not for long, he resisted reading reviews of *The Happy Years*. Christopher Sykes, in *Books and Bookmen* wrote with wounding innocence: 'One must respect the frankness of Miss Garbo in allowing this publication.' Cyril Connolly, in *The Sunday Times*, which serialised long extracts, asked, 'What went wrong? Why is she not now Lady Beaton, mother of some little

Beatons, and gardening among the borders of his Wiltshire home, hiding behind the hedges on the day the public comes?' He concluded it was because of the presence of 'the little man'. Beverley Nichols, unmindful of the sexual secrets he and Cecil shared, wrote in the *Spectator*, 'This is either a true story or it is nothing. I believe it to be true from the first line to the last,' and Auberon Waugh, in *Harpers and Queen*, chided Cecil for snobbism, bitchiness, vanity and name-dropping.

Early in 1973 Cecil toured America, lecturing about his diaries. His television appearances were sandwiched between commercials and the Watergate Scandal. In San Francisco Kin assured him that his qualms about Garbo were unfounded and that he could not have left out such an important affair from his diaries. Garbo, he said, might wish to be private, but she could not expect it, for she had made her career in films.

But Greta haunted Cecil still. On a plane in California the woman sitting next to him seemed exactly like her thirty years back. The woman was sunburned and wearing linen and sandals, her face hidden by her long blonde hair. She 'seemed to exude the same ambiguous sex attraction, half boy, half woman, that Greta had when I first met her', Cecil wrote. The image vanished when a steward asked the woman to move so that a man and his son might sit together. She was Scandinavian but her face quite unlike Greta's.

The next day Cecil flew to New York and a friend told him that he had, that morning, seen the real Greta in an Italian grocery store. She had two bags in which she put the vegetables she was buying. She wore dark glasses but she was smiling and the shop assistants were solicitous, though respectful of her wish for anonymity. The proprietor whispered in Italian as he pointed out the divine signorina to Cecil's friend. It made Cecil feel less guilty to know that Greta was smiling as she bought her vegetables.

On a *Connaissance des Arts* tour in Germany, he met Cécile de

Rothschild. She asked him how much he had made out of Garbo 'on the *McCalls, Times, Oggi* etc. world circulation. I mean how much with *Vogue* photographs *et tout ça* during the past twenty years have you made?' Cecil said that he thought about £4,000.

'Not bad is it? I mean I wouldn't mind being given £4,000 to spend on the kitchen.' She laughed that nasal choking voice. 'Not bad eh? For someone who didn't need the publicity. Even Stokowski didn't sell his story to the papers.'

And at the end the story that Cecil sold was that he had kissed Garbo, wooed and pursued her, been rejected by her, then published all, knowing that to do so was a violation. He had not sold his story merely for money, though everything about himself he turned to money. Nor was it from misogyny, though misogyny lurked behind the impulse in his images of women, to turn them into statues or show ugliness behind façade. Nor was it merely from the desire for self-aggrandisement, for his quest for Garbo failed. It was more that he wanted to say that he had looked into her amazing face and seen his own mirror image transformed. That he had seen reflected back not the self he so scrutinised and tried to disguise, the foppish, fussy bachelor, 'bothering that the Louis Seize was out of place', whose work was ephemeral and who had never been loved, but rather that he saw her face, irresistible in its beauty, with the ability to act with sincerity, and called the Divine for all that the image seemed to promise and provide.

As for Greta, she kept silent, though Peter Viertel, Salka Viertel's son, said she was deeply offended, picked up a copy of *The Happy Years* and said, 'People accuse me of paranoia, but look at this.' But though she did not forgive, she did not resent. She called on Cecil one last time, in October 1975, at Reddish House. By then he had suffered a stroke, which paralysed his right side and left him shuffling with a stick, his speech slurred. 'Well I couldn't have married him, could I – him being like this,' she said to his secretary, Eileen Hose. When she left, she broke one of her rules and in the hall signed her name in his Visitors' Book.

References

Reference is by page number and opening phrase. Provenance
and specific copyright acknowledgment are given where due.
The following abbreviations apply:
BFI: The British Film Institute Library, London.
V&A: The Archive of Art and Design,
The Victoria and Albert Museum, London.
St John's: The Library of St John's College, Cambridge.
Rosenbach: The Rosenbach Museum and Library, Philadelphia.

There are six volumes of Cecil Beaton's published diaries:
The Wandering Years 1922–39 (Weidenfeld and Nicolson, 1961)
The Years Between 1939–44 (Weidenfeld and Nicolson, 1965)
The Happy Years 1944–8 (Weidenfeld and Nicolson, 1972)
The Strenuous Years 1948–55 (Weidenfeld and Nicolson, 1973)
The Restless Years 1955–63 (Weidenfeld and Nicolson, 1976)
The Parting Years 1963–74 (Weidenfeld and Nicolson, 1978)

Cecil's manuscript diaries are more candid than when edited for
print. They comprise 145 notebooks and are in the Library of St John's
College, Cambridge.

The late Eileen Hose gave Cecil Beaton's papers to the College in
1986. She asked for thirteen of the diaries to remain sealed until the
deaths of The Queen, Greta Garbo and Cecil Beaton's sister, Lady
Smiley.

Beaton's biographer, Hugo Vickers, had already quoted from these
now sealed diaries in *Cecil Beaton* (Weidenfeld and Nicolson, 1985).
The word 'sealed' in the acknowledgments that follow, indicates that
those particular diary entries are taken, perforce, from Vickers's book.

1 *The Divine*

1 **offered to one's gaze** Roland Barthes, *Selected Writings* (Cape, 1982)

1 **perfection itself** *Film Weekly*, 21 March 1931. BFI

1 **complex enchanting** Louise Brooks, *Lulu in Hollywood* (Knopf, 1982)

2 **she had something** *Film Weekly*, June 1932. BFI

3 **I am a woman** *Picturegoer*, May 1927. BFI.

3 **I do not want to be** *Sight and Sound*, Winter 1928. BFI

4 **cupping her man's head** Kenneth Tynan, 'Garbo' *Sight and Sound*, Autumn 1953

4 **I practised love** Raymond Durgnat and John Kobal, *Greta Garbo* (Studio Vista, 1965)

4 **The story of my life** Raymond Daum, *Walking with Garbo* (HarperCollins, 1991)

5 **I had never seen** Louise Brooks to Kenneth Brownlow, 19 October, 1968, quoted in Barry Paris, *Louise Brooks* (Knopf, 1989)

2 *Cecil's Quest*

7 **It was to be** Cecil Beaton, Photobiography (Odhams, 1951)

8 **She is at once** Cecil Beaton's Diaries: 1922–39 *The Wandering Years* (Weidenfeld & Nicolson, 1961)

8 **two shades of orchid** Beaton, 'Scrapbook' 1924. V&A

10 **it's absolutely untrue** manuscript diary, 3 December 1928. St John's

11 **We clicked immediately** Gary Carey, *Anita Loos: a biography* (Bloomsbury, 1988) and Hugo Vickers, *Cecil Beaton* (Weidenfeld, 1985)

11 **a mock Moorish conceit** *The Wandering Years*

12 **already somewhat** mss diary, December 1929

12 **at the top** *The Wandering Years*

12 **'Meet Mr Lubitsch'** mss diary, January 1930

13 **She is so casual** *Photobiography*

14 **Hell, Damn Blast** mss diary, January 1930

14 **It is really too awful** *Photobiography*

14 **a man named Adrien** mss diary, January 1930

16 **twilight tandem** Kenneth Anger, *Hollywood Babylon* (Arrow 1986)

17 **She is at no moment** 'Adrian Answers 20 Questions on Garbo', *Photoplay* May 1935 BFI

18 **I feel you are** Anita Loos to Cecil, 15 March 1930. St John's. © The Anita Loos Estate

18 **One day in the lobby** Mercedes de Acosta, *Here Lies the Heart* (André Deutsch, 1960)

19 ***I hope the laurels** quoted in Richard Ellmann, *Oscar Wilde* (London, 1987)

19 **took hold of her** *Here Lies the Heart*

20 **Well that was Mercedes' story** mss diary, 2 February 1930

20 **furious lesbian** mss diary, 3 February 1930

21 **I'd like to change** *Wandering Years*

21 **I adored the Astaires** mss diary, 30 August 1924

21 **going to bed with a nigger** mss diary, 4 February 1930

22 **lesbians and faggots** mss diary, March 1930

22 **It was hard** mss diary, 13 March 1930

3 Mercedes Meets Greta

25 **like a parched camel** *Here Lies the Heart*, first draft

26 **Nothing occurred** ibid

26 **unquestionably had a mother** ibid

28 **You'll get a bad** *Here Lies the Heart*, first draft. Rosenbach

28 **a feeling in my bones** *Here Lies the Heart* (Deutsch)

28 **Every morning** Salka Viertel, *The Kindness of Strangers* (Holt, Rinehart and Winston, 1969)

29 **Books have been written** ibid

31 **Suddenly the doorbell** *Here Lies the Heart* (Deutsch)

32 **Ivor ran down** *Here Lies the Heart*, first draft

33 **It gives me great** *New York Post*, 18 April 1960

33 **She tried to detain** *Here Lies the Heart*, first draft

34 **Only a few hours** *Here Lies the Heart* (Deutsch)

34 **This day she created** ibid

34 **She plucked a handful** *Here Lies the Heart*, first draft

34 **It seemed a chaste room** ibid

35 **But what shall I do** ibid

35 **In the dead of night** *Here Lies the Heart* (Deutsch)

36 **How to describe** ibid

37 **No one can really know** ibid

37 **I want to defend** ibid

38 **To write of Greta** ibid

39 **We used to laugh** *Here Lies the Heart*, first draft

40 **had an appalling habit** ibid

40 **Garbo in pants** *Here Lies the Heart* (Deutsch)

41 **We see Erik's face** mss *Desperate*, Rosenbach

4 *Cecil Meets Greta*

44 **No director has** *Picturegoer*, 18 June 1932. BFI

45 **We would pass** Joan Crawford in conversation with John Kobal. Quoted in Kobal, *People Will Talk* (Aurum Press, 1986)

47 **If a unicorn** *Wandering Years*

47 **Beauty, the most important** *Daily Chronicle*, November 1928. V&A

50 **Why should an oval** *Daily Mail*, 22 November 1930. V&A

50 **intimacies spread** mss diary, November 1928

50 **I'm not ashamed** ibid

51 **Ashcombe – such a lovely name** Stephen Tennant to Cecil, undated 1930. St John's © The Hon. Toby Tennant

52 **I sat gazing** Cecil Beaton, *Ashcombe* (Batsford, 1949)

52 **The place is a paradise** *Wandering Years*

53 **a glance of sympathy** mss diary, 6 May 1956

53 **Oh how I doted** mss diary, January 1931

54 **Peter Watson has bought** Nancy Mitford to her brother Tom 1 November 1930. Quoted in *The Letters of Nancy Mitford*, ed. by Charlotte Mosley (Hodder & Stoughton 1993)

54 **What had formerly** Michael Wishart, *Peter and Others*, ADAM nos 385–90

54 **You have infused** Peter Watson to Cecil, undated. St John's

55 **Titania was never** mss diary, January 1931

55 **No real spark** ibid

55 **the proverbial unrequited** draft letter from Cecil to Peter Watson, undated. St John's

55 **The more you do** mss diary, January 1931

56 **his jacket is displayed** ibid

56 **Please put out** mss diary, February 1931

57 **once more I knew** mss diary, April 1931

57 **terrible rival** mss diary, summer 1931

58 **as completely as I** mss diary, October 1931

58 **like a suckling pig** ibid

58 **But you're so yorng** *Wandering Years*

59 **A rose that lives** ibid

59 **If I were a young boy** mss diary, March 1932. St John's. Sealed

60 **Then this is goodbye** *Wandering Years*

5 *Greta's Wandering Years*

64 **I was born** interview with Ruth Biery, *Photoplay*, April 1928. BFI

65 **She had no** *Here Lies the Heart*, first draft

66 **Your joys and sorrows** *Photoplay*, April 1928. BFI

66 **I don't think anyone** quoted in Frederick Sands and Sven Broman, *The Divine Garbo* (Sidgwick & Jackson, 1979)

67 **Uncle doesn't give a damn** *Here Lies the Heart*, first draft

67 **School?** *Photoplay*, April 1930. Interview with Ake Sundborg. BFI

68 **I see from the papers** Ram Gopal to Mercedes, 12 December 1956. Rosenbach

68 **God what a feeling** *Photoplay*, April 1930. BFI

69 **she thought was as beautiful** Max Gumpel, *Tales and Reality*. Quoted in John Bainbridge, (Frederick Muller, 1955)

70 **boldly and outright** quoted in Fritiof Billquist *Garbo* (Arthur Baker 1960)

71 **As Miss Gustaffson** ibid

72 **When an actor** 'The Man Who Found Garbo' *Films and Filming*, August 1956

72 **I came off the street** *Photoplay*, June 1928

73 **Greta and I** quoted in *Garbo on Garbo*

74 **I am merciless** quoted in the documentary, *Garbo*, directed by Dan Säll

74 **Stiller creates people** ibid

74 **you consider my book** Selma Lagerlöf to Stiller, quoted in 'The Man Who Found Garbo' *Films and Filming*, August 1956

74 **Damn you Stiller** *Garbo*, directed by Dan Säll

75 **In a few years** quoted in Fritiof Billquist *Garbo* (Arthur Baker 1960)

76 **Such a face** Louise Brooks to Ricky Leacock: *Lulu in Berlin* transcript, 1974

76 **we had tea** ibid

77 **I suspect he looked** *Photoplay*, June 1928. BFI

77 **He was so nervous** Victor Sjöstrom, 'As I Remember Mauritz Stiller' *Biografbladet*, No. 4, 1951. BFI

78 **Never mind that** Arnold Genthe, *As I Remember* (Harrap, 1937)

78 **From the moment** Louise Brooks, *Lulu in Hollywood* (Knopf, 1982)

6 Cecil's Wandering Years

84 **When I was three** *Photobiography*

85 **to examine herself** *Here Lies the Heart*, first draft

85 **Among my nightly prayers** *Photobiography*

85 **My inward child's eye** ibid

86 **gilded baskets** Cecil Beaton, *The Glass of Fashion* (Weidenfeld and Nicolson, 1954)

86 **Suddenly out of nowhere** *The Wandering Years*

86 **The tears on his long** Evelyn Waugh, *A Little Learning* (Chapman & Hall, 1964)

87 **I became such a positive favourite** *The Wandering Years*

88 **there could be no** Cyril Connolly, *Enemies of Promise* (Routledge, 1949)

88 **the febrile modernity** *Glass of Fashion*

89 **I felt uncomfortable** *Photobiography*

89 **I must have been rather** mss diary, February 1924. Rosenbach

89 **wretched people** ibid

90 **The only thing you have** *Walking with Garbo*
90 **I'm sick of you worrying** *The Wandering Years*
90 **set about becoming** 'Scrapbook', 1924. V&A
92 **a terrible, terrible homosexualist** mss diary, 9 October 1923
93 **this marvellous step** mss diary, December 1966
94 **a horrible neighbourhood** mss diary, 21 January 1926
94 **He is my living** mss diary, winter 1934
95 **much to her mother's** *Wandering Years*
96 **Edith ate** ibid
96 **The telephone bell** ibid
98 **puffed with pride** mss diary, December 1926
98 **I want to be photographed** Stephen Tennant to Cecil, undated
   1926. St John's. © The Hon. Toby Tennant
99 **Massey, the man** mss diary, 15 January 1927
100 **obviously the home** mss diary, January 1927
102 **rotten, miserable** mss diary, January 1927
102 **Oh I can't tell you** Stephen Tennant to Cecil, undated 1927. St
   John's. © The Hon. Toby Tennant
103 **We swooned at the beauty** mss diary, 1933

7 Cecil's Years Between

104 **There would be no one** mss diary, November 1929
104 **Grief** Stephen Tennant to Cecil, undated 1929. St John's. © The
   Hon. Toby Tennant
105 **Yes let's meet** Stephen Tennant to Cecil, 28 October 1929. ©
   The Hon. Toby Tennant
106 **All his thrilling life** quoted in Hugo Vickers, *Cecil Beaton*
106 **I shall be very catty** Stephen Tennant to Cecil, undated 1930. St
   John's. © The Hon. Toby Tennant
107 **Art is not life** foreword to Willa Cather, *Collected Essays*
107 **pale blue Hanoverian** *Wandering Years*
107 **awfully nice** Selma Hastings, *Nancy Mitford* (Hamish Hamilton,
   1985)
108 **He was looking** press cuttings, October 1933. 'Scrapbook' 1933.
   V&A
109 **it leaves me so cold** mss diary, October 1933

109 **in our black bereavement** ibid
110 **The family has broken** mss diary, Christmas 1934
110 **I know that if** ibid
110 **We are the only two** Mrs Beaton to Cecil, September 1936. St John's
110 **Physically he is maddening** mss diary, 10 July 1933
111 **It is quite easy** draft letter to Peter Watson, undated. St John's
111 **If we cannot see** Peter Watson to Cecil, undated 1932. St John's
111 **Oh dear, how much nearer** mss diary, August 1936
111 **will never be in love** mss diary, January 1933
112 **gross and lecherous** Beverley Nichols, *The Unforgiving Minute* (W. H. Allen, 1978)
112 **It seems so terrible** mss diary, January 1933
112 **quite a charming romance** mss diary, March 1933
113 **It's such fun** ibid
114 **Among those present** press cuttings, 'Scrapbook' 1936. V&A
115 **brawny great cow** mss diary, November 1936
115 **You mustn't put** ibid
116 **Vogue offers me little** mss diary, June 1937
118 **In a city** *Cecil Beaton's New York* (Batsford, 1938)
119 **But it was no joke** *Photobiography*
119 **The Queen smiled** *The Wandering Years*
119 **like a wedding** mss diary, August 1942
120 **Standing before the mirror** Cecil Beaton, *My Royal Past* (Batsford, 1939)
121 **I consider the coinciding** Peter Watson to Cecil, 12 December 1939. St John's
121 **The prospect is for** *Cecil Beaton Diaries 1939–44: The Years Between* (Weidenfeld & Nicolson, 1965)
121 **a riot of fantasy** Olga Lynn, *Oggie, The Memoirs of Olga Lynn* (Weidenfeld & Nicolson, 1955)
122 **travelled with a load** *The Years Between*
123 **Under a lackadaisical** Harold Acton, *More Memoirs of an Aesthete* (Hamish Hamilton, 1970)
124 **very passionate and ardent** quoted in Hugo Vickers, *Cecil Beaton*

124 **a bit like being a sailor** obituary by Adrienne Corri, *Guardian* 31 May 1991

124 **It is a thrilling prospect** mss diary, January 1942

124 **I could hardly** mss diary, May 1942

126 **Most serious gaps** Wire from MOI to British Embassy, Chunking, 27 May 1944. St John's

127 **enough of taking** mss diary, August 1945

8 Greta's Years Between

128 **Under the most** C. A. Lejeune, *Observer*, 18 February 1934

130 **Hollywood seemed empty to me** *Here Lies the Heart*

130 **Please forgive me** Marlene to Mercedes, undated 1932. Georgetown University Library, Washington

131 **I kiss your face** Marlene to Mercedes, 28 July 1932. Rosenbach

131 **As I held the revolver** *Here Lies the Heart*

131 **This might be explained** ibid

132 **She has the technique** interview with Rathbone. Garbo 'Scrapbook', BFI

132 **Before she has even** Alistair Cooke, *Garbo and the Nightwatchman* (Cape, 1937)

133 **The evening was** *Here Lies the Heart*

135 **I never told her** *Photoplay*, April 1972. BFI

139 **There are some who want** press cuttings, March 1938. Garbo 'Scrapbook'. BFI

141 **Soon after Miss Garbo** Gayelord Hauser, *Look Younger Live Longer* (Faber, 1951)

147 **Darling I'm amazed** Ona Munson to Mercedes, 20 March 1940. Rosenbach

147 **You can't dispose** Alice B. Toklas to Anita Loos, 8 May 1960. From *Staying on Alone: Letters of Alice B. Toklas* edited by Edward Burns, courtesy of Liveright and Angus & Robertson, London and Sydney

148 **Why we weren't arrested** *Here Lies the Heart*

171 **One day I might** *The Happy Years*
172 **fooling around** mss diary, January 1952
172 **Well I do** mss diary, 12 December 1947. St John's. Sealed
173 **like a salad** *The Happy Years*
173 **You would say** ibid
174 ***Travesti*** ibid
174 **unsympathetic and recoiling** ibid
175 **I admit** ibid
175 **No, it's not easy** ibid
175 **To my surprise** Tennessee Williams, *Memoirs* (W. H. Allen, 1976)
176 **If the devil's in me** mss diary, December 1947. St John's. Sealed
176 **Have you room** ibid
178 **agonising sounds** *The Happy Years*
178 **It's Mr Thompson** ibid
178 **Our embrace** ibid
179 **I was appalled** ibid
180 **Occasionally we indulged** ibid
181 **the telephone bell** ibid
183 **gathered her into** mss diary, 12 March 1948. St John's. Sealed
184 **I can't think quite** *The Happy Years*
184 **something very violent** mss diary, 12 March 1948. St John's. Sealed
184 **These were done** mss diary, 14 March 1948. St John's. Sealed
184 **Why don't you two** *The Happy Years*
185 **that I had never** mss diary, 12 March 1948. St John's. Sealed

11 Disaffection

187 **It was wonderful** Cecil to Greta, 21 March 1948. St John's. Sealed
188 **in order to keep** *The Happy Years*
188 **That's enough of that** ibid
188 **the rocket went off** Cecil Beaton's Diaries: 1948–1955 *The Strenuous Years* (Weidenfeld & Nicolson, 1973)
189 **I would love you** Maud Nelson to Cecil, 10 November 1948. St John's

189 **Well you can't** Maud Nelson to Cecil, 13 January 1949. St John's

190 **all the same emotions** mss diary, 27 June 1949

191 **He is an amateur** mss diary, October 1949

192 **But on the way** *The Strenuous Years*

192 **I cannot talk about these things** Garbo 'Scrapbook', BFI

193 **How sad a thing** Tennessee Williams, *Memoirs*

193 **I went to see** Jean Rhys, *Letters 1931–66* (Deutsch, 1984)

194 **He said: Go ahead** *The Strenuous Years*

195 **By the end of the evening** ibid

197 **I think you must** Cecil to Maud Nelson, April 1950. St John's

197 **It frankly amazes me** Maud Nelson to Cecil, April 1950. St John's

198 **They did not smile** *The Strenuous Years*

199 **Soon she was on** ibid

199 **When I asked her** mss diary, 1952

199 **It was not surprising** ibid

200 **had fallen in love** mss diary, 1952

200 **Everyone else** *The Strenuous Years*

201 **Who can resist** mss diary, June 1952

201 **She has the most inexplicable** James Pope Hennessy to Nolwen de Janzé, 2 December 1951. Quoted in Peter Quennell (ed.), *A Lonely Business* (Weidenfeld & Nicolson, 1980)

202 **It was not because** *The Strenuous Years*

202 **She was serious** ibid

203 **The way she and Greta** Ram Gopal to Mercedes de Acosta, 1955. Rosenbach

203 **The other day** Alice B. Toklas to Carl Van Vechten, 27 November 1951. From *Staying on Alone*

205 **A lunch together** ibid

205 **Oh I couldn't tell you** mss diary, 1952

208 **a dreadful bathos** Cecil to Mercedes, 19 November 1952. Rosenbach

208 **In a small Madison Avenue** *The Diaries of Judith Malina 1947–57* (Grove Press, 1984)

209 **Hauser had telephoned** mss diary, December 1952

210 **The walls are of a** mss diary, 1954

211 **signed pieces of auction** Cecil to Mercedes, 17 May 1955
213 **Alas! By harping back** Cecil to Greta, draft letter 11 January
1955. St John's. Sealed

12 *Separation*
216 **I feel this to be true** mss diary, 1957
216 **indulged in every nice** Cecil Beaton Diaries: 1955–63 *The
Restless Years* (Weidenfeld & Nicolson, 1976)
217 **let out a moan** mss diary, 6 May 1956
217 **No one has really** Cecil to Greta, 6 May 1956. St John's. Sealed
217 **I was more determined** mss diary, June 1956
217 **wild, ragged** *The Restless Years*
218 **I do love you** ibid
218 **surrounded by half dead** mss diary, September 1956
218 **I was once** ibid
219 **I should have stayed** mss diary, October 1956
219 **She is like a man** ibid
220 **The boys do too much** ibid
220 **When she is settled** ibid
221 **She has gone off** Cecil to Mercedes, October 1956. Rosenbach
221 **I only wish** Ram Gopal to Mercedes, October 1956. Rosenbach
222 **bothering if the Louis** mss diary, May 1958
222 **It is a very sad** ibid
223 **I didn't know I could weep** mss diary, May 1958
223 **she will let me take a hand** mss diary, autumn 1958
223 **was less of a person** ibid
224 **She who used to be** mss diary, autumn 1959
224 **O no, Sissil** mss diary, winter 1959
225 **recovered from the shock** June Osborn to Cecil, December
1959. St John's © The Lady Hutchinson of Lullington
226 **I knew in my heart** mss diary, December 1959
226 **You see dearest** June Osborn to Cecil, September 1960. St John's
© The Lady Hutchinson of Lullington
228 **I do wish you would try** Cecil to Mercedes, undated 1960.
Rosenbach
228 **Guilaroff, pathetic** mss diary, November 1960

228 **terrible pixie woollen hat** mss diary, November 1960

229 **You need to breathe fresh air** *The Restless Years*

229 **this dark, eccentric** mss diary, November 1960

230 **Stephen was lying like a porpoise** mss diary, summer 1961

230 **Can you think of anything** Stephen Tennant to Cecil, undated. St John's © The Hon. Toby Tennant

231 **Cecil dear** Stephen Tennant to Cecil, undated 1961. St John's © The Hon. Tony Tennant

232 **I can't get over** Mercedes to William McCarthy, 31 October 1967. Rosenbach

233 **I have my first intimation** mss diary, April 1962

234 **We have been secretly in love** June Osborn to Cecil, undated 1966. St John's © The Lady Hutchinson of Lullington

234 **violent, big** mss diary, 1962

13 Betrayal

236 **everywhere evidence** mss diary, May 1963

237 **I felt an electric** mss diary, June 1964

238 **They're so busy** mss diary, June 1965

239 **I saw my life** ibid

239 **Can it be Beatie?** mss diary, July 1965

240 **In this cruel** ibid

241 **On the surface** mss diary August 1965

242 **I was determined** ibid

244 **Her cheeks were flushed** mss diary, November 1967

244 **Let her stew** mss diary, September 1968

245 **My heartsearching** mss diary, April 1971

245 **If I have offended** *The Happy Years*

246 **The awful feelings** mss diary, November 1971

246 **utterly against the spirit** ibid

246 **bearing branches** mss diary, January 1972

246 **not for my talent** mss diary, February 1972

247 **a young boy with tiger's eyes** mss diary, April 1972

249 **on the *McCall's*** mss diary, 21 May 1972

249 **People accuse me** Peter Viertel to author

249 **Well I couldn't have** *Cecil Beaton*

Bibliography

Architectural Digest, April 1992, Academy Awards Edition

Harold Acton, *Memoirs of an Aesthete* (Methuen, 1948)

John Bainbridge, *Garbo* (Frederick Muller, 1955)

Abram Chasins, *Leopold Stokowski* (Hawthorn Books, 1979)

Gary Carey, *Anita Loos: a biography* (Bloomsbury, 1988)

Pamela Glenconner, *The Sayings of the Children* (Blackwell, 1918)

Greta Garbo: Photographs 1920–1951 (Schirmer Art Books, 1990)

Anita Loos, *A Girl Like I* (Viking Press, 1966)
    Kiss Hollywood Goodbye (W. H. Allen, 1974)

Olga Lynn, *Oggie* (Weidenfeld and Nicolson, 1955)

Edward Maeder (ed.) *Hollywood and History: Costume Design in Film* (Thames and Hudson, 1987)

David Mellor (ed.) *Cecil Beaton* (Barbican Art Gallery, 1986)

Charlotte Mosley (ed.) *The Letters of Nancy Mitford* (Hodder & Stoughton, 1993)

Edith Olivier, *Without Knowing Mr Walkley* (Faber, 1939)

Graham Payn and Sheridan Morley (eds.), *The Noël Coward Diaries* (Weidenfeld and Nicolson, 1982)

John Pearson, *Façades: Edith, Osbert and Sacheverell Sitwell* (Macmillan, 1978)

Terence Pepper and John Kobal, *The Man Who Shot Garbo: The Hollywood Photographs of Clarence Sinclair Bull* (Schirmer, 1989)

Frederick Sands and Sven Broman, *The Divine Garbo* (Sidgwick and Jackson, 1979)

Sotheby's Catalogue, *The Greta Garbo Collection* (Sotheby's, 1990)

Siegfried Sassoon, *Siegfried's Journey* (Faber, 1946)

Roy Strong, *Cecil Beaton: The Royal Portraits* (Thames and Hudson, 1988)

G. M. Trevelyan, *Grey of Fallodon* (Longman, 1940)

Diana Vreeland, *DV* (Weidenfeld and Nicolson, 1984)

Alexander Walker, *Garbo* (Weidenfeld and Nicolson, 1980)

Evelyn Waugh, *A Little Learning* (Chapman & Hall, 1964)

Laurence Whistler, *The Laughter and the Urn: the Life of Rex Whistler* (Weidenfeld and Nicolson, 1985)

James Woodress, *Willa Cather: A Literary Life* (Nebraska Press, 1987)

Index